YOUTH, SCHOOL, AND COMMUNITY

Participatory Institutional Ethnographies

This book examines how young people's experiences of inclusion and exclusion are shaped by extended social relations, coordinating thought and conduct across time and space. Working with young people and using a range of participatory institutional ethnographic strategies, Naomi Nichols investigates the social and institutional relations that differentially punctuate the lives of youth. While the research begins with what young people know and have experienced, this starting place anchors a deeper investigation of the public sector institutions and institutional processes that remain implicated in the social-historical-economic systems of global capitalism, imperialism, and colonialism.

Youth, School, and Community connects the dots between, on the one hand, the abstract objectified accounts produced by institutions and enabling institutional action and accounting practices, and, on the other hand, the actual material conditions of young people's lives and development, which these accounts obscure. The focus on specific policies and procedures that produce young people's experiences of racialized inclusion/exclusion and safety/risk make this book particularly useful to academics, professionals, and activists who want to ensure that young people experience equitable access to public sector resources and not disproportionate exposure to public sector punishments and punitive interventions.

NAOMI NICHOLS is an assistant professor in the Faculty of Education at McGill University.

Youth, School, and Community

Participatory Institutional Ethnographies

NAOMI NICHOLS

FOREWORD BY DOROTHY E. SMITH

UNIVERSITY OF TORONTO PRESS
Toronto Buffalo London

© University of Toronto Press 2019
Toronto Buffalo London
utorontopress.com

ISBN 978-1-4875-0333-8 (cloth)   ISBN 978-1-4875-2259-9 (paper)

Library and Archives Canada Cataloguing in Publication
Title: Youth, school, and community : participatory institutional
   ethnographies / Naomi Nichols ; foreword by Dorothy E. Smith.
Names: Nichols, Naomi, 1978– author.
Description: Includes bibliographical references and index.
Identifiers: Canadiana 20190128542 | ISBN 9781487522599 (paper) |
   ISBN 9781487503338 (cloth)
Subjects: LCSH: Problem youth – Institutional care – Ontario – Toronto. |
   LCSH: Problem youth – Institutional care – Québec (Province) – Montréal.
Classification: LCC HV866.C32 T67 2019 | DDC 362.7409713/541—dc23

This book has been published with the help of a grant from the Federation
for the Humanities and Social Sciences, through the Awards to Scholarly
Publications Program, using funds provided by the Social Sciences and
Humanities Research Council of Canada.

University of Toronto Press acknowledges the financial assistance to its
publishing program of the Canada Council for the Arts and the Ontario Arts
Council, an agency of the Government of Ontario.

Canada Council   Conseil des Arts
for the Arts   du Canada

ONTARIO ARTS COUNCIL
CONSEIL DES ARTS DE L'ONTARIO
an Ontario government agency
un organisme du gouvernement de l'Ontario

Funded by the   Financé par le
Government   gouvernement
of Canada   du Canada

Canadä

Contents

Foreword

DOROTHY E. SMITH

Being involved in the making of a new sociology, now known as institutional ethnography (a term invented on a beach in southern California), has been exciting. There have been many challenges; overcoming them has led to more and more fascinating possible explorations from where we are, where people are in our/their everyday lives, into the relations that stand over against and overpower us. My experience being part of – and learning from – this shared work as it has gone forward has been of the creative and innovative means, modes, and forms of developing research leading to discoveries that could not have been imagined. And here is the exciting and innovatory work of Naomi Nichols in which we learn from the experiences of young people in racialized communities just how the workings of police, the justice system, and, most especially, the school systems of Ontario and Quebec create for them exclusions that undermine their education, their life opportunities, and indeed more generally their sense of who they are and where they're going.

I found in reading Naomi's book that I was learning about public education in Canada in a radically new way. It's a field I've read widely in and indeed, with Alison Griffith, have contributed research (Griffith and Smith 2005). The specific foci of Naomi's research were students in a Toronto neighbourhood that is predominantly Black and then in a neighbourhood in Montreal with a significant immigrant population. The public school systems of these two provinces differ considerably: Quebec has strict rules designed to accord the French language educational dominance, schooling only to sixteen and provides significant support to private schools; Ontario, on the other hand, is dominated by public schools and has schooling to eighteen. Yet when they are explored from the perspectives and experiences of young people who have gotten into trouble or discovered problems that the "system" did not take responsibility for, there are remarkable institutional properties in common – these young people have experienced the difficulties the school system can create as a side effect of its grand educational project.

It's oversimplifying to tell that what we learn from this book is the damage public education does. But we do learn how deep the divergence is from the experience of middle-class White parents of their children's schooling and what it may be like for children situated very differently. Naomi describes her experience as a middle-class mother getting help for learning problems her eight-year-old daughter was having in her school and contrasts what became available to her with what is ordinarily simply not there for students living in racially defined poverty.

The research in these two provinces, these two cities, differed somewhat. The Toronto project is larger, more involved. Naomi hired and, with her research colleagues, trained some of the young people already subjected to being transferred from their main high school to alternative school as researchers, working along with those from the university. The passages from interviews that are quoted begin to give us pictures of what it has been like for students who could be described as having been discarded – sometimes almost incidentally – as the justice system, its court hearings, et cetera interfered with their school attendance. Sometimes it seems as if the disorganizing if not destroying of an individual student's high school experience is almost auxiliary to its everyday functioning. It does not appear to be intended, even as punishment, though the outcomes appear as intimately tied to the normal functioning of high schools in both these settings.

This is a very different understanding of our public-school system than presented in the literature on education in Canada that I have been familiar with. I cannot claim to be an expert in the field. I am however sufficiently up to date to recognize that this book is a very different way of discovering the workings of the state in this specific area. And, from within the institutional ethnographic approach, it develops and works with a highly original method of inquiry, beginning by learning from those whose lives have been impacted by the normal workings of the provincial governments in ways that are deeply destructive. Naomi does not pretend that those who were interviewed or participated as researchers had not presented their schools with problems; what she does make clear, however, is that, in these neighbourhoods at least, the consequences for the young people of the normal operations that discipline and control students can be serious. And where there are inequities, such as those created by the disproportionate policing of the predominantly Black neighbourhoods in Toronto, standard school practices affirm and intensify inequitable outcomes.

Exploring the workings of the schools in these two sites in the context of the educational institutions of the two provinces enables us to see how this kind of study, beginning with the everyday and local experiences of those who have been in trouble in racially and class differentiated communities, raises issues about how the normal functioning of a formally standardized system may operate in differing settings of class and race. We see here in this book how the actual workings of these two provincial systems of education have outcomes very different from those it was possible for Naomi to bring about for her eight-year-old daughter.

The intimacy of our learning from those young people who speak to us through these pages is powerful, but so is the account of the institutional orders of education, as actually practised, in these two provinces and how they have entered into and damaged these young lives. I have been fascinated too by the discoveries of the workings of the two school systems in these two provinces from a standpoint that simply does not accept the official image but seeks to uncover actual workings as they are happening for young people involved. Of course, there's more to be learned. The fascination of this book is not just in what we learn but also from the doors to further discoveries that it opens. As is always the case for me with institutional ethnographies that introduce me to a new understanding, I want to know more. Institutional ethnographies are not case studies; they do not wrap themselves up into neat packages that put in place only those issues and questions for which there are answers. There is always more to be learned and more to be discovered, which has been opened up by such an exploration as this book brings us.

YOUTH, SCHOOL, AND COMMUNITY

Participatory Institutional Ethnographies

Introduction

The Institutional and Policy Contexts That Shape Young People's Lives

In this book, I investigate public sector interventions that shape how young people grow up, the social relations they participate in, and the ways they come to know themselves and others. I anchor these investigations in the standpoints of young people, diversely positioned by – and in relation to – the range of institutional processes and bodies that comprise the focus of my analysis. Research for this book began with a study (conducted with Alison Griffith and Uzo Anucha) on school and community safety. The study's central lines of inquiry emerge from the experiences and knowledge of young people who live in designated "vulnerable" or "priority" neighbourhoods and/or who attend school in Safe Schools[1] or Section 23[2] Programs in closed custody corrections facilities in the Greater Toronto Area in Ontario. By virtue of where they live, their experiences in school, and/or their involvement with the youth criminal justice system, the young people who participated in the first study were institutionally coded as "at risk" – a category that conceals the ways that state processes produce the grounds upon which the category operates, as well as the racialized, gendered, and classed outcomes of its application. After two and a half years of research in Ontario, I undertook a second phase of the research (with Jessica Ruglis) in Montreal, Quebec, anchoring data collection in the

---

1 I use the term Safe Schools program in this book to account for the array of programs that Ontario schools offer for students completing a long-term suspension or who have been expelled, as well as alternative programs that facilitate educational and other assessments and non-academic support. There are nine Caring and Safe Schools programs for secondary students in the Toronto District School Board (TDSB, 2014).
2 Students in Section 23 Programs are "clients" of an agency funded by the Ministry of Child and Youth Services. Section 23 Programs are found in hospitals, group homes, children's mental health centres, and – of import for this study – in open and closed custody correctional institutions.

experiences and knowledge of English-speaking (although not necessarily Anglophone) youth, from across a range of Montreal neighbourhoods. In the second phase of the project, we deliberately sought to engage with young people who, as a result of their interactions with various institutional discourses and interventions, come to be coded by the state and by people who work in public sector and community-based organizations in a range of different ways – for example, as entitled, at risk, high-achieving, racialized, homeless, immigrant, anxious, learning disabled, gender-nonconforming, and so on. Across the two studies, young people's stories and insights ground an investigation of the educational, social, housing, policing, labour market, and criminal-legal policies, which background and give shape to the stories young people tell. The book reveals the administrative knowledge, activities, practices, policies, and procedures that background and give shape to young people's experiences growing up and coming to know themselves in relation to others and the state. Each chapter offers a focused analysis of a set of political-institutional relations and then illuminates how the focal policies and institutions are part of larger complexes of social activity shaping young people's experiences of inclusion and exclusion, safety, and unsafety across multiple institutional sites.

My analytic foci are the "ongoing socially ordered matrices differentiating" young people's experiences and the extended social relations that can be glimpsed from the actual conditions of their everyday lives. Social relations "arise in the co-ordering of actual activities, and they go beyond or underneath the stories people know how to tell about their lives" (D.E. Smith, 1987, p. 141). These relations connect me to the young people I work with as a researcher and the problems our collaborative work reveals. Like Smith, "I am White, English-speaking, a paid member of the Canadian intelligentsia. I have my place in this same organization of relations that generates the experience of the world of those I observed" (D.E. Smith, 1987, p. 113). Working with young people, using a range of participatory strategies, we investigate the social relations that differentially punctuate our lives. While research began with what young people know and have experienced, this starting place anchors an investigation of public sector institutions and institutional processes that remain implicated in social-historical-economic processes of global capitalism, imperialism, and colonialism. As such, I pay explicit attention to how processes of racialization, class, and gender – as objectified forms of consciousness – figure into the processes of social organization that I am investigating. Unlike other books *about* youth, this book examines how young people's experiences of inclusion and exclusion are shaped by extended social relations, coordinating thought and conduct across time and space. I am not interested in studying young people as members of a socially and administratively constituted category – namely, "youth at risk." Rather, I am interested in understanding how the category is brought into an objectified form of stasis, such that it organizes the provision and management of public sector interventions that target youth and contributes to processes of racialization, classing, and gendering operating through schools. This book provides a cross-cutting intersectoral analysis of the policies, practices, knowledges, and administrative structures that produce material conditions of racialized and gendered poverty and exclusion.

To do so, the book picks up a thread of Dorothy Smith's work that has been insufficiently attended to in most institutional ethnographies. I take up her suggestion that a sociology for people brings into view the general social relations through which our unique experiences are co-ordered. I use as my starting place Himani Bannerji's proposition that the ground of "racist [and other] oppression[s] is the same as the ground of White [and other] privilege[s]" (Bannerji, 1991, p. 72) – that is, the very same social relations that produce one person's experiences of inclusion, safety, and privilege are implicated in another person's experiences of exclusion, risk, and oppression. In some cases, I seek to do this by illuminating how the same institutional processes implicated in the severing of a young person's relation with education can produce my own child's continued – if tenuous – attachments to this same institution. The dissimilarity in outcomes is not based on a differential institutional savvy, resilience, or some other individualized explanation; rather, the differences reveal just how the organizational structures that comprise the public education system support and protect the interests of those who have historically held privileges in these institutional environments. Working in this way, the book reveals how processes of racialized, gendered, and classed exclusion/inclusion are organized *across* institutional contexts; in, for example, social housing, education, and neighbourhood policing. The cross-sectoral organization of the problem of social exclusion/privileging makes it difficult to see and disrupt the relations through which privilege is protected for some and denied others. Because public sector interventions have been designed by and normed against a particular segment of the population and then applied universally, they produce social relations that reflect and maintain historically situated patterns of privilege, oppression, invisibility, surveillance, suffering, and entitlement. My aim is for this book to crack open the assumptions of neutrality and objectivity upon which the public sector operates and continues to defend its legitimacy.

I have written this book to get underneath abstract theoretical concepts like institutional violence and institutional racism to reveal the actual social relations that the theorizations obscure. Racial-ethnic disproportionalities across institutional contexts make it clear that public institutions and institutional processes are not equally accessible or useful to all people living in Canada (Contenta, Monsebraaten, & Rankin, 2014; Galabuzi, 2014; Maynard, 2017; Rankin, Winsa, Bailey, & Ng, 2014; Winsa, 2014). Robin Maynard's (2017) and Jaskiran Dhillon's (2017) books, in particular, document the legacy of anti-Black[3] racism and White settler colonialism that have been central to the formation and ongoing operations of the Canadian state. But neither the statistical documentation of the problem nor its theorization as institutional betrayal or violence enables us to figure out how social and institutional settings – increasingly guided by policy, practice, and legislative moves ostensibly designed to enable equality – are actually organized to produce these disproportionate outcomes. In this book my aim is to systematically connect the dots between the abstract objectified accounts produced by institutions and enabling institutional action and accounting practices and the actual material conditions of young people's lives and development, which these accounts obscure. The specificity of the analysis (i.e., focusing on specific policies and procedures that produce young people's experiences of racialized inclusion/ exclusion, safety/risk) make it particularly useful to academics, professionals (across sectors), and activists who want to ensure that young people experience equitable access to public sector resources and not disproportionate exposure to public sector punishments and punitive interventions. I also hope it rattles people's convictions that their good *intentions* outweigh the clearly racist, classist, and gendered outcomes of their work, particularly in the "helping" sectors: education, social work, and child welfare.

Outline of the Book

The book begins with the central ideas that have organized my approach to research and my thinking about the social relations the research reveals. Chapter 1, "Experience, Ontology, and Sociologies of

---

3 In this book, Black and White are capitalized when the terms are used to reference a racial category. This decision conforms with APA style guidelines, but also with my own intention to present Blackness and Whiteness as categories – constructed, disputed, contentious, and evolving categories – that coordinate consciousness and activity at the level of the social body.

Resistance," describes institutional ethnography (or IE), which is the sociological approach that I have chosen to use, and it situates IE within a broader critique of dominant ways of working in the social sciences and a history of problematic applications of social science knowledge. Much of the thinking conveyed in chapter 1 can be linked to a course I teach at McGill on the educational implications of social theory as well as a series of public talks I have given in the last couple of years about institutional ethnography and what it offers, sociologically speaking, to those seeking to work against the grain of traditional sociological research. Although chapter 1 describes my sociological approach, I see it as conforming to what would typically be a theory chapter in other books. This is the chapter where I illuminate the conceptual resources that have fundamentally grounded the analysis I put forward in the book. From here, I describe the two studies through which data for this book were generated. Chapter 2, "Participatory Institutional Ethnographics of the State," describes the two projects – Schools, Safety, and Urban Neighbourhoods and Sampling Youth Development. This chapter is rich in detail because I want this book to be useful to others embarking on an institutional ethnographic investigation of their own. My intention in beginning this book with a chapter on institutional ethnography, followed by a chapter on my methodological orientation and methods, is to illuminate how institutional ethnography's epistemic and ontological commitments can be upheld in multiple ways. In much the same way that I seek to bring particular institutional and policy processes into view, ethnographically, for the reader in subsequent chapters, here my aim is to make visible the relations of participatory research with young people. I intentionally do not gloss over the more challenging aspects of this work; rather, I focus on what can be learned from these moments about the institutional relations that are the book's focus.

Chapter 3. "The Neo-liberal State and the Creation of Race, Class, and Gender," sets up the analyses that comprise the book's central empirical offerings. Focusing specifically on policing practices and uses of institutional evidence to legitimize state activities, it reveals how relations of race, class, and gender are produced, maintained, *and* obscured in these complexes of institutional activity. Consistent with an institutional ethnographic approach, analysis emerges from and remains faithful to the ordinary things that young people say they do every day and night. The chapter began with my efforts to understand how Black youth, living in social housing in an economically disenfranchised Toronto neighbourhood, come to the shared conclusion that the state doesn't care about them. To produce my analysis, I build from people's divergent accounts of their experiences with various state authorities to show how young people's ordinary daily work to avoid state institutions – that is, the police, social, and immigration workers – is connected to the work of other young people across the country seeking to bring the state into their lives to keep them safe and enable further access to public resources. Because these complexes of social action – which shape highly unequal outcomes in young people's lives – are the product of bureaucratic institutional and policy processes, they are presented as rational and fair. On the contrary, chapter 1 shows how these seemingly rational cross-cutting bureaucratic processes select for or exclude people in highly unequal ways, setting the stage (for instance) for precariously housed Black youth to conclude that the state doesn't care about them. The chapters that follow adopt a similar approach. Each chapter seeks to address a particular research problematic, which was evident in people's accounts of their lives, but which they could not fully explain. This focus on political and institutional relations that are present in and give shape to our lives, but which we cannot fully see or comprehend from where we are situated in them, distinguishes IE from other modes of inquiry and makes it useful to my efforts to explain how seemingly benign institutional processes produce disastrously unequal effects. Chapter 4, "Evidential Practices in Education and the Negation of Race," explores how the same young people who produce astute race and class analyses of social housing and policing struggle to hold on to race analyses when they talk about their experiences in school. Drawing on the experiences of young people in Toronto and Montreal, chapter 4 illuminates the general policy and institutional organization of schooling in the two cities, which shape the negation of race in people's talk as well as the racialized, classed, and gendered disproportionalities that the same policies and institutional contexts produce. Chapter 5, "Risk, Safety, Inclusion, and the Inter-institutional Organization of Educational Interventions," begins with young people, youth workers, and educators' embodied knowledge of their own lives and experiences – particularly their experiences being moved or coordinating moves for young people across a range of educational environments. The movement of young people from one institutional site to another constitutes a key form of discrimination – rationalized by educational and/or correctional organizations as evidence of bureaucratically sanctioned actions meant to address a young person's "complex needs." Having studied these processes for the last decade, I am left with the conclusion that young people become vulnerable because we (adult decision makers in youth sector institutions) do not know how to meet their needs. These young people are subject to multiple, often poorly coordinated and destabilizing institutional moves, which fail to produce the outcomes they need, but which serve as a justification that "the system" has done what it can for these youth.

Finally, chapter 6, "State Surveillance and School Discipline," focuses specifically on forms of state surveillance and punishment shaping disproportionate educational and social outcomes for youth. It begins with a deep dive into suspension and expulsion policies, practices, and programs in Ontario and Quebec, interrogating these from the standpoints of youth in both provincial contexts. Young people's stories illuminate interconnections between school discipline policies and the other relations of surveillance, targeting, and dislocation within which young people's lives unfold. Across all of the chapters, the research reveals purportedly objective institutional processes, increasingly grounded in the generation and use of institutional data, that produce a range of material conditions and conceptual frames illustrating and entrenching inequalities along racialized, classed, and gendered lines.

Chapter One

Experience, Ontology, and Sociologies of Resistance

The weapon of criticism cannot in any case replace the criticism of weapons, material force must be overthrown by material force, but theory too becomes a material force as soon as it grasps weapons. Theory is capable of grasping weapons as soon as its argument becomes ad hominem, and its argument becomes ad hominem as soon as it becomes radical. To be radical is to grasp the matter by its root. Now, the root for mankind is man himself. (Marx, 2010)

This book describes an institutional ethnography (D.E. Smith, 1987b). Institutional ethnography is an alternative sociology, which seeks to generate knowledge that can be used to improve the conditions of people's lives. Like other progressive approaches to research (e.g., participatory and community-based research approaches), institutional ethnography is committed to generating knowledge for/with – rather than about – people. Unlike other approaches, institutional ethnography offers a method of social analysis that begins with what people know and have experienced to discover something about how the social is "put together" (D.E. Smith, 1999, 2005) in the coordinated social and intellectual practices people describe. One's line of inquiry emerges from people's experiences and insights, but the ethnographic and analytic foci are the modes of social coordination (the relations of ruling) that give shape to the experiences and insights people have shared with you.

The ethnographic focus is the first point of departure institutional ethnography makes from traditional ethnographic forms of qualitative research. Traditional ethnographies produce rich descriptive accounts, through which researchers attempt to convey the lived realities and cultural practices of people who have been – or will be – classified and grouped (e.g., young mothers in an urban environment). In contrast, the ethnographic focus of an IE is the political-institutional terrain that is present in, but obscured from, the everyday local settings of our lives (D.E. Smith, 1999). In an institutional ethnography, the everyday world of embodied action and experience represents a project's starting place or foundation, rather than its analytic focus. George W. Smith (1990) – a former student and collaborator of Dorothy Smith and one of the scholars that has most influenced my work over the years – identified six key features of his own research endeavours (which inform my work):

> (1) start from the actual lives of people and undertake an analysis of a world known reflexively; (2) stake out an ontological commitment to a social order constituted in the practices and activities of people; (3) take, as their analytic, the notion of "social relations"; (4) are based on the use of meetings with government officials and professional cadres as ethnographic data; (5) analyse texts such as media reports, legislation, internal agency memoranda, and annual reports of government departments, in developing a description of how a ruling regime works; and (6) illustrate the necessity of bracketing ordinary political explanations – the technique of the materialist epoche, as I call it – in order to provide a scientific account of the social organization of a ruling regime. (pp 629–30)

For example, the investigations at the heart of this book began with and remain faithful to the experiences and insights of the first group of young people with whom I spoke – that is, young people living in racialized, economically marginalized, and criminologically stigmatized neighbourhoods in the Greater Toronto Area. The social world that their accounts begin to bring into view in this book is one that each of us has come to know (and to know differently) by living in it. The foci of analysis (i.e., one's sociological problematic) emerges from actual people's accounts of their work and typically requires that one refocus her ethnographic attention on describing institutional modes of work and thought, which are implicated in producing the problems that people have described. The coordination of this social world – what institutional ethnographers describe as social order or social organization – is a function of the co-ordered thoughts, activities, and practices of actual people. The concept of social relations, which Dorothy Smith has developed and George Smith points to above, directs an institutional ethnographer to pay attention to the ways people's practices and ideas constitute "reflexive courses of action" (G.W. Smith, 1990, p. 635), whereby people's work practices are knitted together – not deterministically, but interdependently across time and space – to produce the objective modes of consciousness and concerting that comprise the observable patterns of social life. In my own research, young people's accounts directed me to investigate mainstream and alternative schools, child welfare, social housing, neighbourhood policing, the youth justice and mental health systems, and the intersecting institutional and policy relations, which suture each of our individual experiences into a broader social matrix. Particular aspects of this "politico-administrative regime" (G.W. Smith, 1990, p. 634) were brought into view by field notes produced by me and research assistants (often documenting meetings we have attended and our own participation in particular institutional courses of action), as well as interviews with young people and the adults with whom they work. By stitching together people's accounts of their work in particular institutional contexts and situating these descriptions of people's coordinated activities against an analysis of the textual and policy relations that background them, I was able to bring into view the objectified institutional relations that connect young people to one another and give shape to their divergent experiences of and in the public sphere. Instead of relying on theoretical explanations for young people's differential outcomes in standardized politico-administrative processes, I followed George Smith's suggestion that one bracket theoretical explanations, in an attempt to show how these outcomes are the result of actual relations among people, socially organized to produce and rationalize the experiences young people describe.

The second way institutional ethnography differs from other qualitative approaches to social research is its relationship with theory and theoretically constituted systems of classification. Institutional ethnography is often misunderstood as being resistant to theory. But this is an oversimplification of an institutional ethnographer's relationship to the production and use of theoretical ideas. Institutional ethnography is simply resistant to the use of theory to name, model, and interpret various sociological phenomena, such that the theoretical construct acquires an objectified status, which obscures the actual intellectual practices that go into the production of an abstract objectified mode of thought. This move reflects IE's epistemological and ontological stance. Epistemologically, institutional ethnographers conceive of knowing as a social process. One doesn't simply assimilate an objective knowledge that exists "out there" into an individuated consciousness. Rather, how we come to know and think is through a social – and hence dialogic – process. One learns to name and make sense of the world with others. The social character of knowledge production, acquisition, and use, therefore, represents grounds for sociological inquiry. Ontologically, institutional ethnographers uphold a materialist conceptualization of reality and social life. This means that even those things that appear to have a metaphysical dimension (e.g., beliefs, ideas, perspectives) can be revealed to have a material (social) origin that can be brought into view. Theoretical models, premises, and explanations are produced by people as part of organized methods of intellectual activity (D.E. Smith, 2004). Increasingly, this work represents and feeds into other institutionally organized sequences of activity that contribute to the management and commodification of academic labour, through research funding and citational processes, as well as intellectual property designations.

Of interest to me and the research I do are the ways that the generalized systems of classification and explanation produced and substantiated by academic research are adopted by and go on to organize how institutions operate. Theoretical explanations for the problems people encounter in their everyday lives are produced by academic researchers as part of an institutionally regulated work process (e.g., through academic disciplinary norms and standards and ethical review processes). As abstract concepts and explanations are embedded in other institutional processes operating in and shaping universities (e.g., academic teaching and training, the production and testing of models and interventions) as well as any number of other institutional settings (e.g., courtrooms, police stations, schools), they are taken up and used by people working in a variety of professional capacities, informing how they interpret, code, and respond to actual people and the unfolding social relations of their personal and professional lives. These processes of knowledge production and use are ideological processes, as D.E. Smith (2004) understands Marx and Engels's conceptualization of ideology.

Social Research and Ideology

Rather than conceiving of ideology as a thing (e.g., a false consciousness), a materialist orientation to ideology directs a researcher to pay attention to the social processes through which knowledge is produced and used. Critical scholarship, pushing back against the reification of Marx's thinking, suggests how one might explore and understand the intersections of knowledge and social life, such that research is used to discover precisely "*how* a particular set of ideas comes to dominate the social thinking" at particular points in history (Hall, 1986, p. 129, my emphasis), or how a particular set of sense-making practices and dispositions are lived and naturalized (Crehan, 2011; Bourdieu, 1990; Gramsci, 1971). For her part, Sarah Ahmed (2011) plays with Engels's use of the term "false consciousness" to explore the ways that people's beliefs – their adherence to or rejection of particular normative ideals or narratives – coincide with their interests. Ahmed's phenomenological investigations suggest "how the social is arranged through the sharing of deceptions that precede the arrival of subjects" (Ahmed, 2011, p. 165). Her analysis of revolutionary and other forms of consciousness addresses something that remains unnamed in most institutional ethnographies – that is, how it happens that normative ideas and ways of relating "precede the arrival of subjects" or *appear to* exist over and above us, acting on and through our lives. Institutional ethnographies have tended not to illuminate how the objectified status of mass consciousness – the sense that consciousness exists independently of actual thinkers, speakers, and listeners – is a function of how social life is organized. D.E. Smith's (1999) work on ideological codes suggests how we might attend to the actual social processes through which ideas acquire objectified status, such that they seem to "precede the arrival" of the people they influence.

Ideological explanations and ideological codes (D.E. Smith, 1987; D.E. Smith, 1999) are developed out of people's observations and experiences at particular times and places. Over time and use they gain an objectified status, which makes them appear as though they exist in their own right, and, as such, their active production from the actualities of people's intellectual work is concealed. Ahmed's sense that the arrangement of the social is predetermined or heritable is a consequence of the ongoingness of social life. Once ideological abstractions are embedded in the textually mediated fabric of social life, they coordinate conduct and consciousness at the level of ongoing social relations: "Though ideology may begin with the real world, it proceeds by constructing a concept or theory that supplants the original and treats the original actualities as expressions or effects of the concept or theory" (D.E. Smith, 2004, p. 453). Elsewhere Smith has described this process as an ideological circle. I imagine it operating more like a feedback loop, where the more the ideological (re)presentation of a social relation is used, the greater its effect on our interpretation of the actual conditions of our lives. Ideology refers to the ongoing social processes – coordinated through language, especially in textual forms – that people use to perceive and interpret their lives and experiences; the shared phraseology and interpretive schema of specific ideologies correspond with and protect the interests of those who produce and use them. These social processes of knowledge production and use are constituted in people's practices, and as social scientists, our research often builds from and contributes to these highly coordinative processes (e.g., police officers who participate in guns and gang training that is based on gang typologies and criminological theories, which are generated academically).

One way to engage critically as a social scientist, then, is to open up for analysis the taken-for-granted, common-sense, or objectified modes of thought that organize our everyday sense-making practices. In my own research (Nichols, 2017b), for instance, I've sought to show how people are participating in discourses of racialized masculinity, shaped by their ongoing engagement with (production and critique of) media and popular cultural texts (news headlines, music videos, movies) and their interactions with dominant institutions like policing. These social practices come into view when a police officer tells a young man that he only stops youth wearing "Crooks and Castles" sweaters and not youth wearing Gap. In this interaction, the racially and culturally coded meaning of this point is not lost on the young man (or the officer). The officer need not explicitly link Crooks and Castles to race, class, gender, or culture for knowledgable participants in the discourses of racialized masculinity to make these connections (D.E. Smith, 1993).

When one anchors her analysis in theory – rather than in the actual experiences of people's lives – the fact that the theoretical phenomena one seeks (e.g., race and gender) were produced in the world where one looks to find them is obscured. In the end, then, when research findings get shared, it appears as though race and gender are naturally occurring things that people can go out in the world and find. From here, a series of abstractions become possible that take us further and further from the actual social relations one was attempting to understand in the first place. Scales and systems of classification are created, variables and models are tested, and knowledge is produced (and vested in texts), all of which gets taken up and engaged by people all over the place, shaping how people come to think and act across a number of seemingly disparate contexts. As theoretical concepts get drawn into work processes across institutional and social contexts, they obtain an objectified status that obscures how the concepts are produced through the ordinary professional practices associated with social science and other forms of research. In this way, objectified systems of thought – that is, ways of knowing that transcend and link individual knowers at particular moments in history – appear to exist independently of the actual material practices of their production and use. As D.E. Smith (2004) observes, the result is the treatment of people's actual lives and experiences as "expressions or effects of a concept or theory" (p. 453), alienating us from the people we work with and the problems we seek to resolve together.

Beyond Alienation: Ideology and Processes of Domination

Beyond alienation, the production and use of abstract universalities plays a key role in social processes of exploitation and domination. The production of abstractions, which enables commensurability among and exchange of non-like things (e.g., money and labour) within a single system of organization, is key to the operations of capitalism and the democratic, constitutional, juridical, and bureaucratic organization of the state. And, as Ahmed (2011) reminds us, the production of normative standards conceals how those who create and maintain them do so in their own best interest. Marx suggests that the processes of abstraction, which permit the establishment of general principles, universal norms, standards, and laws, are also essential to the activities of ruling. In order for one group of people to legitimate its governing status, it must create a "wave of enthusiasm in itself and among the masses, a wave of feeling wherein it would fraternize and commingle with society in general and would feel and be recognized as society's general representative, a wave of enthusiasm wherein its claims and rights would be in truth the claims and rights of society itself, wherein it would really be the social head and the social heart. Only in the name of the general rights of society can a particular class vindicate for itself the general rulership" (Marx, 2010, p. 16). One must read Marx, D.E. Smith, Michel Foucault, and Franz Fanon in conversation to fill out the rest of the picture that Marx begins to paint in the above statement. The establishment of "universal" social, legal, and economic standards and norms always reflects and serves particular historically contingent interests and values, and the work of establishing – that is researching, drafting, reviewing, discussing, revising, and implementing – juridico-institutional standards, norms, and policy is always done by actual people, at particular moments in time. Like Ian Hacking (2004) situates his thinking in conversation with Michel Foucault and Erving Goffman (as well as Sartre and Bourdieu) to provide a fulsome philosophical treatment of the role of systems of classification in "making up people," I do my best thinking in the interstices of social theory and method.

When Foucault (Foucault & Gordon, 1980a) writes about power-knowledge, he is interested in the ways that knowledge serves a ruling or coordinative social function. The power-knowledge relation rests on two social moves: first, the presentation of certain knowledges as objective, natural, and universal, and second, the production, circulation, and application of these knowledges in various institutional and social contexts, which solidify their universalized status and simultaneously the subjugation of other forms of knowledge. Foucault's critique of the "tyranny of globalizing discourses" (Foucault & Gordon, 1980a) enabled a postmodern turn towards a genealogical practice – that is, an "attempt to emancipate historical knowledges from that subjection, to render them, that is, capable of opposition and of struggle against the coercion of a theoretical, unitary, formal and scientific discourse"(Foucault & Gordon, 1980b). By illuminating how interrelated practices and ideas emerged at distinctive periods in time to serve a particular social and political function, Foucault systematically demonstrates how the emergence and dominance of particular knowledges are historically, institutionally, politically, and economically contingent – rather than universal.

Similarly, mechanisms for surveillance, documentation, measurement, and intervention emerge at specific points in history and for political, social, and economic utilities. Foucault observes, "It is only if we grasp these techniques of power and demonstrate the economic advantages or political utility that derives from them in a given context for specific reasons, that we can understand how these mechanisms come to be effectively incorporated into the social whole" (Foucault & Gordon, 1980a, p. 101). Foucault's conceptualization of power as a technique or technology – an exercise, rather than an entity – prevents us from treating power as a static generalized theoretical phenomenon. He intimates the role that people play in exercises of power when he suggests one pay attention to the "manifold relations of power which permeate, characterize and constitute the social body" and how "these relations of power cannot themselves be established, consolidated nor implemented without the production, accumulation, circulation and functioning of a discourse" (p. 93). Foucault's conceptualization of discourse as disciplinary practices or power-knowledge relations suggests the presence of actual people who think, write, and speak. But people are only ever implied in his work as the "targets," "vehicles," or "extremities" of power. Precisely *how* people participate in and evolve discourse is left unexplored.[1]

---

1 It is at precisely this juncture that Hacking (2004) positions Goffman's work as necessary for illuminating how the forms of discourse Foucault points to shape the habits, dispositions, and everyday lives of ordinary people.

The result is a tendency to position power as the subject or the agent of Foucault's analysis. It is as though power acts, rather than people. The result is that discourse appears to float freely above us all, coordinating how we know ourselves, our experiences, one another, truth, and right, but ignoring how discourse is continually being produced, negated, contested, evolved, and circulated by actual people (like the police officer and the young man on the streets of Toronto). This absence of people, situated in the actual, multiple, and diverse conditions of their lives, lends a sense of universality and generalizability to Foucault's own work, despite his efforts to resist this force. Indeed, Gayatri Spivak observes that Foucault is subject to the very universalizing impulse he seeks to avoid, that is: "the bestowal of the name power upon a complex of situations that produce power 'in the general sense'" (Spivak, 1993, p. 28). This tension, which she – citing Jacques Derrida – describes as the "curious relationship between the narrow and the general senses" (Spivak, 1993, p. 28), is for Spivak both necessary and irreconcilable. But the tension is only necessary and unavoidable if one adopts a deconstructionist approach to theory-building. If, in contrast, one's aim is to produce an analysis that builds from the particularities of people's lives and experiences to investigate the social relations that link and separate us, the particular and the general can both be kept in view.

Beginning with Experience

Before D.E. Smith began problematizing the available discourses and methods for understanding how the grounds of women's oppression is socially organized, other scholars were coming to similar conclusions about the limits of traditional epistemic and methodological practices for discerning how their experiences of racial oppression were organized. In the middle of the twentieth century, anticolonial scholars began producing a body of knowledge that has resonance with D.E. Smith's. Superficially, the resonance reflects a shared Marxist influence and a rejection of the posited neutrality and universality of Western knowledge. More than this, I recognize a similar struggle to interpret their own lives and experiences when they suspect that the very intellectual tools afforded to them for this purpose are implicated in the processes of subjugation they seek to investigate. There was no language from which to begin. And so, people began with their own experiences and observations of the world.

In writing about the development of a sociology that treats women as subjects rather than objects of inquiry, D.E. Smith observed that mainstream sociological "concepts and frameworks do not work because they have already posited a subject situated outside a local and actual experience ... [People] are readily made the objects of sociological study precisely because they have not been its subjects. Beneath the apparent gender neutrality of the impersonal or absent subject of an objective sociology is the reality of the [White, straight, able-bodied] masculine author of the texts of its tradition" (D.E. Smith, 1987, p. 109). Similarly, in *Black Skin, White Masks*, Frantz Fanon traverses the dominant forms of knowledge of his time to show us how this knowledge – produced by White Europeans in the context of imperialism, colonialism, and global capitalism – defined the world and his experiences as a Black man in it. Fanon (2008) writes of the experience of being produced as an object of medical curiosity, intellectual analysis, and economic exploitation:

"Look! A Negro!"

I came into this world anxious to uncover the meaning of things, my soul desirous to be at the origin of the world, and here I am an object among other objects.

Locked in this suffocating reification, I appealed to the Other so that his liberating gaze, gliding over my body suddenly smoothed of rough edges, would give me back the lightness of being I thought I had lost, and taking me out of the world put me back in the world. But just as I get to the other slope I stumble, and the Other fixes me with his gaze, his gestures and attitude, the same way you fix a preparation with a dye. I lose my temper, demand an explanation ... Nothing doing. I explode. (p. 89)

Like Marx and like D.E. Smith, Fanon wants a social method to "uncover the meaning of things," to bring into visibility the social processes through which his subjugation is organized. His efforts to reconstitute himself as a subject – as a knower of his own life and experiences – meet the vast bodies of intellectual work spanning disciplines that "fix" Fanon like a "preparation with a dye."

Fanon analyses what Aimé Césaire calls thingification and what Marx calls ideology – that is, the social processes through which objectified forms of consciousness are (re)produced. Fanon vacillates between the material world where he experiences his blackness – listening to the child on the train, crying, "Look! A Negro!" – and the bodies of knowledge whereby processes of racialization operate. Fanon shows how every attempt to "make himself known" hits up against a "history that others have fabricated for" him. Both his knowing of himself and his efforts to communicate what he knows are mediated by an objectified knowledge about the Black man, already produced, circulating, and exerting its organizing effects on thought and conduct: "The white gaze, the only valid one, is already dissecting me. I am *fixed*. Once their microtomes are sharpened, the whites objectively cut sections of my reality" (Fanon, 2008, p. 95).

The processes of objectification that Fanon points to require the disarticulation of his embodied life and experiences into discrete sections – preparations that can be fixed on a slide to enable scientific study. Fanon moves systematically through various bodies of knowledge, showing how thoroughly White scholars have determined the parameters for knowing race. None of which have been built from experience. As part of his archeological study, he includes the work of Césaire and other Black artists and intellectuals associated with the Negritude movement. He also engages with the White European establishment's critique of Negritude, showing just what Black intellectuals were up against in generating of a body of knowledge that attended to what Black people know and have experienced and that challenged the dominance of the knowledge produced about – and to objectify – blackness. Fanon observes, "At the very moment when I endeavoured to grasp my being, Sartre, who remains 'the Other,' by naming me shattered my last illusion ... While I, in a paroxysm of experience and rage, was proclaiming this, he reminded me that my negritude was nothing but a weak stage"(Fanon, 2008, p. 116). Not only did scholars and political leaders refrain from challenging the violence of colonialism in the way that they protested – cried out against – the violence of anti-Semitism associated with Hitler, no one (and this is Fanon's point) grasped the magnitude of damage experienced by people whose histories have been written for them by others. Processes of "thingification" – ideological proceedings of abstraction, central to bureaucratic forms of rule – have also been central to the conjoined social and economic practices described as colonialism and capitalism. The institutionalization of these knowledges through various academic disciplines; professional discourses; and actions, treaties, policies, and laws was essential to their legitimation, reach, and efficacy.

In Césaire's (1972) poetic indictment of colonialism, he calls out the vast network of social practices through which colonialism operates. Here, Césaire names as responsible the people whose labour is implicated in the production and dissemination of the ideological knowledges that solidify colonialism and capitalism: "Therefore, comrade, you will hold as enemies – loftily, lucidly, consistently – not only sadistic governors and greedy bankers, not only prefects who torture and colonists who flog, not only corrupt, check-licking politicians and subservient judges, but likewise and for the same reason, venomous journalists, goitrous academics, wreathed in dollars and stupidity, ethnographers who go in for metaphysics, presumptuous Belgian theologians, chattering intellectuals born stinking out of the thigh of Nietzsche" (Césaire, 1972, p. 54). Knowledge is produced and used by people. Its production and use are *part of people's labour*, directly and indirectly hooking them into relations of capital and exchange. Colonialism has been and remains a central feature of capitalism, connected to – and enabled by – objectified modes of thought produced and circulated by academics. It is a system that is drawn into and coordinates myriad institutional and political processes.

Objectified knowledge about and classifications of people enable and legitimize methods of managing a population through the bureaucratic organization of the public sphere. The characteristic principle of bureaucracy is "the abstract regularity of the execution of authority, which is a result of the demand for 'equality before the law' in the personal and functional sense – hence, of the horror of 'privilege,' and the principled rejection of doing business from 'case to case'" (Weber, 1993, p. 116). Bureaucratic forms of state organization were developed to level social and economic difference (Weber, 1993). But bureaucratic organization depends on general principles and standards, which are unable to reflect the varied needs and interests of actual people. Marx argues that the "modern State makes abstraction of real men or only satisfies the whole of man in an imaginary manner" (2010, p. 11). Abstractions and generalities, encoded in law and other institutional processes, allow states to administer the lives of real people living at particular moments in time, and with particular needs, desires, and experiences as though none of these particularities matter. For Marx, this means the state is only able to satisfy "the whole of man in an imaginary manner." When viewed from an anticolonial perspective, it is clear that these same processes of abstraction legitimize genocide and violent forms of colonial rule.

The legitimization of rule through bureaucratic forms of institutional organization, accounting mechanisms, policy, and law represent ongoing social processes, evolving across time and space. For example, Edward Said's (1979) work illuminates how the emergence of Orientalism as a discipline and a body of art and thought was key to the social processes through which the invasion and occupation of

Egypt was legitimized: "The Napoleonic invasion of Egypt in 1798, an invasion which was in many ways the very model of a truly scientific appropriation of one culture by another, apparently stronger one … [it] provided a scene or setting for Orientalism, since Egypt and subsequently the other Islamic lands were viewed as the live province, the laboratory, the theater of effective Western knowledge about the Orient" (1979, pp. 42–3). Said goes on to trace out the emergence and solidification of Orientalism as a distinctive disciplinary paradigm within the humanities and social sciences, which intersected with and was expanded by other dominant fields of thought at the time. Ultimately, Orientalism became a discipline unto itself, with its own "'paradigms' of research, its own learned societies, its own establishment" (1979, p. 43). This institutionalizing process led to a growth in professorships in a field titled "Oriental Studies" and, consequently, a surge in texts produced from these experts in the field. What's more, avenues for disseminating this disciplinary knowledge across time and space intensified (e.g., via classrooms, journals, conferences). As the discipline expanded and grew, conceptual categories were developed and used to stand in for actual people and the particularities of their lives. Through extended use, the conceptual frames developed and promulgated within the discipline became *the* interpretive devices whereby all people construed as members of this identity category were classified.

Said maps how over time and use, the concepts – and the relations they express – took on a static quality. The bluntness of these categorical sense-making practices led towards the types of polarizing Manichean analyses that Fanon observed and critiqued. Said notes: "When one uses categories like Oriental and Western as both the starting and the end points of analysis, research, public policy … the result is usually to polarize the distinction – the Oriental becomes more Oriental, the Westerner more Western" (1979). In the (1979) foreword of the twenty-fifth anniversary edition, he draws parallels between the discursive techniques used to rationalize and organize the colonial occupation of Egypt and people's participation in discursive constructions of the (Oriental) Other elsewhere and for other purposes; for example, the rationalization of foreign occupations, as well as the production and imposition of laws and policies internally (the recent travel bans in the United States, the banning of the Burka in France, and the proposed ban of religious symbols [e.g., the Hijab] among public servants in Quebec, Canada). Of contemporary policies, military actions, and the insurgence of academic tomes on "Islamic fundamentalism and American foreign policy" (p. xxi), Said observes that the textual construction of the Orient in opposition to the West remains an essential social political move: "Without a well-organized sense that these people over there were not like 'us' and didn't appreciate 'our' values … there would have been no war." As much as state-sanctioned violence is about commodities (land, resources), exploitative international relations also depend on ideological productions of "the Other" and "us," against which an array of institutional policies and other forms of institutionally organized action operate. Processes of alienation and abstraction are requisite for the construction and enforcement of policy and law, as well as acts of state violence.

Conclusion: A Feminist Method of Inquiry

In D.E. Smith's efforts to understand how the sociological tools of her training failed to produce a knowledge that was useful to women, she points her readers toward the "problem of the concealed standpoint" in academic and other forms of writing. But unlike any of the other people whose ideas are explored in this chapter, D.E. Smith provides both a theorizing of the erasure of women's knowledge and experiences from sociological discourse *and* a method of inquiry, which might allow us to begin to find out how our lives have been organized such that we live them as we do. She proposes standpoint as a method for re-establishing the absent subject of sociological discourse, "to be filled with the presence and spoken experience of actual women speaking of and in the actualities of their everyday worlds" (1987, p. 107). This invitation for people to speak "of and in the actualities of their everyday worlds" is to be the *starting place* for interrogation, rather than the final research product that one seeks to produce. The work of social scientists cannot be to make generalities that reflect different experiential realities of artificially constructed groups (e.g., homeless youth); rather, our work is to produce from people's actual experiences an analysis that might be useful in helping them live the lives they need and want. Our "business" as social scientists (D.E. Smith, 1987, p. 110) is to produce an account of social life that is not visible from the grounds of experience alone. Otherwise, we are not offering people more or other than what they already know. Our ethical and intellectual responsibilities as social scientists demand that we produce knowledge that will improve the conditions of our interconnected lives. To meet this demand, Smith proposes an examination that begins "where actual people are in their own lives, activities and experiences to open up relations and organization that are, in a sense, actually *present* in them but are not observable" (D.E. Smith, 2006, p. 4). The aim – in beginning in this way – is to discover how the things we experience in our everyday lives are connected to and shaped by extended social relations, which transcend and connect individual experiences across time and space.

In the beginning of the *Criticism of Hegelian Philosophy of Right*, Marx observes: "Man is no abstract being, squatting outside the world. Man is the world of men, the State, society" (Marx & O'Malley, 1970). Rather than creating and testing theoretical generalities that arise from and are meant to represent actual people's experiences, Marx proposes that analysis remain on the ground, so to speak, in the "actual situations" of people's lives. Where "the Idea is made subject, then the real subjects ... become unreal, and take on the different meaning of objective moments of the Idea" (Marx & O'Malley, 1970). Earlier, I talked about ideology and ideological processes of abstraction; this is the process that Marx draws our attention to here. In producing an abstract account, the actual social relations about which one writes are subsumed in – that is, they become substantiating examples for – the general explanations. Coupling this insight with Marx's observation that the bureaucratic forms of rule (what he called bourgeoisie forms of rule) depend on these processes of abstraction, which allow for the presentation of the interests of a particular group to stand in for the interests of all, one sees traces of the thinking that inspired the theorists whose contributions have been the focus of this chapter.

Chapter Two

Participatory Institutional Ethnographies of the State

Like all projects, this one begins somewhere. This project begins in a community organization in a Toronto neighbourhood – a neighbourhood that has received considerable negative media and institutional attention for being dangerous. It begins here for no other reason than it is where I was working when the project started to come together in my mind and in the minds of my collaborators. Halfway through the research in Toronto, I got a job at McGill and so I moved with my family to Montreal. In Montreal, I began a new project with new collaborators and another community partner organization. The project in Montreal is not an extension of the project in Toronto. The projects followed different research designs and were shaped by the insights of different collaborators and different groups of youth researchers. But both projects are institutional ethnographies, and the second project builds from the process and research outcomes of the first. In both, the objects of investigation are the institutions shaping the lives and experiences of youth living in large urban centres. I bring the two studies together in this single volume in order to more clearly reveal the racializing, classing, and gendering effects of the disproportionate distribution of public sector resources and punishments in Canadian cities. Young people's diverse stories of their institutional work and the divergent research interests of youth researchers expose how public institutions differently enter into and shape young people's lives.

In Toronto, for example, the research began with and remained attentive to the knowledge and experiences of the largely Black young men and women, from the city's designated "vulnerable neighbourhoods" learning on the very fringes of the education system. These were youth transitioning between Section 23 programs in open and closed custody facilities and in Safe Schools alternative education programs. Their institutional work differed considerably from the largely White young men and women going to school at McGill University. This finding is of course unsurprising given the role the Canadian state has always played in the norming and privileging of White, middle-class, straight bodies (Maynard, 2017). Young people's own stories, though, help to explain the mechanisms through which the same social processes produce the various inclusionary and exclusionary conditions of young people's lives.

Project One: Schools, Safety, and the Urban Neighbourhood

When colleagues and I designed Schools, Safety, and the Urban Neighbourhood, I was a new PhD, cobbling together full-time work as a research associate on several research projects – all of which shaped the direction of Schools and Safety. One of the projects was a knowledge exchange initiative co-led by Alison Griffith (my former doctoral supervisor), and the other was a complex community-academic research partnership led by Uzo Anucha. Both Alison and Uzo were York University professors at the time. Alison's project allowed me to work with, and learn from, Safe Schools educators working in Long-Term Suspension and Expulsion programs across the Greater Toronto Area (GTA). The project combined research on the social organization of school discipline (grounded in conversations with educators, youth workers, social workers, psychologists, and administrators working in Long-Term Suspension and Expulsion programs across three school boards) with opportunities to convene and learn about what everyone was doing in these small, generally disconnected learning environments on the margins of the mainstream educational system. This opportunity for people to gather and share – and hear from us what we had been learning from them about how their work is organized – was important. As this book reveals, the programmatic landscape of Safe Schools programs – and alternative and adult education more broadly – makes it difficult to coordinate and implement meaningful professional learning and sharing opportunities.

People working in alternative education sites are often working off-site from mainstream schools and may be one of only two people on staff in the building. In small towns, the educators responsible for teaching students completing long-term suspensions and expulsions often end up working in libraries and coffee shops with small groups of young people to progress through independent learning courses. As such, there is little opportunity for ongoing collegial sharing of promising pedagogical practices, identification of common struggles, or possible solutions. Based on my work on this other project, I developed relationships with some of the Safe Schools administrators and a growing understanding of the complexity of the policy and programmatic landscape, which shape Safe Schools sites. The more I learned about how Safe Schools programs were legislated and how they operated as part of a larger educational response to school climate and risk mediation, the more curious I became about the implementation and oversight of educational interventions for students who were seen to threaten school safety. Based on the research I had done with young people who were experiencing homelessness (Nichols, 2014), I knew that the classroom experiences of youth implicated in multiple institutional interventions would be shaped by an array of social relations that educators and educational researchers could not see from where we were positioned within the institutional frames and relevancies of public education. If we started an investigation of school safety with what young people knew, I suspected that we might learn something new and useful about the social relations coordinating schools' responses to safety and how these differentially (dis)advantage youth in schools.

The other project that was pivotal to Schools and Safety was the community-based youth participatory action research (YPAR) project that Uzo was leading: Assets Coming Together (ACT) for Youth. Participating on this community-university partnership was the first time I had seen a YPAR project in action, and as a former teacher and outdoor educator I relished an opportunity to spend more time learning with young people again. In this second project I had two roles, which shaped Schools and Safety. The first was to analyse the data from an internal evaluation of the project and bring a report to the group for reflection. As I combed through the qualitative data to evaluate whether the community-university partnership had an equitable process, I could see that it was important that academic members of the team were perceived to be accessible and active on the ground in the settings where the research was taking place. It was also clear that young people wanted opportunities to contribute to changes in their own lives and communities and saw projects like this one as offering avenues through which they could contribute to the kinds of changes they wanted to see. But young people – like everyone else who contributes to a collaboration – needed to see how their individual expectations, experiences, and knowledges were being incorporated into and guiding the research and action processes as these were unfolding. The ACT for Youth evaluation results suggested that facilitated opportunities for learning and engagement throughout a project strengthen people's commitment to a collaborative process and promote mutually desirable community changes (Nichols, Anucha, Houwer, & Wood, 2013).

The second role I had on ACT for Youth was to lead a participatory "social impacts" evaluation of a community youth organization – an organization that I refer to in this book as Rosewood. As part of this process, I developed and implemented qualitative research and evaluation training for three youth researchers, and – under the guidance of a community advisory body – we designed and implemented an evaluation of the "social impacts" that the organization could claim it contributes to in the neighbourhood and the outcomes it creates for the young people who participated in its programs. The three youth researchers and I coconducted a series of focus group discussions with various stakeholders who had a stake in Rosewood's activities: young people who had participated in the Safe Schools alternative education program (the Assessment and Support program on-site at Rosewood), young people who participated in the studio arts program, educators from the school board, community leaders, current and former staff, and mothers who had historically participated in a group for parents with children in Safe Schools programs.

This was the first time I led a participatory research process, and I learned important things about how these exercises unfold. Two of the youth coresearchers were chosen by the community organization, while the third was completing a voluntary university service-learning experience. For the two who were being paid, this research job constituted their first paid work opportunity within the taxable economy. At the time, I failed to recognize the practical significance of this. I remember showing up to Rosewood one day to be greeted by a very angry young woman, demanding to be paid for her work. I had failed to explain how payroll and university accounting processes work – particularly that there is an initial lag between the work itself and the receipt of your first pay cheque. Having participated in the formal economy since I was sixteen years old, myself, and having gleaned some awareness of how these processes work from watching my parents do so, it hadn't occurred to me to explain the conventions. Now, the payroll conversation is one of the first discussions I have with new youth researchers – and we usually have it again throughout a project – to make sure that these processes are transparent. The work of making things navigable to everyone involved is ongoing in participatory research projects, as we begin to enter into and learn about one another's lives. Facilitated opportunities to think, engage in dialogue, and ask questions can change how we understand each other's lives and experiences. As such, the research process itself, if learning is a shared goal, can be transformative for all participants – be they youth or adult researchers, community professionals, or graduate students.

As participants in a research process, young people pose rather than simply respond to interview questions. During the evaluation, my coresearchers offered insights and asked probing questions in focus group discussions that deepened the conversation and held people – particularly adults – accountable in ways that I would not have been able to do. When the research is about how well institutions are bringing positive changes to young people's lives, it is important to have young people at the table coming up with and asking the difficult questions. Of course, like all social processes, participatory research can also be silencing and oppressive. In this chapter, I seek to elucidate what I have experienced that seems to work as well as places where things fell apart. One thing that works for me is to create a program of research that is continuously building from what I'm learning through the research itself. A humble and inquisitive stance is central to this approach; this attitude requires one to be an active listener and learner, rather than an expert. Sincere interest in and curiosity about people's lives and experiences is important, as is the conviction that there is something more to be discovered than what people can tell you, based on their own experiences.

The content of the focus group conversations we held directly influenced the project that York University professors Alison, Uzo, and I would go on to propose. It was during one of these focus group conversations where the first layer of the problematic we would go on to investigate came into view. During the focus group with school board staff, I was surprised to hear people at the table suggest that the school system worked for 98 per cent of Toronto's youth. They observed that a minority of youth experienced difficulties with achievement and discipline, and as such, they went on to reason, the issues were individuated rather than systemic. During a subsequent focus group discussion, a leader of a community youth arts initiative articulated her concern that conversations at community safety tables constructed an us-them distinction between the community and a minority of dangerous youth, citing the same statistic that I had encountered during the earlier discussion. Her efforts to advocate for young people's safety and inclusion in the aftermath of recent police raids was met with pushback from people she described as the "higher-ups on the table." Much like they did in the focus group I'd conducted the week prior, the "higher-ups" argued that the young people swept up in the raid represented only 2 per cent of the school population; therefore, they posited, when 98 per cent of students are doing what the school requires, the remaining 2 per cent don't warrant the school board's attention. As she reflected on this experience, she recalled that she and her colleagues had been described as *thug huggers* – a racially coded term that implies she and her colleagues care about the wrong group of people.

As I listened to and participated in these conversations, and thought back to the work Alison and I had done with Safe Schools educators across the GTA, I began to catch glimpses of a world of activity – just outside of my direct field of view – influencing Rosewood's efforts to generate what its funders described as "social impacts." These included Safe Schools educators' tireless work to support "sustained transitions" to mainstream school for their students and young people's experiences of inclusion and success in schools – what schools describe as "student success." Across institutional settings, investigative processes, metrics, and scales, calculative procedures and policies were used to designate people and places as unsafe or at risk. These designations acted like on-switches for a range of institutional processes. For example, these designations allowed principals and Safe Schools coordinators to move young people from school program to school program, across the GTA. They were also part of a larger complex of institutional activity, which made it difficult for community advocates to persuade their public-sector colleagues (e.g., people who work in community housing, policing, and education) that the safety and inclusion of *all* young people (even "thugs") mattered. As I paid more attention to the ways discourses of safety and risk were operationalized in the context of larger programs of institutional action meant to create school and community safety, I began to wonder whether the various interventions we had devised to produce and manage safety as an institutional and policy phenomenon were implicated in (re)producing and obscuring the interconnected conditions of exclusion that shape the material conditions (e.g., isolation, poverty, racism, and perceptions of systematic unfairness) most commonly associated with youth violence (Wortley & Owusu-Bempah, 2011). Schools, Safety, and the Urban Neighbourhood was born out of this suspicion.

To write the proposal for this project, we engaged in a number of ideational conversations with community youth workers and community leaders at Rosewood and at the university. Each time, we brought forward questions and ideas, received and incorporated people's feedback – not all of which was positive. I remember one woman – a doctoral student and the former executive director of an alternative education site in the neighbourhood where the research took place – telling us that this project wouldn't make a difference. At the time, I was frustrated by her lack of hope. Now, I better understand the magnitude of what we are up against, and I recognize that our different orientations to the possibilities of a project like this one reflects our own raced, classed, and gendered experiences of the world. This former doctoral student is a Black woman who had spent her life working in a Black neighbourhood, one that historically and continually bore the brunt of systemic anti-Black racism in the form of intersecting punitive immigration, policing, educational, and child protection policies (Maynard, 2017). I, on the other hand, am a White woman from a small town outside the city. My optimism reflected my thirty plus years of experience growing up and working in institutions normed by and for people like me; her scepticism, however, reflected her own thirty plus years of experience growing up and working in these same institutions. In fact, having spent some time at Rosewood early in 2018, I was dismayed to learn from staff that young people in the neighbourhood are experiencing more educational marginalization than ever, including more violence in one of the main secondary schools, school principals actively conveying to youth workers that they are simply waiting for young people to age out of the system, fewer board-supported opportunities for alternative education, and more youth being sent OT (out of town) to work in the drug trade in other cities. The research we did together has not yet contributed to positive systemic changes for youth in this neighbourhood.

I hold on to the memory of these conversations as a reminder to be humble and truthful about who research usually benefits – namely, not the communities that are its focus. Surprisingly, perhaps, none of these grounding reminders inspire me to quit. Quite the opposite, I see social action – in the many and varied forms this will take – as the only way forward. One project won't make a difference. But I am inspired by the many people I know who are participating in multiple and diverse initiatives to directly improve the material conditions of people's lives, cultivate dialogue, demonstrate solidarity, and directly oppose exploitation and oppression at various levels of social organization – surely *this* work makes a difference. Particularly as this research has revealed the limitations of state-led interventions as a mechanism for destabilizing status quo relations of access, inclusion, dispossession, and dislocation, small targeted collective approaches to research and action strike me as one of the only just ways forward.

Project Two: Sampling Youth Development

Within months of having moved to Montreal, I was invited to join the board of a youth organization (Chalet Parc) in the city's most densely populated racially, linguistically, and ethnically diverse neighbourhood. Like the neighbourhood in Toronto, this one is also home to a university, but unlike the Toronto locale (especially at the time of the research), it is well-connected to other parts of the city via a comprehensive public transit system. Sampling Youth Development originated in response to concerns young people brought forward to the director of Chalet Parc about experiences of overt and implicit racial discrimination at school. The project emerged out of a series of conversations between me; a McGill colleague, Professor Jessica Ruglis; and different groups of young people who participate in the organization's studio arts program. The conversations began with an invitation to talk about people's experiences going to school in Montreal. Talking with people about the actual conditions of their lives – that is, the things that they have experienced and that concern and/or inspire them – is central to community organizing efforts (Warren & Mapp, 2011). Moreover, it is the backbone of institutional ethnographic ways of working (D.E. Smith, 2005). People's actual lives and experiences – not theorizations of youth development – always constitute the starting place for a project.

In our case, as we were learning, we took notes – using notebooks and chart paper – that were accessible to anyone who was sitting at the table. The notes served as an important reflexive guide. Jessica and I shared a big black notebook, and the youth also each had their own notebooks. Two musicians and youth workers (Jakarius and Malik) also participated in these weekly sessions, as part of their work to coordinate the studio arts program at the youth organization. Each week when we met, we would summarize the main points of the discussion from the week before in order to check that we had accurately captured what we'd discussed. Sometimes the young people shared insights and song lyrics they recorded in their personal journals in between meetings. From here, we would ask people to reflect and move the conversations forward using prompts like, "What has happened (in the world and in our lives) since our last meeting that we should all know about/ consider?" and "Where does the conversation/work need to go next?" Talking with people in the ways that we describe here does not represent formal data collection. Rather, these grounding conversations ultimately comprise the foundation for research we will go on do together (DeVault & McCoy, 2006; McCoy, 2006; D.E. Smith, 2005).

For young people who have had racist and racializing experiences in school, who have experienced or witnessed discriminatory treatment, or who have had experiences in school that promoted a feeling of discomfort or disquiet, these conversations are also important opportunities to see personal experiences as connected to – and reflecting – social and institutional relations shaping the provision and management of public schooling more broadly. That is, in conversation with adult allies (e.g., community youth workers, artists, and researchers), as well as in conversation with one another, young people develop and experiment with new vocabularies and theoretical insights for identifying and interpreting structural forces that shape how individual experiences unfold.

For our team, these general conversations quickly began to gather focus. And a single group of five young people began meeting biweekly and then weekly with community youth workers / artists, researchers, and graduate students to deepen our collaborative analysis of the social and institutional relations that influence how young people group up. We proposed that our work together serve two purposes: inspire artistic production and a new research proposal. To provide a framework for thinking and dialogue, and to move us towards our two objectives, we engaged in artful approaches to critical social analysis. Inspired by the use of found poetry techniques to work with and analyse interview data (Butler-Kisber, 2010), we designed opportunities for our intergenerational team to examine the world using the content of our earlier conversations. We curated a collection of words and phrases from various print media sources – for example, McGill student newspapers, fashion magazines, the *Montreal Gazette*, and old conference program listings – to create found poetry. In an attempt to relay what found poetry is to the group, one young person drew a comparison to music making practices: "It's like sampling," they said, the practice of taking small clips of songs, vocals, beats, or instrumentals and using them to create a new song or recording. We all (adults and youth) worked on creating poems together, using images and words and sharing what we were working on as the night wore on.

In a subsequent week, we invited young people to read through blinded interview transcripts from Schools and Safety and talk about what stood out for them. Participants read silently, pausing from time to time to read something out loud to the group for people to think about and discuss. These became opportunities for me to talk about findings from this first project and for my colleague Jessica and me to teach key research terms, principles, and techniques (e.g., what is an interview and why does one do it) to the group. The next time we met, we brought more transcripts, glue, and scissors, and young people were invited to cut these up and experiment with creating lyrical poetry out of the written copy of the anonymized interviews with youth in Toronto.

As the weeks progressed, encouraged by one of their adult artist-mentors from the studio program, the young people also performed the poetry and songs they'd been working on, and we would talk about these creations as a group as well. People brought music and videos to share with the group, and we explored other interesting arts- and research-informed projects happening in the world. One evening, as we sat quietly reading transcripts, artist-mentor Malik jumped up and asked whether people wanted to listen to music. The transcript he was reading was reminding him of Kendrick Lamar's new album, and he thought we should listen. When I admitted I hadn't heard it yet, I was promptly told by one of the younger artists that I was a "lacker" and then given explicit instructions to listen to the entire album twice, without interruption, to let the magnitude of what the artist had done sink in. Against this backdrop of informal knowledge exchange, we talked about what it was we wanted to do together. One night someone asked, "Is *this* a project?" and another person responded, "Let's call it a mixed tape." In this case, the "project" in question ("Is *this* a project?") is musical in nature – as in, Are we producing an album out of this work we are doing? The answer ("Let's call it a mix tape") was suggested to enable us to carve out a number of distinct – but connected – smaller projects that we could work on as a collective. Each week we met, we spent part of our time together engaged in ideational work – brainstorming possibilities for collective enterprises. Many of these brainstorms, and the early stages of research ideation, were captured on scraps of paper, notebooks, and chart paper. Ultimately, these all became resources by which we designed our research.

After a few months of these meetings, we moved energetically into conceiving a participatory research project and ultimately into proposal writing. This action constituted a shift in our collective work. We began by looking at other research tools (e.g., large-scale survey instruments) that had been developed and are commonly used in research about youth development. As a group we reviewed these tools, discussed, and unpacked them together. Young people candidly revealed that any survey research distributed in and through schools is met with considerable scepticism by them. They and their friends would not, for example, accurately answer questions about their substance use or sexual, mental, or physical health practices despite researcher assurances that survey data would not be linked to individuals. The fact that the surveys were administered in schools, by school administration and teachers whom they did not trust, undermined their faith in the instruments and meant they did not complete the questionnaires in good faith. This review and discussion about survey tools led to a discussion of the utility and validity of youth survey research, considering that many policies related to youth health and development are constructed by way of research that is conducted in schools. In light of these conversations, our research design began to emerge. We decided that youth-to-youth anonymous interviews would be central to our methodology.

We talked about how to ask research questions and began working on developing queries ourselves.

Not all of this work was done collaboratively. Just like people worked on music, writing, and video projects on their own and in small groups, bringing their work into the larger groups to share and discuss, on many occasions, McGill Professor Jessica Ruglis (the study colead) and I would take the chart papers and black notebook back to our offices in order to transform the emerging ideas, questions, and concerns of the group into the beginnings of a research design. During the formalizing research design phase, we would bring draft research questions and instruments back to the group for feedback, returning later to our computers to continue to try to stitch all the pieces together. This occasion was the first time Jessica and I had sought to bring our own programs of research into alignment. Further, the entirety of our work had to be brought together within the parameters of the Research Ethics Board review process. This dialogic and constructive proceeding took considerable time and energy. Traces of early conversations found their way into the project title – Sampling Youth Development (a play on the concept of sampling in music and in research) – and into our first two panel presentations at academic conferences (we titled the panel "Let's call it a mixed tape"). The concepts of sampling and mixing resonated with our desire to use a range of data collection methods to generate samples of the developmental contexts shaping how young people grow up.

Research Participants

Aligned with the principles of youth participatory action research (YPAR) methodologies (Kirshner, 2010), young people in both projects participated in study design, data collection, analysis, and dissemination. For these two studies, young people were defined as anyone between the ages of fifteen and twenty-nine years of age (Gaetz, 2014). In the first project, all of the youth researchers, as well as most interview participants, lived or hung out in the neighbourhood where this research took place. In the second project, the youth researchers lived in a number of different Montreal boroughs. During the street interviews in the second project, we deliberately attempted to speak with youth from a number of the city's communities – seeking out interviewees at subway entrances, parks, and on campuses. None of the youth we were working with spoke French very well (if at all), so interviews with French-speaking youth were often conducted by French-speaking graduate students, most of whom also fell within the age range used to delineate youth as a research category for these projects.

In both projects, the research teams were comprised of a mix of graduate students, community professionals, youth, and university professors. Of the nineteen young people who participated as youth researchers over the term of these two projects, fifteen identified racially as Black, two as White, and two as Asian. Seven are women, and twelve are men. All are cis-gendered, and none of the youth identified as LGBTQI*. A number of graduate students have been peripherally involved in these projects (e.g., doing background research on policy and organizational mapping), and a smaller number (n = 10) have been actively involved in the project for years at a time, working in the field with me, the youth researchers, and my professor colleagues. The projects span enough years that some of these team members have graduated (notably Jessica Braimoh, Alison Fisher, and Camisha Sibblis, who are now done their PhDs or are "all but dissertation," and Stephanie Mazerolle, who finished her MA in 2016 and has worked as a community collaborator at Rosewood ever since). Most graduate students (six) identified as White, two as Black, one as Brown, and one as Asian. Three of these graduate students were cis-gendered men and nine were cis-gendered women. Three graduate students identified as LGBTQI*. We also worked closely with a range of community professionals (e.g., youth workers, executive directors) at Rosewood and Chalet Parc, and only two of these people are White. I am a White woman, and one of my professor colleagues is a Black woman and the other two are White women. We are all cis-gendered, and three of us are straight. I include these categorical descriptions for the sake of transparency and because they matter to a central argument I'm making in this book: studies of social organization can reveal how complexes of institutional activity produce the range of experiences people have.

Philip Howard (2006) refers to the interrelations of experience as "the juxtaposed surfaces of the same wrinkled fabric. The valleys in the one side of the cloth are the mountain peaks on the other." I describe the research team categorically here not because these classifications comprised the starting place (or the explanations) for this research, but because the same social grounds that produce the experiences of racial profiling among the youth research team in Toronto shaped my own lack of interactivity with the police in all facets of my life. While our embodied experiences are in marked opposition, we are connected by the grounds that shape them.

In Toronto, over two and a half years of field research, we interviewed fewer than five individuals who described themselves as White. The Toronto District School Board school census indicates that the highest numbers of Black students live in the Neighbourhood Improvement

Areas (NIAs) where the research takes place, as well as those nearby (TDSB Census Report, 2011). NIA designations are themselves established using fifteen indicators adapted from the "Urban Health Equity Assessment and Response Tool" (Urban HEART), which measure health equity across the following five domains: (1) physical environment and infrastructure, (2) social and human development, (3) economic opportunity, (4) governance, and (5) general population health. Economic opportunity indicators tracked by the Urban HEART tool (including unemployment, low-income, and social assistance usage rates) suggest low-levels of economic opportunity across the adjacent NIAs where this research occurred. Many research participants lived in social housing, and most youth suggested that "a little money in their pockets" would make life easier.

Between 2014 and 2015, we interviewed sixty-three youth for Schools and Safety. Of the sixty-three interviews conducted with young people, forty-eight were with young people who live, work, and/or attend school in one of four adjacent NIAs, including the one where Rosewood, our community-partner organization, is located. We also interviewed young men (n = 15) detained or serving sentences at a youth justice facility outside of Toronto. Beyond this, we interviewed and/or engaged in focus groups with forty-eight professionals who work with youth. For two and a half years, the research team spent between one to five days per week in the field. Part of this time was directly oriented to data collection and analysis; part of it was dedicated to fostering reflexive learning and critical socio-political analytic processes among youth and adult participants (Cammarota & Ginwright, 2007; Ginwright & Cammarota, 2002; Ginwright, Cammarota, & Noguera, 2005; Krishner, Hipolito-Delgado, & Zion, 2015).

In Montreal, we deliberately recruited youth from all over the city to participate in interviews. As well as conducting more than sixty anonymous youth-to-youth street interviews across the city in the fall of 2016, we produced field notes, recorded sound samples of the public spaces where these interviews took place, and drew/photographed the visual contexts for each interview location. Youth interviewers were asked to invite their interviewees to reflect on the ways race, class, gender, sexuality, and/or ability shaped their responses to the questions they'd asked about safety, immigration, and so on. But when we began coding the transcripts in 2017, I noticed that this wasn't a question that most people asked during the street interviews, and so we don't have a consistently clear sense of the how young people we interviewed identified. During the street-interview phase of this project, interviewees were recruited very informally on the streets of Montreal and interviews took place on street corners and parks directly following the invitation to participate; this context does not lend itself to rapport building or in-depth probing.

While the street interviews were being conducted, Professor Jessica Ruglis and I met biweekly with the graduate student and youth researchers in the field to debrief the experience, but we did not – at that time – listen to the audio recordings. As such, we didn't realize that the data did not contain demographic information about participants until the following spring. The debrief meetings were used to enable ongoing reflexivity, critical social analysis, and planning, rather than fidelity to our field instruments. Indications of the ways experiences in the public sphere shape young people's gendered and racial identities thus appear inconsistently across our data. For example, a Black youth researcher pointedly asks another Black youth whether the police make them feel unsafe because of racism: "Is it like racism, do you think?" He is met with a single word answer: "Yes." It is clear in this interaction that race – as an objectified form of consciousness or shared interpretive schema – structures the way the researcher asks the question, the respondent's answer, and the way they both experience safety/ unsafety with the police. In other street survey transcripts, however, questions about identity are not posed by the youth researchers and are thus unlikely to surface in the ten-minute interview context. The street interview context may not have always been conducive to complicated conversations about identity – that is, how young people see themselves in relation to others and the institutions that they engage with in their lives.

As such, these relations were not always evident in interviews. At other times, they were brought into view by the research team themselves in the form of field notes and during the team debrief conversations. Jessica and I often developed specific prompts to guide the meeting discussions. We asked questions like: What is the most poignant, surprising, saddening, inspiring, or interesting story you've listened to so far in the field? What themes are you starting to notice across the stories you are listening to? What experiences have you had in the field that have taught you something or that have revealed something to you about the contexts of youth development? In response to the question about the contexts of youth development, our research team told us that the field work itself revealed the ways that our public systems interact with social relations of race, class, gender, sexuality, and ability to shape experiences. These discussions helped to illuminate the intersecting relations our research intended to reveal.

For example, after the first week of data collection at a popular metro station in a gentrified centrally located Montreal neighbourhood, a graduate student told the group that within fifteen minutes of being there, "police were circling the metro. A group of young Black men were listening to music, and the police were waiting for them to do anything. There were about a million cigarettes on the ground, but as soon as one of the youth flicked a cigarette, the cops descended." After the police left the area, the graduate student talked to the young man; he said that he's at this station every day and sees interactions like this regularly. The biweekly debrief conversations also allowed people to talk about how challenging the street can be as a context for interviewing, particularly in a bilingual French and English context. During one of these meetings, another graduate noted that the week prior, she and her team had had only two successful interviews all week: "We were curbed. Depending on where your head is at in life, this [rejection] can be tiring and isolating."

In addition to the short anonymous street interviews, we also conducted twenty-seven in-depth interviews and two focus group discussions with groups of youth. One focus group took place at a community organization serving young people seeking employment (n = 7) and another with a small group (n = 3) of newly arrived refugee youth living in a Maison des jeunesse (i.e., subsidized housing for youth experiencing housing precarity or homelessness). Young people were recruited with the goal of maximizing the diversity of our respondents. We actively sought to interview racial, gender, and sexual minority and majority youth; youth with varying levels of education; and youth from different neighbourhoods in the city. In addition, we conducted five pilot interviews and a focus group debrief at the end of the first summer institute (in 2016) with our youth research term. The in-depth interviews were conducted during the winter, spring, summer, and fall of 2017, with a few final interviews occurring in the winter of 2018.

Methods

Fieldwork for both projects involved extensive participant observation and ongoing reflexive analysis, which guided our efforts to refocus the research. In the first project, for example, older youth researchers (post-secondary, school-aged) volunteered as mentor-tutors in a Safe Schools program, cofacilitated workshops on research and critical issues with the adult researchers on the project, and participated in community events (e.g., community dialogues regarding police practices in the neighbourhood). Fieldwork also involved institutional outreach, in-depth interviewing, and focus group facilitation. I did much more institutional outreach in Toronto, where I speak the dominant language. I met with people who work in programs for young people involved in youth justice and Safe Schools processes to learn how their work was organized. These were not formal interviews; rather, these experiences constitute what institutional ethnographers call "talking with people" (DeVault & McCoy, 2006), which is essential to learning how institutional processes and/or settings works. Formal interviews and focus groups for both projects began with people's descriptions of their everyday work (in school, at home, in their places of employment), but these conversations ultimately sought to bring into view the co-ordered work activities that compose various organizational courses of action (e.g., school suspension and expulsion processes) (DeVault & McCoy, 2006).

Rather than use an interview schedule, we also organized formal interviews around a series of conversational prompts, which interviewers would invite people to speak about. Interviews were developed with the hope that people would discuss their experiences with different institutional processes, associated with (and linking) education, youth justice, housing, health, child welfare, policing, and urban neighbourhoods. In other words, interviews did not focus on young people, but on the public and institutional contexts that shape their lives – for example, schools, public transit, housing, policing, and health services. Even in the street interviews, which focused on a single institutional context (e.g., education), interviewers asked interviewees to consider the intersections between education and other institutional contexts (e.g., public transit and youth criminal justice). For each project, the youth researchers' own interests fundamentally guided the direction of the research.

For example, while Schools and Safety began with a desire to learn something new about community safety, Andy, the first youth researcher to join the project, immediately identified that young people don't talk about safety and would be unlikely to admit to feeling unsafe:

ANDY: Yeah, no one really comes out and says, "Oh man, I feel unsafe." You know, I think there's like a little bit of pride ... But I mean they would always talk about like, "Oh man, I saw two cruisers pulled up and I had to out quick, I had to run out quick," and "I had to move a different way because of this and because I had this on me, and blah-blah-blah." They're not expressing [feeling] unsafe or any fear, but it's more like those variables, those factors are out there ... And they will always be out there, no matter what. That's a definite. And it's always on their minds, as it is on mine, because I guess when you grow up in that type of environment, it's like sometimes say you're smoking or you're drinking outside, your mind is always still on six, like to keep six, you know?

NAOMI: What does that mean, "to keep six"?

ANDY: "To keep six" is like to always be on lookout in case police come or anything like that. So I mean like it's a constant thing, and I'm sure it's a constant thing with them too, like thinking like that. But I mean they never expressed any type of unsafeness to me. They tell me about cops who roughed them up and everything and treated them like dirt, but they've never expressed unsafeness.

As such, the conversational prompts we used did not explicitly address issues of safety; rather, we invited young people to talk about their experiences of institutional processes, associated with the production of community and school safety as institutional phenomena. As more youth researchers joined the project – many of whom were growing up working the streets in the neighbourhood where the research took place – their interest in understanding why the police were "always harassing them" shaped how the project evolved. In the end, we focused much more on relations between young people and the police than we initially envisioned doing. Because we were seeking to understand community safety from young people's standpoints, young people's experiences (e.g., being "roughed up" by the police) were understood in a new light (e.g., as promoting safety by preventing a young person being labelled a neighbourhood snitch). As we began to investigate and understand policing practices, it became clear that the police tactics to promote disclosures (e.g., telling young people their coaccused had "sung" on them or ratted them out) were conducted with knowledge of the norms guiding young people's actions on the streets (e.g., the abhorrence of snitching). Initially interviews with youth were coconducted by me and youth researchers or graduate students, as part of the training process and then later by youth researchers. Two of our youth researchers – Andy and Chantel – were in their twenties and worked with us all year. After considerable training, they cointerviewed with younger youth (eighteen years or younger) who were hired in the summers. Interviews and focus groups with adults were conducted by graduate students, me on my own, or in conjunction with a youth researcher.

Interviews with practitioners sought to reveal how their work with young people was organized: what policies and processes they used; what discourses they participated in; what other professionals they interacted with, why and how; what seemed to be working well for them; and what difficulties they encountered in their work. In the interviews and focus groups, we invited people to help us understand the material conditions of their lives, by asking them to provide us with detailed accounts of what they actually do, think, and say, rather than high-level abstract descriptions of their work. It was a common practice for us to check out our emerging understanding of a particular complex of institutional relations during an interview or focus group discussion. Because our aim was not to generalize about the people we interviewed, but to bring into view general processes that background and connect their work, we were transparent about our emerging understanding and the gaps in our knowledge with participants.

Other than fifteen interviews that we conducted with young people serving detentions or sentences in a youth justice facility, all other interviews and focus group discussions were audio recorded and transcribed verbatim. Due to institutional restrictions, we were unable to audio record the interviews with young people in jail. These interviews were live transcribed by two observing researchers, while a third researcher conducted the interview. Single versions of each interview were produced immediately after leaving the field each day by comparing and combining the transcripts. Each transcript was also reviewed for accuracy by the interviewer. It would have been ideal to have each interviewee review his transcript after we had had a chance to consolidate them. Unfortunately, we were not able to communicate directly with young people in the jail and sending the transcripts to them through the facilities staff would have undermined our commitment to confidentiality. Youth research assistant, Andy, conducted most of these interviews, while a graduate student and I transcribed; even still, the experience of being interviewed in jail, with two observer-transcribers frantically recording the content of the conversation, seemed to limit the degree to which some participants were comfortable sharing their experiences. In general, these interviews were shorter than the ones conducted in non-carceral settings.

In addition to interview and focus group data, we also collected and analysed policy, legislative, organizational, and media texts. Text data include policy, legislative, and institutional texts in the fields of education, housing, youth justice, child protection, and policing. In an institutional ethnography, texts (i.e., a reproducible and dispersible communicative media, such as a paper or digital document) are key to understanding how people's thoughts and actions are coordinated across time and space. Institutional ethnographers see texts as essential coordinators of ongoing courses of action, which allow researchers to trace from the local sites of listening, reading, writing (or typing), and watching to translocally organized systems of thought and classification whereby subjectivities are coordinated (D.E. Smith, 2005, 2006). The identification and investigation of key institutional texts and textually mediated social processes allows the researcher to move, analytically, from the grounds of experience into the textually mediated relations (the objectified forms of knowing and doing) that comprise the objects of one's analysis – the relations of ruling.

Analysis

The goal in analysing interview data for an institutional ethnography is to "make visible the ways the institutional order creates the conditions of individual experience" (McCoy, 2006, p. 109). As well as regularly speaking with people about what they were learning during interviews and focus groups, all interview and focus group data were coded using codes derived from our initial research questions, through ongoing conversation with the youth researchers, and arising from our collective engagement with the data themselves. Analytically, the coding directs the researcher's attention to particular aspects of an account that suggest the institutional organization within people's stories (McCoy, 2006). To achieve this analytic aim, the field research teams developed a range of "generous" codes that aimed to bring the work organization of a setting into view (e.g., emotion work, moving through space, making money, monitoring, and measuring) as well as to draw our attention to key institutional sites, processes, knowledge, and policy (e.g., housing, treatment, probation). To achieve coding consistency and accuracy, we test coded transcripts together in order to develop an annotated code book, which was organized into code groups (e.g., education) and individual codes within each group (e.g., alternative and safe schools, attendance, codes of conduct). We then piloted and revised the code books. The coding served as a uniform method of labelling the interview transcripts, which enabled subsequent analysis of the institutional relations the interviews pointed us toward. This feature is essential to institutional ethnographic analysis. People's experiences do not constitute data to be analysed; rather, they illuminate points of friction or rupture, which show a researcher where she needs to stop and determine how institutional relations are organized to produce this outcome.

   As central coordinators of thought and action, texts are essential links between the things people do and how these activities are coordinated institutionally. Textual analysis is used to reveal extended social relations that are not initially visible in people's experiential knowledge of their lives, but these nevertheless shape their personal experiences in ways an institutional ethnographer wants to bring into view (D.E. Smith, 2005). The development and testing of the code book served as an important process – across both projects – for engaging in critical, social analytic work with the youth research teams. Here, we would talk about traditional forms of sociological research and how/why we were working differently. I would also often introduce central institutional ethnographic concepts that I have found useful. For example, in my previous book, I used D.E. Smith's generous notion of work to orient myself to the coordinated complex of relations connecting young people's work to one another and to the institutions that govern their lives. This concept has been particularly useful and accessible to youth and community researchers in our efforts to bracket or suspend theoretical interpretations and/or judgements of the things people tell us in interviews (G.W. Smith, 1990). Fidelity to the idea that young people are engaged in work – that is, coordinated practices of thinking and acting with others – helped us to avoid making assumptions about drug use as an escape mechanism, for example, which is how our research team originally made sense of it. It was important for us to begin to see drug use as a work (deliberate and effortful activity) that young people undertake and that connects their activities to others, to institutions, and to relations of capital and exchange. For instance, young people's drug use is connected to, and shaped by, the people they buy from/ sell to, the schools that they get caught high in, the police who frisk and charge them, the dealers who profit from their hustling and consumption, and all the commercial contexts where the cash generated via transactions on the street is used to buy goods (e.g., new sneakers or a meal).

Once I moved into the writing phases of this project, I struggled to hold on to a race, class, and gender analysis throughout my engagement with the data. I wanted to show how race, class, and gender are embodied and experienced as objectified forms of consciousness and relating, rather than simply labelling people's activities and experiences as representative of pre-existing race, class, or gender categories. Analytically, I found it helpful to hold genderraceclass together, as a complex of relations, such that I did not rupture "the complex and constitutive mediation of an entire social organization" by disaggregating one "relation – '[for example,] gender' – and conferring on it an autonomous status and transcendent universality" (Bannerji, 1995, p. 69). Otherwise, I found myself dropping threads, so to speak, and losing site of the social organization of race, gender, or class in my analysis. Even with this concerted effort on my part, one shortcoming of the book is that I have not sufficiently revealed the ways that young men and women are experiencing and participating in social relations of gender. For example, young Black women talked about expectations that they hide a weapon or drugs in their bras and underwear during encounters with the police, given shared knowledge in this heavily policed neighbourhood that they would be less likely to be physically searched than their Black boyfriends. These accounts illuminate how relations of race, femininity, and masculinity are coconstitutive – and how young people come to participate in shared sense-making practices with respect to their race, class, and gender identities, in their ordinary encounters with public sector institutions.

Another way that the social relations of gender come into view in this project is by paying attention to my own, my colleagues', and graduate students' caregiving work within and beyond the summer research internships. I have a vivid memory of watching my one- and five-year-old children play in the yard, while (via telephone) I walked a graduate student research assistant through a daily crisis at Rosewood with our first summer youth research team in 2014. I felt torn between whatever was happening in my own yard (some minor conflict between the children) and the pressing needs of the youth we were working with in Toronto that summer, who were struggling with acute mental health issues, homelessness, and involvement in the criminal legal system. In both Montreal and Toronto, our teams hosted lunches and dinners and brought food with us into the field. We cared for sick youth research assistants, supported young people through familial and intimate relationship conflicts, and supported one another by debriefing and listening. In Montreal, I watched my colleague Jessica Ruglis help youth get access birth certificates, social insurance numbers, and glasses. This caregiving work was always done by women graduate students and professors. And I know for myself, sometimes there was very little caregiving energy left for my own children and spouse at the end of the summer. While this book focuses more explicitly on the social relations of race and class, people are simultaneously participating in social relations of gender. My sense of responsibility for the experiences and well-being of the teams I was leading *and* my sense of having failed to be sufficiently present and available to my own children are suggestive of the ways in which my own activities and analysis are punctuated by and constitutive of White middle class hetero-femininity.

Youth Summer Research Internships

All of the research activities described above have been facilitated, directly or indirectly, by annual paid youth summer research internships. Originally proposed by Professor Uzo Anucha based on her work with ACT for Youth, these internships became the cornerstone of each project – even though every summer I promise my own children that I will not facilitate another one, given the sheer amount of energy they require. In this, the last section in this chapter, I seek to illuminate different ways we have organized these internships, as well as critically reflect on the limitations of each approach. I do this deliberately so as not to overstate the political or transformative potential of a participatory practice, particularly those processes that involve the inclusion of young people in state structures (e.g., education) that have operated as exclusionary forces in their lives (Dhillon, 2017).

In Toronto, while I worked with the same post-secondary youth researchers for one to two years, we hired different youth to participate in each summer internship to ensure that the largest number of youths received an employment experience. This approach was a direct response to community concerns about a lack of meaningful employment opportunities for youth in the neighbourhood. The shortcoming was that most of the young people we worked with did not participate in all aspects of the project, from conception through data collection, analysis, dissemination, and action. To attend to this issue, we ensured that each summer included aspects of each of these research techniques.

Funding for the internships for both projects was secured through the Canada Summer Jobs Program, which allowed us to hire young people for seven-week full-time employment opportunities. These young people join a team of older youth researchers from the community (also hired through the Canada Summer Jobs Program), graduate students, community youth workers, and university researchers. In response to Rosewood teachers' concern that their students were short on high school credits, in the first summer, we arranged for the project to serve as a two-credit co-op education experience for the students as well as their first paid work experience in the formal economy.[1]

We advertised the four internships at Rosewood, and the school board teachers and Rosewood staff helped the youth create covering

---

1 In the second year (2015), the school board was not willing to agree to this arrangement. By 2017, there was no longer a school board–supported alternative education program at Rosewood at all, despite community demand.

letters and resumés. We formally interviewed every single student who applied, and one of the project doctoral assistants gave each young person extensive written feedback on their interview with clear accounts of what they did well and what they could work on for future interviews. The following year, a former MA research assistant on the project in year one was employed full-time at Rosewood and coordinated the entire hiring process. While we had only four full-time positions each of the two years we conducted research in Toronto, we offered every young person who applied the opportunity to join the project and receive a $500.00 honorarium for their participation. One young man took us up on this offer.

In the first year, all five of the young people we hired were (or had been) involved with the youth justice system, had been expelled from school, and were enrolled in Rosewood's alternative education program. One was also navigating the mental health system. In the second year, two of the young people had been students at Rosewood and two had been connected to the organization's youth work program. Three of the four young people hired in year two had been expelled or de-enrolled from the mainstream school system and involved in the youth justice system; the third youth remained enrolled and on track to graduate the following year. In years one and two, the young women we hired had children, although only one was actively parenting. We deliberately sought to hire youth with employment barriers during each of the four years we offered internships in Toronto and also in Montreal. In Montreal, while we remained committed to hiring youth who experienced difficulties finding work, the youth had far fewer obvious barriers to employment (e.g., no one had a youth justice record). The positions were not advertised at the organization; rather, in conversation with the director, we hired a group of young people who were in a hip-hop group that consistently made use of the organization's studio arts program. The design and delivery of the youth research internships in Toronto and Montreal reflected the interests, dispositions, and needs of the different youth in the two cities as well as the larger research teams and project interests in both sites. The dynamics within the teams were also quite different, year over year, and in the two cities.

In both settings, graduate and community research assistants and I took field notes documenting and reflecting on what we were learning together. In the last part of this chapter, I turn my ethnographer's lens towards the internships themselves as a way of bringing the programs into view for the reader. I do this for two reasons: first, to ensure that I don't gloss over some of the difficulties I have encountered doing this work; and second, to make it clear that I appreciate the humanness and complexity of front-line youth work. The more time I spend in the university, the easier it is for me to get disconnected from my own roots as a youth worker and teacher and the people who are doing this important work today. I want to convey the feeling of never quite getting it right, which characterizes a lifetime of working with children and youth.

Toronto: Schools and Safety

To provide young people with a full-time training and employment experience and ensure that they completed the assignments for their co-operative education credits meant that we maintained a ratio of two or three staff to five youth. This ratio is, I realize, totally unrealistic in most community organizations or educational settings, which is why I want to be clear about what it took for us to be successful. In the first year, post-secondary-aged youth researchers from the community, graduate students, and I coordinated and delivered the entire internship – operating like a satellite program between Rosewood and the university. In year two, the community organization took the lead and the organization's project manager (the former MA research assistant) and senior youth worker provided essential leadership and oversight.[2] In year one, I spent the first two weeks of the internship in the field almost every day. Additionally, I spent one morning per week meeting with the graduate student and older youth researchers, while the youth were participating in a co-operative education class. Also, I spent one afternoon a week alone with the team of youth researchers in order to give the graduate students and post-secondary-aged youth researchers an afternoon to regroup, reflect, plan, and prepare. The weekly check-ins with the high-school-aged youth researchers were dedicated to ongoing research training, emerging analysis of the data, and the preparation of a presentation on our findings for teachers and youth workers in GTA schools and communities at the end of the summer. These opportunities also served as times to meet individually with youth about issues in their lives, and occasionally to review the terms of their employment.

A powerful tension in the project, especially during the first year when we explicitly hired youth with significant employment barriers, was how to provide an employment opportunity that prepared them

---

2 After I left Toronto, Rosewood continued to adapt the original proposal to seek funding through the Canada Summer Jobs Program to hire and train young people from the community to engage in community research to action processes (e.g., a community asset mapping exercise in 2016).

for success in other workplaces, while also ensuring we were attentive to and understanding of the complexities of their lives. For example, we knew that Tayah was often up late at night with her infant daughter and Omar and Aaron were involved in late-night work on the streets. In Kenneth's case, we knew that there were violent conflicts at home and that he was often unable to sleep there. Ahmed had a history of psychosis and was undergoing psychiatric care, including the use of medication, which had physical side effects (e.g., headaches, dizziness, and once a loss of vision). Young people had also been honest with us about their drug use and the role it played in their abilities to deal with the stresses they encountered in their everyday lives.

During an analytic conversation about young people's identity work, Omar explained how much mental and physical energy went into being fierce and calm – two characteristics necessary for street work. Given the effort that goes into maintaining this active state, smoking weed (marijuana) was the only way he could prevent himself from "snapping on people" (especially his teachers) when they irritated him by focusing on "little things" like being late for class. We strove to not only have high expectations for the young people we worked with but also to exercise extraordinary flexibility so that each young person completed the summer internship.

A central finding from Professor Uzo Anucha's Assets Coming Together for Youth project, which I participated in as a research associate, was that young people in the neighbourhood experience systemic violence in the form of low institutional expectations. As a team, we sought to actively destabilize this trend. A recurring conversation among the full-time field research team contained two thrusts: (1) we wondered if our commitment to flexibility undermined our desire to express high expectations for youth and (2) we questioned if our hope to create a supportive employment experience meant youth would be unprepared for the demands of a "real job." I understood and respected these concerns, which I could also see raised methodological and ethical tensions given the tenets of a Youth Participatory Action Research (or YPAR) process.

The concept of coresearcher – central to a participatory process – suggests a flattened hierarchy, which is at odds with an employment and school-based educational situation. Without the employment component, however, the internship would have been inaccessible to young people living in poverty who are expected to earn their own way. We had explicitly attempted to hire youth with significant employment and educational barriers; it was important to ensure they had the supports they needed to complete the internship and participate in the project as researchers. On the other hand, it was becoming increasingly difficult for the two senior youth researchers to coordinate and implement the weekly schedule, when people were showing up late, showing up but refusing to participate, and/or showing up having smoked so much weed that participating was impossible.

During the first week of the internship, we had collectively established a disciplinary process, so that the terms of the employment experience were clear and people understood what would happen if these terms weren't met. The process was reviewed with each of the high-school-aged youth researchers to make sure they understood and to invite their suggestions for modifications. In a number of the weekly check-in meetings with the older youth and graduate student researchers, people expressed concerns about (youth researcher) Kenneth's drug use and diminishing interest in doing work for his co-operative education credits or the research-related tasks that needed completing. According to our disciplinary process, people (mainly the two older youth researchers, Andy and Chantel) had spoken privately to Kenneth on numerous occasions. I volunteered to meet with Kenneth to review his contract and establish a plan with him for moving forward. We arranged for Kenneth and me to speak when Andy brought his field team to the university to do an interview. In my field notes about the conversation, I have recorded the following:

> When everyone arrived, I checked in with people about the day prior – what had they done and what had they learned. [Youth research assistants] Tayah, Aaron, and Kenneth had been with Andy in the field doing some recruitment. Andy had already debriefed with me over the phone about this, so I knew that it had been a bit challenging for him to ensure that they didn't spook anyone (people in the neighbourhood are hesitant to speak with strangers) and put themselves in danger. He had to negotiate private conversations in alleys with the folks they ran into, while simultaneously keeping one eye on the youth to ensure they were ok. He admitted that it was more challenging than he had thought it would be. From Tayah's and Aaron's perspectives, however, it had gone really well. Tayah said that people were nice to them and wanted to talk to them and were interested in the project. When I asked her whether people were "working," she said no. I asked Andy the same question and he said that they did, indeed, have "work" with them. Kenneth was being very quiet. When he finally spoke, it was to tell me how "cheesed" he was about yesterday and how unfair everyone was being with him. He blurted this out, seemingly out of nowhere, but clearly front of mind for him. Based on the state of agitation – leaning forward, raised voice, interrupting the

flow of the conversation – I surmised that yesterday was laying somewhat heavily on his mind. I told him that he and I would have a chance to have a private conversation about it shortly.

With the rest of the youth research team working on another task, Kenneth and I sat and talked. I began by asking him to tell me about what happened in the field the day before. In my field notes, I wrote:

> He said it was ok, but he got really nervous and when he started to talk to the youth about the project, he made some mistakes and one of the "staff" cut him off (the staff must have been Chantel, Andy or one of the graduate student researchers), and this made him feel embarrassed. He explained that given some time, he could have explained about the project on his own and even recruited some people to participate in interviews, but because he was interrupted he felt embarrassed and anxious. I was surprised to hear him say this, and it made me wonder whether our expectations of him are too low, and we are not allowing him to take enough risks.

From here I invited him to tell me more about why he was feeling so "cheesed" with everyone. He explained that

> everyone except Andy is hassling him all the time and treating him unfairly – because he hasn't ever done anything wrong. I shared a few of the examples of the things I'd heard he was doing that were frustrating people and getting in the way of the learning of the group (e.g., distributing YouTube videos and refusing to contribute to any of the work for the project) ... From here, we attempted to come up with a plan for him to stay connected to the project. It was very hard. He had lots of things staff could do differently (e.g., stop hassling him, let him just work with Andy, not make him go to any of the neighbourhoods he doesn't feel safe in). He had some difficulty coming up with anything that he could do differently to make things work.

One of the things we knew when we started this project is that young people feel safe in some parts of the neighbourhood and not in others. Their experiences of safety/unsafety are often connected to where they live, work, and go to school (e.g., what social housing complex they live in; whether they are from "up top" or "down bottom"; whether they or their relatives are involved in the drug, sex, or arms trades). So, if you tell us you are unsafe somewhere, we don't ask any questions, we simply organize our work so that you never have to be there. Rather than interpreting an expression of unsafety as a sign of weakness, admitting that you are not safe somewhere was seen as a coded admission that a young person was involved in street work – an admission that conformed to the standards of masculinity the youth shared.

But as the team moved into participant recruitment for interviews, Kenneth began explaining that he felt unsafe everywhere – in all the neighbourhood schools and social housing complexes (including his own). Based on an interview Chantel and a graduate student had done with him earlier in the project – before he joined the team as a researcher – I knew that when Kenneth had moved from an east-end suburb to this north-west-end neighbourhood, he had gone to his assigned high school once, and then stopped going for an entire year because he felt uncomfortable there. Kenneth clearly felt less at ease in the neighbourhood than the other members of the team, less confident about his role on the team, and displeased about his interactions with senior members of the team, who he felt were disrespecting him. In combination, these experiences undermined Kenneth's willingness to participate in scheduled activities – although he desperately wanted to remain involved in the project.

In addition to his reluctance to be part of any recruitment or data collection efforts in the neighbourhood, he also refused to do any of the other tasks people suggested. He was also unable to suggest any alternative activities that would support the project aims. I tried to illuminate our dilemma for him and invite him to troubleshoot a solution with me. I explained:

> "It is difficult to keep you hooked into the project when you say you can't go anywhere to do any fieldwork. It's starting to feel like you are messing with us. It was totally fine for you to go to W-school for the co-operative education training. Why is [it] not safe for you to be there now? Why not [D. housing complex] – this is where you live? We need to come up with a compromise where we can both feel good moving forward." Having both had a chance to say our piece, we came up with a smaller list of places Kenneth is really unable to go. Surprisingly, many of the places were other "notorious" neighbourhoods in Toronto, quite far from where we were working, so it was simple to agree that we would not go there as part of our research.

In addition to gaining clarity about where Kenneth felt safe to work, I used this private time to have a conversation about other things going on his life, as well as to strategize with him about how our team could best support him to remain actively involved. The next phase of the disciplinary process was to develop an employment agreement with Kenneth, and this conversation would comprise the basis for this work. In this case, the conversation was utilitarian insofar as it was oriented to producing an agreement between Kenneth and me; but it was also illuminating in other ways. Clearly, Kenneth and the other youth research assistants are not the objects of this study, but I still learned much from one-on-one conversations like the one I had with Kenneth, which helped me understand how the demands, expectations, and institutional organization of dominant youth-serving institutions are at odds with the actual circumstances of their lives. As the following conversation with Kenneth illuminates, ordinary aspects of institutional organization conflict with the experiences, desires, and needs of actual youth:

> I asked Kenneth whether it is difficult to focus when there are things on his mind, and he said yes. We talked about the fighting that has been going on at home between him and his mom. I asked whether Burt (his youth worker) has helped them access conflict mediation supports (which was the plan), and he said no. I asked whether his mom had a new boyfriend, and he said yes. I ask whether there is anything we can do to help with the stuff at home, and he said "no, it's been this way for too long." As we talked, I thought about the crumpled-up paper that Andy found on the classroom floor with Kenneth's reflections on the things he'd said and done that he regretted (e.g., past conflicts between him and his mother), and I feel pretty helpless and sad for Kenneth and his mom. Throughout this entire conversation, Kenneth didn't make eye-contact with me – which is fairly typical of all conversations with him – and provided a lot of one-word answers to my questions. I asked whether it would be useful if we put into his plan that staff were willing to chat with him about this stuff at home and support him in sorting it out – whenever he was ready to speak with us about it – and he said yes. We went back to the discussion about how difficult it is to focus when things in his life start to preoccupy him, and I asked what we could do to help him re-engage when this occurs. He shrugged. I asked about how he is feeling when he has trouble focusing – anxious? Frustrated? Tired? And he explained that he got really angry. I asked what he could do to cool down, and he suggested a walk. We came up with a plan for this to be arranged between him and Andy or Chantel to allow him to cool-down when he got angry, so as to remain engaged in the project. I explained that one thing I feared was that he would use this walk to go smoke up because he was often coming back to work high after lunch. He agreed that this was likely. I told him what I observed about his behaviour when he was high – referencing his inability to hold on to the thread of the conversation during the first part of the presentation

on Tuesday from three racial profiling researchers and activists who had come to speak with us. I observed that when one of the researchers asked him a question, he was unable to answer because he couldn't remember what had been asked of him. I contrasted this with his ability to engage – and his willingness to take the sunglasses off – during the latter part of the talk. Kenneth admitted he had been high and he didn't want people to know.

During our chat, I introduced Kenneth to the concept of harm reduction. In his case, we came up with a harm reduction goal to ensure Kenneth's substance use did not interfere with his employment. Smoking weed was not the issue; the problem was smoking so much that it interfered with Kenneth's ability to meet and interact with new people and do his job. We agreed that if he showed up at work unable to participate (e.g., wearing sunglasses inside, falling asleep, or unable to make eye contact), he would be sent home for the day. This standard became one of the terms of our agreement, and Kenneth remained employed for the duration of the summer. But our continuous efforts to keep Kenneth employed for a seven-week internship reveal the inadequacy of the standard institutional responses offered to youth.

Many conditions create friction in some young people's lives: the size of youth workers' caseloads, timelines for accessing urgently needed services, class sizes, standardized curricula and testing, the organization of the school day, inadequate and/or poorly timed psychometric assessment processes, insufficient accommodations and supports for students experiencing learning difficulties, normative ideas about youth development, abstinence-only substance-use policies/discourses, the criminalization of drugs, and expectations for the work organization of families. Many teachers and youth workers recognize these disconnects, but they seldom feel institutionally empowered to address them. In a busy classroom, in a large school, the actualities of Kenneth's life will not be acknowledged, let alone addressed; in our short-term, highly staffed summer internship, we could acknowledge young people as living full and complex lives, but we were not able to substantively address any but the most urgent of problems with them. In fact, when we attempted to do so, court-appointed youth workers accused us of overstepping.

While I undertook the first summer youth research internship largely to support the youth and youth workers at Rosewood, these intensive experiences keep my feet firmly planted in the material world where actual young people and youth workers of various stripes are hard at work. The concept of youth work, as developed in my first book

(Nichols, 2014), remains a useful heuristic in this regard. The notion draws our attention to the actual activities of young people and adults actively and deliberately working to accomplish particular things in various organizational contexts. People are working hard, but all too often, their work is co-ordered such that it fails to result in the outcomes young people want or need. My own efforts to situate my work within these complexes of socially organized action remind me how challenging it is to try to improve the actual conditions of people's lives using the existing institutionally sanctioned channels for doing so. These channels, as Maynard's recent (2017) work shows, were not designed for the purposes of actualizing the dreams of economically disadvantaged Black youth.

In the second year of the internship, one of the former research assistants on the project was working at Rosewood full time, and she and another Rosewood youth worker took on the role of internship coordination and field supervision. My role was to help them and the new youth research team design a research project that would allow young people and staff to answer a question that was important to them (about what services youth in the neighbourhood used and/or wanted and why). Together, we designed and implemented a youth-to-youth survey, and under the guidance of a Rosewood board member, the youth learned how to map the results using a free participatory mapping software. Graduate students and I delivered weekly research training sessions, and one of our senior youth researchers and a graduate student designed and cofacilitated weekly critical analysis sessions on issues that youth and the youth workers wanted to discuss (e.g., gender and sexuality). We all participated in field work – collecting, analyzing, and mapping data. We shared the findings in a community knowledge mobilization event and celebration at the end of the summer. Still, I did not have the same type of intensive relationship with the youth researchers as I'd had the year prior when I was in the field many days per week with them and more actively mentoring the graduate student and older youth research assistants. By the second year, our research team had been working together for two years and had a rapport with one another and better integration with Rosewood staff. Another interesting dimension in year two was the regular involvement of Rosewood's full-time youth worker and the inclusion of two adult youth worker trainees from a local college: Jeremiah and Gillian. Based on their enthusiastic participation, the research training and social analytic conversations were clearly as useful and interesting to them as to the youth research trainees. Our field notes capture multiple social and pedagogical dimensions, which distinguished this group from the one the year prior. Graduate student Alison Fisher writes of her experiences cofacilitating a session on research ethics with Andy, one of the older youth researchers, whom I had worked with on and off since 2012. In Alison's field notes, some of the social and pedagogical dynamics characteristic of the second internship experience come into view. She writes:

I told youth we would be watching a clip from the show *The Wire* ... I gave a description of the scene they would be watching between a Social Work researcher who wants Bunny Colville (an ex-cop) to help him engage with youth involved in the drug trade. We watched the clip. Both [youth worker-trainee] Jeremiah and [Rosewood youth worker] Warren vocally reacted to various parts of the script (laughing or murmuring in various moments) while the kids watched. After the clip, I asked about their impressions of the scene and what was happening. [Youth researcher] Neville summarized the clip. I asked what Bunny the ex-cop thought was a problem with the social worker's approach. The kids were quiet. Warren spoke up to suggest that the character Bunny felt that the researcher was trying to work with kids who were too "deep in the game" to help (18- to 21-year-olds). I pointed out the issue of language and how the social worker/researcher was using certain terms (e.g., "epidemiology," "inoculate"), which Bunny was uncomfortable with. I asked the group whether they ever had experience of someone using words that they didn't understand even though the person was speaking the same language. Everyone nodded and responded to that. I showed the group the next clip where Bunny returns to his old police department, in order to introduce the academic to an 18-year-old youth involved in the drug trade. After the clip, I asked students what was making the youth so angry about the researcher in this clip? This clip definitely evoked more response and discussion afterwards. [Youth researcher] Ekon pointed out that the researcher kept writing even though the youth had told him to stop and that this wasn't very respectful. The youth also noticed that the researcher in the clip didn't make very much eye contact with the youth or introduce himself. Warren pointed out that the youth in the film knew immediately that the social worker was not a cop and that the young person in the film was probably very knowledgeable about what his rights were and who was supposed to be present in an interrogation room. I think Andy brought up the issue of consent and whether the researcher had ever asked for the youth's consent to be present. We also talked about body language and the ways in which the ex-cop used his body to get in the youth's face to provoke a reaction. The group identified that the ex-cop Bunny was provoking the youth by talking about his sister. Jeremiah suggested that the youth was hand-cuffed to the table, so this was also creating a context where the youth was not given a choice to participate, making the experience feel forced rather than voluntary. I introduced the idea of research ethics again and indicated in the next part of the lesson we would be speaking specifically to informed consent as an ethical condition for research involving people. (Field note, 2015)

As well as conveying the various insights and extensions offered by people in the room, (graduate student) Alison's field notes capture the pedagogical organization of their work. She and Andy had clearly designed a pedagogical encounter: it began with a "hook" (analyzing the clips from *The Wire*) that connected back to the previous lesson on the classed and racialized dimensions to historical research ethics violations and ended with opportunities to engage in structured role-play scenarios. At times, Alison describes the young people as students and the training as a lesson. She is a high school teacher, and I used to be one. It is easy for us to slide back into these roles in the training sessions, which shapes the tendency among the youth researchers to slide into similarly well-worn student roles. Particularly given the historically entrenched raced, classed, and gendered divide between teachers and students in the neighbourhood, we needed to interrogate the roles we assumed as emblematic of the same complex of institutional and social relations we were investigating.

Two White women in our midthirties (at the time), with similar colouring and build, both wearing glasses and speaking in ways that reflect a shared educational trajectory and similar political disposition – new youth researchers could not immediately tell Alison and me apart. We appeared to be two more White women teachers among many in a neighbourhood of largely Black families. We talked about this stuff with one another and with the youth, but maybe not as much as we should have. For instance, while graduate students (Jessica Braimoh and Alison Fisher) and I often talked (and wrote) about race and the racialized identities of our team – as a large group – we did not talk about how the team itself echoed the racialized distribution of labour more broadly in the community: Black youth workers, White and biracial teachers, and Black youth. Later in the same field notes, Alison describes herself walking in on a youth work encounter, structured by youth worker and youth worker trainee Warren and Jeremiah, who were speaking with youth research assistant Trishelle. According to Andy, a friendly exchange between Trishelle and Jerrick (another youth research assistant) had quickly escalated into a heated encounter and the two youth were separated – Andy taking a walk with Jerrick, while Warren and Jeremiah spoke with Trishelle in the classroom. Conflicts over territorial loyalties, which neither Alison nor I would have likely noticed as quickly and therefore might not have been able to de-escalate, were quickly addressed by Andy, Warren, and Jeremiah. They were trained as social service or youth workers, and Andy and Warren had grown up in the neighbourhood and understood that these conflicts run deep for youth. With ample and engaged staffing and lots of time to debrief, opportunities for meaningful learning and respectful dialogue were not difficult to cultivate over two years of offering summer internships; with one teacher and thirty students with a range of needs, interests, and passions, however, I have trouble seeing how it would be possible.

For example, over the second summer most of us were involved – to lesser and greater degrees – in supporting Trishelle to maintain a safe place to live. In my own field notes, towards the end of the summer, I have written that Trishelle is not coming to work that day because, according to Stephanie (my former research assistant and the current program coordinator at Rosewood), Trishelle had "something to sort out." My field notes from that day recount a conversation where Stephanie tells me she

> has been working hard to get Trishelle into housing, so that she no longer has to crash at her boyfriend's house. Trishelle had confided to Stephanie that her boyfriend was being physically violent with her. She no longer wanted to stay with him, but she was unsure how to leave. Having lost all of her possessions during a previous breakdown in housing, Trishelle did not want to leave them behind again. She was also keenly aware that if she packed up her things, her boyfriend would know she was leaving and get angry. (Field note, Naomi, 2015)

Although Stephanie had looked into different housing options for youth in Toronto, Trishelle was reluctant to pursue these. When I spoke with Trishelle about housing a little later that week, she explained that she did not want to stay in congregate supported housing, nor was she interested in staying temporarily at a youth shelter, both of which constitute traditional pathways into permanent housing for youth. She said she was tired of people saying they would help her, when no one seemed to be able to get her what she wanted: a studio apartment near school. Because she had been expelled from the Catholic School Board, she was required to attend school in a program for youth who are expelled or completing long-term suspensions. There were only two of these programs in Toronto at this time (within the Catholic school board), making it even more difficult for youth workers to help secure housing.

Youth research assistants Ekon, Neville, and Jerrick were also difficult to engage towards the end of the internship. They were thinking about going back to school and talking about applying for another job between the end of the internship and the start of school. Although they were supposed to be in the lab mapping survey data the day Trishelle was absent, it was difficult to keep them focused on this task:

> After Stephanie's explanation of their work for the day, no one got to work. Neville's energy had perked up and he had much to say, but it was all about e-bikes and clothes – he was "window" shopping online – and not beginning the task he'd been asked to do. Later, it became clear that he didn't understand the instructions. Jerrick, for his part, forgot his login information and needed to get this from Steph, but even with the login information, it took two adults to help him log in. I think eventually they rebooted and started again. Even Ekon just sat and stared at his computer. This is unlike him. Typically, he would just tuck right into work with very little instruction or even offer to do things without being asked … Once Neville and I knew what was being asked of him – to interpret the data from the question about what resources for youth are needed in the community – he and I set to work. I brought my laptop over and attempted to draw out and synthesize his interpretation of the numbers for the question about what resources for youth the community needs and record his verbal answers on my laptop. As Neville talked, he simultaneously kept looking at clothing – primarily backpacks and shoes. He and Jerrick were both heading to schools this week to see about registering. (Field note, Naomi, 2015)

Through the use of descriptive accounts, bolstered by the generous inclusion of team member's field notes, I have been attempting to bring the Toronto youth research internship programs into focus for the reader. Not because I think we did an exceptional job, but because most of the YPAR accounts I've read do not offer up the research process itself as data, which reveals something about the intersecting institutional and social relations one is investigating. Nor does enough YPAR research attend to the difficult balance I've faced each year between pedagogy, paid meaningful work opportunities, and what feels (at times) like summer camp programming. Although some of the contexts of the internships in Montreal differed significantly from those in

Toronto (e.g., the youth in Montreal finishing or close to finishing high school, they knew each other, they were of mixed races and ethnicities, and they were slightly older), in both scenarios we maintained high expectations and even higher flexibility in seeking to achieve our collective and individual aims.

Montreal: Sampling Youth Development

In Montreal, we reserved the summer youth research internship opportunities for the youth we'd been working with at Chalet Parc all winter and spring, rather than posting a general call for applications at the agency. Although I had written the Canada Summer Jobs application for Rosewood, my coinvestigator on Sampling Youth Development, Professor Jessica Ruglis, took the lead on the application for Chalet Parc. Having worked with the same group of young people one night per week for several weeks prior the start of the internship, we had intended to use the summer experience for research training and fieldwork. Unfortunately, due to holiday schedules in the Research Ethics Board review office that summer, we did not receive ethical approval until the end of the summer. As a consequence, we revised the summer institute to focus on cultivating skills along four domains: critical social science research; community development (e.g., community gardening); the arts (e.g., music and creative writing); and mixed media communication. The institute combined training and skills development in research and critical social analysis, mixed media (e.g., video, photography) production, writing, and music production, as well as community-building opportunities within the team and within the city more broadly (e.g., developing a community garden; cooking and delivering food to local activists holding a vigil).

Research training began before the internship with the development of generative research questions and brainstorming about methods. This work took place all spring and allowed Jessica and me to develop the research design and submit it for ethical review. In the summer, the research training became more deliberate and focused as we had to ensure we all had the skills required to carry out the research project we had designed together. Like we had done in Toronto, the research training began with an exploration of a range of research approaches, aims, objectives, methods, and orientations. This set up a lengthy exploration of research ethics and participatory, activist, and systems-oriented approaches to research. We learned about the Tuskegee Trials, where syphilis was left untreated in poor Black men to allow White scientists to track the "natural" (i.e., untreated) progression of the disease. Like he'd done at other occasions, Malik (a Chalet Parc youth worker and musician) deepened the discussion by introducing us to a powerful song, written by jazz clarinetist Don Byron. In my field notes, I've written the following about this experience: "First, Malik told us about the instrument we'd be hearing (a clarinet), and he gave us a sample of the type of sound we could expect, using his own voice. He does this a lot – uses his voice to represent a beat or an instrument and it always blows me away. We listened to the piece, which included spoken word and music. It was powerful – cacophonic noises, making me cringe at the squealing clarinet and wildness of the piece. Everyone just had their own moment with the music. People didn't make much eye contact or engage with one another" (field note, Naomi, 2016). An abstract discussion of the racist and objectifying tendencies in research took a profoundly more affective turn as we listened, stunned, to the cacophonic sounds of Byron's Tuskegee Experiments. Again, like we'd done in Toronto, at Chalet Parc we engaged with pop-culture representations of research in "marginalized" urban communities (e.g., from music and TV) as we learned about the concepts of subjectivity, objectivity, insider/outside issues, and the politics of evidence and representation. In this way, our research training began with an exploration of the historical and present-day relationship between knowledge production, epistemic (in)justice, race, and processes of racialization.

Over the next couple of weeks, young people also completed Canada's Tri-Council Panel on Research Ethics Tutorial Course on Research Ethics (CORE) together in McGill's computer lab. Because we completed the tutorial together, young people could help one another, and we could – as a group – pause as we made our way through each module to discuss what we were learning. As we wrapped up the course, we moved into working with particular methods. By this time, we had been trying to document and keep track of our process a little more diligently and so we had begun to talk to one another about how we wrote field notes. Young people were provided with structured opportunities to practice listening, observing, and asking questions. Sometimes they were asked to close their eyes and listen. At other times, they were invited to go out in the world and pay attention with all of their senses. They walked along busy streets full of shoppers and stood in line at fast-food restaurants, soaking in the experiences, jotting notes in their books, and returning to the university to produce and share their field notes and the experience of producing them. They talked about what it felt like in their bodies to be completely still, mindful, and observant in the context of so much movement and – they noted – so much consumerism. Thus, we circled back to a conversation we'd return to over and over again: how to be present in our lives, by identifying and seeking to resist the forces that turn us into "clones" and "zombies" (words used by the young people to describe the pressures of a consumeristic culture). Because we were working together regularly at this point, different aspects of our work had begun to run together. I accompanied the group on the days they'd do creative writing workshops with a local playwright. The themes that emerged in these writing sessions ran through the research training components and allowed us to pick up on and respond to the things young people really cared about.

That fall when the internship was done, most of the young people we had been working with went back to school. The project shifted again, as the team swelled to include a number of new graduate students who – with the youth researchers – comprised the field teams for the street interviews that were conducted that fall. After a winter of slowly working on cointerviewing (youth/graduate student and adult researchers) young people, recruited during the street interviews and through the youth researchers' social networks, youth researchers participated in a second summer institute in 2017, which focused much more on recruitment, interviewing, coding, analysis, and action. Prior to the second summer institute, and to prepare us for another summer of intensive work, we facilitated a week of training (half-days) on coding and analysis. This grounding enabled the production of our team's code book and coding strategy as well as an analytic framework or heuristic device, designed to direct our attention to the social processes through which identity development occurs. These two tools guided our work that summer to complete a final set of in-depth interviews and code the existing interviews collected over the prior year. Our collective and reflexive engagement with this work also shaped the actions that the youth elected to pursue. In addition to three presentations to academic and professional audiences (teachers), the action phase focused on learning how to create podcasts. Under the coleadership of Jessica and a graduate student named Rakeb Tesfaye, the youth produced two podcast episodes. The first episode was about our project, and the second was about an issue that emerged from our data as important to youth in Montreal: racial profiling. Both podcasts required additional research on the parts of youth – largely comprised of interviews with members of the team as well as anti-racist activists in and beyond Montreal.

The longer I do this work with young people, the more I appreciate what participatory research offers me: opportunities to return to my roots as a teacher and youth worker; meaningful connections with community organizations and non-academic collaborators; links to policy decision makers; opportunities to speak with and learn from young people who might otherwise be wary of interacting with a university researcher; occasions to check my own understanding and ongoing analyses with knowledgable experts; and chances to share and/or apply the information we generate to create policies, tools, and programs that will actually be useful and used. I am also increasingly convinced that the acquisition of critical social analytic skills – that is, the development of an analysis of the social forces acting on and through their lives – is the central benefit for young people participating as researchers.

It is also true that young people were paid for their contributions and acquired an employment experience – and for those few youth who we were able to hire, the internship alleviated some of the acute pressures of poverty, at least in the short term. But a focus on basic needs, at the expense of people's holistic development as soulful, imaginative, questioning, and thinking beings, seems like one of the ways we participate in the making of class. Time spent hanging out under the shade of a tree on a university campus, learning about and supporting other community research processes, questioning the police about their own questioning practices, watching and discussing films, and participating in intellectual conversations does not contribute to the resolution of pressing material needs. However, like the other relations young people participate in, these connections contribute to how young people come to see themselves as knowledgable experts of their own lives. This acknowledgment is at the heart of an institutional ethnographic research process; people's knowledge of their own lives and experiences illuminate social ruptures, which methods of institutional analysis seek to reveal.

Chapter Three

The Neo-Liberal State and the Creation of Race, Class, and Gender

When E.P. Thompson (1966) wrote about the making of the working class in England and Michael Omi and Howard Winant (1994) described the making of race in the United States, they did so by drawing attention to the active, historically situated social processes through which race and class categories and identities were produced and solidified over time and space. Many scholars since then have grounded their work in the foundational assumption that race, class, and gender are socially contingent (rather than natural or objective biological) categories, which are (re)produced in and shape ongoing social relations. My own work is grounded in a similar set of propositions. But it departs from these other important foundational studies in terms of the data that I am using to anchor my investigations. Beginning with the ordinary things that young people say they do every day and night – rather than historical and political analysis – the studies in this book show how raced, classed, and gendered identities get produced. I show how some young people's ordinary daily work to avoid state authorities – that is, the police, social, and immigration workers – is connected to other young people across the country seeking to bring the state into their lives to keep them safe.

While the things we do, think, believe, and say are not *determined* by the institutional, political-economic, and discursive structures of social life, our everyday worlds are continually conditioned by these things – and in ways that are not evident upon first glance. In fact, this is the reason why we tend to operate as though the choices we make, our beliefs and behaviours, *are* a reflection of internal processes, rather than the outcome of the continuous interplay between the self and the social spaces we occupy. People's conscious and unconscious thoughts, feelings, and motivations, and the actions that they give rise to, are habituated by the specific forms of social organization that punctuate our lives. The environment structures development – from the ways we see ourselves in relation to others; to the sizes and shapes of our bodies; and the ways we metabolize, think, and talk about stress. This observation does not reflect structurally deterministic ways of thinking; rather, it reflects my work with Social Paediatrics specialists at the Hospital for Sick Children, where I had a year-long research contract shortly after I finished my PhD.

Medical research has generated a substantive body of evidence linking exposure to abuse, neglect, trauma, instability, and loss (i.e., adversity) with "myriad chronic conditions associated with premature mortality: smoking, substance abuse, obesity, cardiovascular disease, depression, and attempted suicide" (Brent & Silverstein, 2013). Health researchers have identified causal pathways between the conditions of early life, neurobiological functioning (e.g., the neurological and endocrine systems), and long-term health and social outcomes. In the face of this overwhelming body of evidence, we are well-served by critical sociological research, which illuminates just how the institutional, political-economic, and social forces that saturate and give shape to daily life structure what young people are able to do and be; how they know themselves in relation to others; and how they end up thinking, speaking, and acting in the ways that they do. While my own research does not identify *causal* pathways between particular developmental outcomes and the generalized conditions of social life, I do endeavour to bring these generalized conditions more clearly into view for the reader, to make evident how social, institutional, and political-economic relations structure how young people know themselves and others in raced, classed, and/or gendered ways.

Racism without Intent

The inspiration for this particular chapter comes from an experience seeking to prepare an oral and written deposition about racial profiling in schools for the Ontario Human Rights Commission. I was working with two colleagues and a youth researcher to prepare the report. We had reams of ethnographic data that conveyed the exclusionary processes underpinning the movement of young Black men and women out of mainstream school programs. These students were moved into alternative programs and struggling schools with low enrollment, as well Section 23 educational programs available to youth serving sentences in open and closed custody environments. We were well acquainted with the growing body of quantitative research confirming unequal educational outcomes for economically disadvantaged and racial minority groups across North America (Fine & Ruglis 2009; Morris & Perry, 2016; Ofer, 2011/2012; Skiba, Eckes, & Brown 2009/2010; Skiba et al., 2014), as well as research pointing specifically to academic disparities for Black and Indigenous students in Canada (Abada & Lin 2011; Caldas, Bernier, & Marceau, 2009; Bhattacharjee, 2003; James, 2012; Maynard, 2017). We had also seen and felt these disparities first-hand as we stood in the middle of the windswept field in Canada's largest youth jail, watching as line after line of young Black and Brown men in maroon tracksuits trekked across the field from the sleeping units into the school. Clearly, our public institutions were systematically producing disproportionate outcomes, structured along raced, gendered, and classed lines. But I struggled for weeks to try to convey the findings from our own and others' research, as instances of racial profiling in schools.

I now understand this difficulty as having two interconnected roots: first, institutional relations are largely organized to obscure the ways they contribute to entrenched raced, classed, and gendered outcomes; second, our efforts to find evidence of racial profiling in our data was at odds with IE. In all of my work, I try not to treat institutionally derived and institutionally actionable concepts like race and class as naturally occurring and measurable phenomena. Race, from this perspective, is not something that you have or are; rather, it is a category that gets produced, used, and has an effect in and through relations among people, as these relations are mediated institutionally (Maraj-Grahame, 1998; Ng, 1988, 1993; D.E. Smith, 1999). Institutional ethnographers attempt to problematize the production of abstract accounts of, or categories for, social problems that are produced as issues in and through academic and professional discourse. Our desire is to reveal how esoteric institutional conceptualizations of a problem are actually implicated in people's experiences of injustice and inequality. For all of these reasons, my efforts to begin with the concept of racial profiling as a central orienting frame and then apply this conceptual clamp (D.E. Smith, 2005) to the data after the fact proved problematic.

Racial profiling is a term that – as it is constructed in institutional settings – implies intent. That is, the concept of racial profiling suggests an active process of sense-making on the part of individual practitioners, based on racial stereotypes.[1] No doubt, racial profiling happens.

---

1 I use the Ontario Human Rights Commission's definition of racial profiling as "any action undertaken for reasons of safety, security or public protection that relies on stereotypes about race, colour, ethnicity, ancestry, religion, or place of origin rather

And where these occurrences become visible, individualizing responses are produced – individuals or groups are required to participate in "cultural sensitivity training," conduct may be investigated, and disciplinary actions may be meted out. But this leaves unaddressed the larger systemic forces through which institutions are producing processes of racialization, class, and gender in the absence of social practices, which can be coded as racial profiling. Had we only looked for instances of racial profiling, I may have missed all of the subtle processes of racialization and criminalization operating in and through institutions like schools. Further, narrowly constructed institutional definitions of racial profiling as visible instances of discrimination, for instance, make it challenging for people who are experiencing a lack of access or fairness to prove that it has anything to do with how their bodies are read and responded to, institutionally. Finally, this orientation distracts from the norming of Whiteness, cis-gendered maleness, and middle-classness – social processes that are fundamental to the racializing, classing, and gendering forms of inclusion and exclusion that the research seeks to address. As such, in this chapter, I begin in another place. Rather than starting with the concept of racial profiling, I start with the experiences and knowledge of actual and diverse young people. I also look to my own experiences operating within these same institutional relations to get things done for my own children.

This chapter seeks to show how race, class, and gender – as objectified forms of consciousness (e.g., categories, coded language, and shared discourse) and material relations among people – are produced by public sector institutions and institutional processes described as objective, evidence based, or intelligence-led. Analysis for this chapter is grounded in young people's descriptions of their experiences moving in and through their neighbourhoods. Building an analysis from young people's encounters with the police, I show how interactions between young people and the police are connected to and organized by the provision and management of social housing as well as the distribution and management of municipal resources (e.g., through "priority" neighbourhood funding designations). The chapter explicates how young people come to know that they are perceived as a threat to "community safety"; how they come to learn that interfacing with the police is dangerous – even where they have been criminally victimized;

---

than on reasonable suspicion, to single out an individual for greater scrutiny or different treatment" (Bhatteracharjee, 2003, p. 6).

and how these cumulative experiences shape a profound sense that the state doesn't "care about poor Black kids."

To build this argument, I draw on analyses developed across a range of recent articles (Nichols, 2017a, 2017b; Nichols & Braimoh, 2016; Nichols, Fisher, & Braimoh, submitted 2018), which reveal raceclassgender as a "central axis of social relations" (Omi & Winant, 1994, p. 61) – a shared mode of consciousness – constituted through specific (identifiable) ideological practices. Starting from young people's experiential knowledge of the institutional contexts directly and indirectly shaping their lives, this chapter illuminates a range of institutional relations as they appear in and structure people's lives, shaping how they grow up, and how they come to know themselves in relation to others and the state. This chapter sets the stage for subsequent chapters that offer deeper and more focused analyses of the education system. Here, young people's accounts provide a glimpse into the intersecting relations of access, surveillance, punishment, inclusion, privilege, neglect, and exclusion that actively shape the outcomes of their lives and experiences in school: the housing, policing, and criminal legal systems.

The Police "Don't Care about Us"

All of the interviews we conducted with young Black people who live in Toronto's NIAs are punctuated by stories of their ongoing encounters with the police. These young people describe a public sector that clearly and relentlessly fails them, and in so doing, produces a shared sense among them that the state doesn't care about poor Black youth. For those who also lived or hung out in social housing, the interactions with the police were particularly relentless. We were struck by how young people described these interactions as ordinary aspects of life in NIAs and social housing, in particular. Morris, a young Black man and old friend of Andy's we interviewed, describes the type of ordinary interactions he got used to growing up in the neighbourhood, coming and going from school and work on his bike:

> It was night. And it was late at night [around 2:00 a.m.] because I come home from work, right? I ride my bike … And somebody stole my bike seat at work, so the bike I was riding looked sketch. It looked like I almost stole it, right? But I had no choice. I had to ride that home. I couldn't even sit down because there was no seat. So I was pissed off, and I was trying to get home fast. And I rode my bike through this little stop sign. And I know the area, and I know no cars really come through there, but there

was a police car waiting there. And they stopped me … They told me to get off the bike, put the bike down. And one officer was talking to me, but the other officer was looking like he was already upset at me, kind of. And what did he do? Oh, my bike was on the ground, and he kind of kicked it. And the next guy just started … you know, "Can I see your bag? Is this your bike?" That kind of stuff. "Where are you going?" And they interrogated me, and only at the end of it, they said – like, once I proved to them I'm coming from work, blah, blah, blah – only at the end did they say, "Okay, well, be careful. You can't run a stop sign."

The interview with Morris was littered with stories like this – interactions that he described as annoying but did not otherwise strike him as terribly unjust. Indeed, the police do catch Morris riding his bike "through this little stop sign." Elsewhere I've written about young people's encounters with the police because of Highway Traffic Act violations like the one Morris describes above (Nichols, 2017). The traffic violation enables the police to engage in what would be otherwise be considered unlawful investigative detentions (e.g., requests to see ID and dump out the contents of their backpacks). In Morris' neighbourhood, biking on the sidewalk, riding a bike without a bell, failing to wear a helmet, or running a stop sign at two o'clock in the morning are likely to lead to an unwanted encounter with the police.

Through these encounters with the police, young Black men and women grow up learning a refusal to comply with the police is more likely to result in a characterization of their behaviour as "suspicious" and therefore as grounds for an investigative detention. Early on a Sunday morning on an empty dead-end street or late at night in a deserted parking lot, young people are less likely to stand up for their rights – even where they are aware their rights are being violated – than they are when they are in the public eye. They learn that they are unable to freely and safely walk away from these encounters and that their best approach is to play the part of the officer's "little bitch" (Tyrique). In other words, when it comes to interactions with the criminal legal system, young people come to expect that neither the process nor the outcomes will be fair. In the context of diminished relational fairness during all interactions with the police – the front line of the justice system – young people come to learn they will be denied rights that others take for granted. These experiences translate into other aspects of a young person's life, substantiated by the experiences, observations, and advice of older siblings, parents, and other important adults in young people's lives, who reaffirm that the police are not working to protect their safety. They are also constitutive of a shared race, class, and gender consciousness. To play an officer's "little bitch" is to assume a submissive role in the face of oppressive state power. That this submissiveness is at odds with hegemonically masculine norms is conveyed in its characterization as being a "little bitch."

Chris is a young man who was living in one of the city's NIAs that was being "revitalized" into a mixed-income neighbourhood at the time of this research. In an interview, conducted with Chris while he was in jail, he described a typical interaction with the police that occurs as he is moving through his neighbourhood: "When I'm walking in my community and I'm going to the [community] centre it's basically – [the police] will just drive up and ask, 'Where you going?' and ask a lot of questions. When I answer them, it's like they don't believe me ... even if I did know what's going on I couldn't tell them. I wouldn't want anyone I know to get into trouble. The police aren't really helping us; they're trying to help people who are not in my community." Chris goes on to explain that the police are there to protect the wealthier members of the neighbourhood from economically marginalized people, like him. Young people we interviewed expressed a belief that they are targeted by the police because they are poor and not White. Indeed, the intersections of race and class are conditioned by State interventions – whether these be the policing and neighbourhood "revitalization" efforts Chris describes or the organized program of alignment between Toronto Police Services and Toronto Community Housing (Nichols & Braimoh, 2016).

Kaneesha, who lives in social housing in a different NIA on the other side of the city from Chris, described a violent interaction she witnessed between the police and her brother that helps to illuminate how young people grow up to understand that the police are not there to bring safety into their lives, but to protect others *from* them and their families:

> KANEESHA: [The police] came with long guns like deuces, like, big, long guns. Through the neighbourhood with kids, dogs, everybody's out there ... they walked with their big guns, through the neighbourhood and asked my brother for his name. Said his name, then they turned his neck, looked at his tattoo and just started fighting him. So then my brother and everybody started jumping in [and fighting back].
>
> INTERVIEWER: Is this a normal thing that you would see when police come into the area?
>
> KANEESHA: Yeah, they don't care about us.

Young people growing up in public housing describe the police as relentlessly present in their lives. Whether the police are riding or walking through the neighbourhood on bikes (doing what they describe as "community outreach"), riding into a housing complex on ATVs ("waving the flag"), or streaming out of a van with weapons raised (in the context of an arrest or raid), they are an ordinary feature in NIAs and in public housing in particular.

The justification for increased presence in the neighbourhood is constructed through crime analytic and other municipal data, which suggests the neighbourhood is vulnerable and unsafe. Increased police monitoring is meant to address the problems of safety that the crime analytic data reveal. But increased policing numbers (what police describe as "boots on the street") and policing activities (described by police as "outreach" and "intelligence-gathering") in designated NIAs bring the young people who live there into an organized relation of surveillance with the state. Police interactions – and their criminalizing impacts – constitute the background noise in young people's lives. But not all young people or all neighbourhoods grow up with this background noise.

Differential Policing Practices: Producing Race, Class, and Gender

As I write this, I am sitting on my couch in the west-end Montreal neighbourhood where I live, thinking about the policing I witness in my everyday life here. Historically a working- and middle-class neighbourhood, it is – like many urban neighbourhoods in Canada – becoming increasingly and homogenously White and middle to upper class as the cost of housing continues to rise. I walk around the neighbourhood all the time on my own and with my two children, and it is common for the police to drive by. They never stop. They do not even slow down, and we rarely see officers traversing the neighbourhood on foot or by bike. The policing practices in my neighbourhood stand in stark contrast to the policing I witnessed around Rosewood, where I also often walked. There it was a regular occurrence to see groups of officers riding through the neighbourhood on bikes, talking to people at bus stops and in parks, parked at intersections pulling people over, and slowly circling the neighbourhood in cars that would periodically peel out of parking lots in a burst of noise, lights, and dust.

These contrasts are important to keep in view because the raceclassgender relations this book seeks to make visible cannot be fully comprehended by only paying attention to relations of exclusion and neglect. "Noticing" relations of inclusion and privilege are important because of the ways they tend to disappear in people's descriptions of their experiences, concealing how these social relations are organized in ways that make them hard to see. The analysis produced in this chapter is informed by Sarah Ahmed's (2007) phenomenology of Whiteness and her interest in uncovering how "whiteness is lived as a background to experience" (p. 150). This chapter shows how Whiteness and Blackness are effects of racialization (like masculinity and femininity are effects of gender), which shape "what it is that bodies 'can do'" (Ahmed, 2007, p. 150) and what institutions and laws do to bodies.

Kaneesha's description of the police in her neighbourhood (showing up armed and without warning to arrest her brother) stands in sharp contrast to the experiences of a group of young White women we interviewed at McGill. These young women actively sought to bring the police into their lives after a spree of break and enters in their sorority. Their embodied experiences and the history of race, class, and gender oppression in Canada orient them differently to the state than Kaneesha, Tyrique, and Chris, the youth we interviewed in Toronto. "What comes into view" as a possibility for action for the youth in the Toronto NIAs and youth in McGill's "student ghetto," is a consequence of their divergent orientation to the state – an orientation that arrives as an inheritance and that is conditioned through experience (Ahmed, 2007 p. 152). Kaneesha and Nadia inherit the history of French and English settlement, colonization, and slavery in Canada – a history that differently conditions their present-day experiences and engagements with the state. "Such an inheritance can be re-thought in terms of orientations," whereby Whiteness "puts certain things in reach" (Ahmed, 2007, p. 154). While Kaneesha would not actively pursue a police intervention as a form of protection, Nadia (one of the McGill students we interviewed) does just this. For Nadia, reaching out to the police seemed as natural and obvious as avoiding the police was for Kaneesha.

The sorority where Nadia lives is located in a neighbourhood on the edge of campus, dubbed "the McGill student ghetto" by the economically privileged and largely White students who occupy it. Even the university itself positions it in that way.[2] Nadia describes what happened to prompt her interactions with the police like this:

> Okay, so, me and my six other roommates, we moved into a seven bedroom in the McGill ghetto area, super close to campus ... We're

---

2 For example, the 2017–2018 Summer Studies Programs, Courses and University Regulations manual states: "The New Residence Hall (NRH) also offers hotel-style accommodation in the heart of the *McGill student ghetto* [emphasis added]." (McGill University, 2017–2018, p. 49).

actually a sorority, so we're always having girls moving in and out of the house for meetings and stuff. So, in the beginning of the year, we had our recruitment … So, over the course of the last semester, we've had four incidents – like, one every month. That's when I posted it [on McGill Reddit] … The first one was when we had our recruitment event in September. So, there's three floors in our house. We were all on the main floor, and one of my roommates, she lives in the basement. She had left her window just open a little bit, and during the time that we were having our recruitment, we were all upstairs, super loud, and somebody had come in through her window and stole her camera. And it was a really expensive camera – like, $2,000–3,000 – so that was really hard on her because she's super into photography. So, after that, I mean, obviously, she started closing her window religiously, but she no longer felt safe because she felt so invaded on. We knew that with safety in the McGill ghetto – we knew that these things always happened … we did call the police. And we also notified our sorority headquarters. We started talking to our landlord about maybe putting bars on the windows. I mean, obviously, we started locking everything, clearly not well enough for the second [break-in to have occurred], but, yeah, we called the police. They came, but they didn't really [do anything]. They just said, "If it happens again, call us."

When Nadia references the "things [that] always happened" in the "McGill Ghetto," she is referring to the prevalence of minor property thefts in the neighbourhoods around the university (Rocha, 2018) – where considerable foot traffic, unlocked doors, and a wealth of personal electronics create conditions for "crimes of convenience."

In this context, Nadia is part of the community, whose safety the police work to preserve. Nadia speaks dismissively about the police and their efforts to keep her neighbourhood safe, but there was no sense during my interview with her that the police represent a material or symbolic form of violence in her life; rather, they are a semi-useless state intervention, which Nadia seeks to access largely out of convention rather than an expectation that they could contribute to her safety. She neither links the inefficacy of the police intervention to her Whiteness nor does she interpret the police inaction as a sign that the state doesn't care about White people. Indeed, she doesn't signal race at all in her account. As Ahmed (2007) observes, Nadia's Whiteness goes unnoticed and this is "what allows whiteness to cohere" and disappear as a social relation of privilege. You have to hold Kaneesha's story of the police in her neighbourhood next to Nadia's story to take in the weight of the genderraceclass relations shaping and being produced in and through their interactions with the state. Kaneesha's belief that the police "don't care about us" *and* Nadia's orientation to the police, the landlord, and sorority headquarters as tenable avenues through which to pursue her safety are socially organized relations that produce and are shaped by race, class, and gender consciousness. The relations that appear in young people's own analyses of their experiences in/with public sector institutions show us how they understand themselves in relation to others and the state.

Most Black youth growing up in the NIA where the research in Toronto occurred were clear that their interactions with the police were shaped by and reflected relations of race and often also gender and class. In contrast, the young White women we interviewed about neighbourhood safety at McGill did not speak about race, even when prompted to do so. Exemplary relations of race in purportedly post-racial times, Whiteness disappears for White youth interacting with institutions normed for White settlers. But "whiteness is only invisible for those who inhabit it" (Ahmed, 2007, 2004). These surfacing and disappearing relations – the individual threads of the complex of relations I described above as raceclassgender – are important analytic signposts. Paying attention to young people's negations of raceclassgender relations in their talk is as important as the places where these relations are actively brought into view by them.

Housing, Policing, and the State

Like people orient themselves differently in relation to the state through repetition and normative practices, institutions do the same (e.g., helping, protecting, surveilling, or punishing) towards people (Ahmed, 2007). As I am using it in this book, orienting is not simply a theoretical abstraction; rather, it is an accomplishment of actual embodied people, participating in institutional and social practices of knowing and doing. Over time and through repetition, these orientations acquire an objectified status and appear to exist independently of people's direct experiences of them. Race, class, and gender identities work in similar ways. They are theoretical abstractions, which encode and organize an unfolding history of material inequality. When prompted to tell the interviewer a little bit about himself, a young man named Felix described himself as "a young male living in a low-income area" and later in the interview as someone who grew up in a "priority neighbourhood." Across Canadian municipalities, socio-economic data are used to produce low-income, vulnerable, or priority neighbourhood designations, which connect economic disparity and vulnerability in the public imagination. The economic data themselves are presented as objective indicators of the relative distribution of economic and social opportunities across a geographic area. But the data depend on and conceal historically unequal social relations through which patterns of income and racial inequality are (re)produced.

In our interview with him, Felix reflected on what it meant to grow up in social housing in one of Toronto's designated NIAs. His description reveals the classed and raced social relations – but class and race do not describe naturally occurring and measurable phenomena. Race, poverty, and desperation are linked conceptually as economic data get drawn into other socio-political processes such as the state regulation of subsidized housing and the use of economic data to guide the distribution of public sector interventions across a municipality. Felix observed that living in social housing is like living in a "lobster cage, bro. They all want to get out. But they're all hands tied, they're all stepping on one another trying to get out or get some space. But you ain't getting no space." It is in the lobster cage of public housing, inhabited largely by people of colour living with poverty, that young people who live here (and those that don't) come to know what it means to be poor and Black in Canada. These institutionally mediated relations *are* the social relations of raceclassgender – not as three discrete sets of intersecting or aggregative social positions, but as a spectrum of actual material relations among people, structured by institutional knowledge and activity, and generative of both the experiences of race, class, and gender categories and the production of race, class, and gender consciousness.

Stories about public housing were always also stories about the police and often also stories about the paid and unpaid work of mothers and children. The social relations of gender and class are evident in young men's stories of their relationships with their mothers and their desires for economic independence to ease their mother's financial hardships. Another youth we interviewed, Tyrone, observed that no matter how hard his mother worked, she never had enough money to be able to move out of social housing: "It's like all you see is your mom working, working, working her ass off … Working, working, working, years on years on years, but you're still in Ontario Housing. She's saying, 'I want to move out of here.' Every year, 'We're moving out this year, we're moving out this year.' But she's not moving. Like little stuff like that. Like you just realize it's fucked." In this passage, Tyrone notices that it's the "little stuff" that makes him realize that he and his mother are unlikely to move out of public housing. The interview with Felix brings some of this "little stuff" Tyrone alludes to into greater visibility. He notes that economic eligibility criteria for housing subsidies perpetuate welfare dependence, criminality (working "under the book"), and the inability to transcend socially organized class difference:

> If you're in community housing, right, Toronto Metro Housing, you can't make certain amounts of money. You have to stay on welfare. So how are you going to liberate a man from poverty when everything he has to do is under the book? If I want to make an extra dollar, I got to make it under the book. If I'm making a certain amount of money, say I got a better job, I make more, and my rent will go from like eighty bucks to, like, might as well put a down payment on a million-dollar house than buy this piece of shit home.

Establishing and maintaining eligibility for social housing subjects an *applicant* or *resident* of social housing to ongoing economic monitoring. The desire to maintain access to housing subsidies becomes the justification for making money "under the book." Otherwise, the gains made through labour market participation are lost to market rents, which cannot be met if one is only making minimum wage. The abject conditions of the housing itself represent the only motivation to "liberate (oneself) from poverty." The poor quality of subsidized housing is a key juncture whereby class difference and human worth are coconstructed.

These are the social relations that shape Felix's belief that the state "don't give a shit about the houses with all the roaches and shit. I've been living in that motherfucking shit. That motivates (my ass) to go out there and go hustle. Because then I go home and lay my head down and I'm like, 'Fuck.' Slap myself, fuckin' roach crawling on my arm or some shit." Felix is a fourth-year university student. But his ability to support himself and his family depends on the degree to which he can "go out there and go hustle" – or make money "under the book." The underground economy in social housing environments, which is linked to housing subsidy eligibility monitoring practices and the inaccessible cost of market-based housing in the Greater Toronto Area, is recorded in crime analytics as elevated crime data in NIAs and public housing environments. The crime analytics reflect and guide ongoing field-based data collection and reporting processes used by the police. The Toronto Police Services rely on crime analytics to make decisions about how and where to deploy additional officers through the Divisional Policing Support Unit. This unit allows additional police officers to be stationed in areas where crime analytics suggest a need for increased police activity (field note, key informant, 2015). This ahistorical interpretation and use of crime analytics enable a rationalized (evidence-based) police response, which negates historically situated race-, gender-, and class-based experiences of institutionalized oppression.

Conclusion: Technologies of Evidence and the Construction of a Post-racial, Post-gendered, Post-class World

Administrative and other forms of institutional data and the evidential basis they inform connect to and serve the interests of institutions and institutional administrative and governing processes. The data collected and used by public sector organizations convey information about those individuals and families who have historically been the objects or targets of increased public sector interventions (Eubanks, 2018). As such, the data that inform predictive and other "evidence-based" practices in the public sector (e.g., intelligence-led policing) disproportionately reflect the racialized, classed, and gendered groups who historically and currently rely most heavily on public sector supports and/or who are most likely to experience unwanted public sector interventions (Eubanks, 2018). In the context of increased public sector interest in big-data solutions, it is important to reveal how biases get built into the data sets, which then permeate predictive and other evidence models. This chapter begins to bring these processes into view.

Public sector institutions – like the criminal legal system – operate through the collection and use of data that fit with and enable particular institutional courses of action that have material effects in the neighbourhoods where young people live and work; for example, issuing a warrant, approving a police raid, or laying a charge. But these are not neutral processes, and as this chapter illuminates, they create differential effects depending on how the data are collected and used to inform evidence-based decision-making (or intelligence-led policing practices). Crime analytic data collected in both cities reveal that Nadia's and Kaneesha's neighbourhoods have elevated rates of criminal activity, compared to the rest of the city. But in Nadia's neighbourhood, the thefts are described as "crimes of opportunity" committed against the middle to upper class, largely White student body at McGill by people living in poverty and struggling with addiction outside the neighbourhood. Nadia is able to report the theft of the camera to the police because theft is a recognizable and institutionally actionably threat to public safety and because there is an institutionally organized process (a call for service) for her to do so. She is also able to demand a response – however futile she perceives this act to be. Nowhere, in Nadia's recollection of her experiences do the police intimate that she or her White sorority sisters represent a threat to the other people living in her neighbourhood, to themselves, or to the state.

In contrast, Kaneesha describes the police showing up in the context of a raid, carrying long guns, threatening and then physically fighting with the largely Black residents who live in her social housing complex. The character of policing differs in the two neighbourhoods, justified in both cases by the collection and use of crime analytic data. In Kaneesha's neighbourhood, the police are always present – continually generating the data that can validate their presence in the neighbourhood as legitimate. For example, the sheer number of police on the streets in Kaneesha's neighbourhood, coupled with their presence in and access to community housing properties (Nichols & Braimoh, 2016) and neighbourhood schools (Nichols, Fisher, & Braimoh, submitted), as well as the higher incidence of stop-and-search procedures (Logical Outcomes, 2014), increases the likelihood that the police will find and charge young people carrying drugs (Alexander, 2012). All of this then elevates the crime statistics for the neighbourhood. The collection and use of administrative and other data are meant to substantiate the objectivity and neutrality of policing and other institutional practices of the state. But the discourse and practice of data- or intelligence-led policing obscures how these data have historically been produced through differential policing practices and data gathering techniques (e.g., community policing, stop-and-search processes, profiling) in different Canadian neighbourhoods. For example, where Black men in Toronto reported an average of 3.4 police stops in the last two years, White men reported 0.7 stops on average for this same period (Wortley & Owusu-Bempah, 2011). Significantly, Wortley and Owusu-Bempah found that racial differences in police contact remain statistically significant even where they controlled for age, income, driving patterns, alcohol and marijuana use, and criminal history. While there are not statistically significant differences in prevalence rates for marijuana possession between young White and Black men (Alexander, 2012), the disproportionality of stop-and-search practices will uncover higher rates of possession (i.e., chargeable crimes) among young Black men, thus legitimizing targeted stop-and-search practices (Wortley & Tanner, 2005). The move towards data-led policing thus operates like a feedback loop; as Black people are subject to more frequent stop-and-search processes, they are "more likely to be detected and arrested for illegal activity than people from other racial backgrounds who engage in exactly the same behaviour" (Wortley & Owusu-Bempah, 2011, p. 403), which rationalizes the deployment of more officers in neighbourhoods with higher numbers of Black people. An institution's divergent effects result from the ways people differently orient to the institutions of the state as well as how state institutions differently orient towards people. These social and institutional orientations are conditioned by and condition people's race, class, and gender consciousnesses and identities.

Chapter Four

Evidential Practices in Education and the Negation of Race

Canadian scholarship points specifically to academic disparities for Black and Indigenous students (Abada & Lin, 2011; Caldas, Bernier, & Marceau, 2009; Bhatteracharjee, 2003; Daniel & Bondy, 2008; Dei, Mazzuca, McIsaac, & Zine, 1997; James, 2011; James & Turner, 2015, 2017; Solomon & Palmer, 2004). Research also confirms racial minority youth perceive and experience proportionately more school-based interventions in the name of school safety compared with White youth in Ontario (Ruck & Wortley, 2002; Bhattacharjee, 2003, 2003) and in other Western nations (Gilborn, 2005, 2008; Ofer, 2011/2012; Rios, 2011; Skiba, Eckes, & Brown, 2009/2010; Skiba et al., 2014). Alongside ongoing research documentation of race-, class-, and gender-based disparities, claims continue to be made about the objectivity and neutrality of the public sphere. In the context of evidence-based policy-making and practice, the dominant narrative of public policy and programming neutrality has access to new discursive tools. These discursive practices condition people's interpretations of the results of particular institutional processes. For example, while the concept of race was frequently activated by Black youth to make sense of negative encounters with the police, they were less likely to activate the concept of race to make sense of similar experiences of targeting and exclusion in schools. This, despite the body of evidence cited above suggesting that Black children and youth in Canada experience disproportionately poor rates of academic success and higher rates of suspension and expulsion (Abada & Lin, 2011; Caldas, Bernier, & Marceau, 2009; Galabuzi, 2014; TDSB, 2013; Zheng & De Jesus, 2017). Differences in the institutional organization of schooling and policing background young people's differential assessment of these parallel processes of institutional exclusion. In fact, my sense is that negations of race in people's talk about schools tell us something important about processes of racialization operating there.

Education has long relied on testing as a means of measuring and ranking people. Indeed, Bourdieu and Passeron's (1977) research illuminates how education, culture, and the political economy structure each other. Far from determining the natural intellectual capacities of students, academic assessment practices select for the communicative norms and knowledge of those currently in power. Because access to education determines many forms of labour market participation, accepted links between entrance examinations and access to educational opportunities obscure how systems of pedagogic communication and assessment entrench (and naturalize) economic and cultural dominance.

The translation of educational success into labour market opportunities continues to shape contemporary meritocratic narratives and educational assessment practices – including international testing regimes – that effectively stitch young people's experiences in schools into a wider politico-economic order. The long history of dependence on evidential practices – in the form of standardized entrance examinations, ongoing student assessment, recorded observations, and psychometric testing – to make decisions about access to educational opportunities and interventions makes it difficult to imagine schools functioning in any other way. Despite research that confirms that standardized tests only reliably measure test preparation, while generating gender and race gaps in academic achievement (Nguyen & Ryan, 2008; Good, Aronson, & Inzlicht, 2003), or research that demonstrates intelligence quotient (IQ) scores increase with access to health care and education (Bradley & Corwyn, 2002; Duncan, Brooks-Gunn, & Klebanov, 1994), nation-states, governments, schools, and families continue to depend on standardized metrics to evaluate and compare educational performance and make decisions. Although Bourdieu and Passeron (1977) limit their analysis to class and gender, their studies suggest why young people may be less likely to link their experiences in school to any form of unfairness: academic standards, assessment practices, and processes of academic sorting continue to be commonly understood as objectives means for differentiating merit and potential.

For instance, when I was explaining the thinking behind this book to a colleague, she responded by telling me a story about her grandson, who is the first in his immediate family to graduate from university. In order to pay for school, he – like many young people – worked part-time and lived at home. He is now thinking about graduate school, and he has begun looking at admissions requirements for graduate programs in clinical psychology at the University of British Columbia (UBC), which would allow him to continue to live at home. In so doing he has discovered that successful completion of an undergraduate degree is not sufficient to apply to a clinical psychology program; applicants are required to demonstrate their interest in the field by completing (typically unpaid) research assistantships in large clinical labs. Indeed, a quick review of the UBC website confirms: "Research experience in psychology is required for admission to our graduate program" (UBC, 2018a). The website further affirms that the admission process at UBC "is similar to any research-intensive psychology department in Canada or the USA" (UBC, 2018b). The number of applicants to the program far exceeds the number of available positions each year, and, as such, the department unequivocally states that "preference is given to applicants who have demonstrated interest in the scientific basis of clinical psychology as well as practice" (UBC, 2018c). Some young people enter university with a mind to the admissions requirements for entry into subsequent graduate or professional programs. This thoughtfulness is neither a natural precociousness nor a predisposition to planning; rather, it reflects a set of learned practices cultivated in the social spaces of their lives (e.g., the home, school, and within their friend groups) that solidifies race, class, and gender stratification and obscures the university's implication in producing these relations.

The irony is that departments that include service and field experience often do so in order to diversify the criteria upon which admissions are based – that is, not just cumulative grade point average. Unfortunately, rather than basing admissions on holistic demonstrations of competence within the field, the criteria are aggregative and the expectations for admissions simply rise – one now needs to demonstrate field-based *and* academic competence. In doing so, departments limit entry into the field to those students who have the economic capital and institutional know-how to acquire the experience base and grade point averages (always much higher than those stated on the university web pages) required for admissions. In other words, university admissions processes anchor and produce the social relations of class. And because relations of class are "shot through" (Bannerji, 1991) with, and further productive of, relations of race and gender, we catch a glimpse here of the ways that everyday institutional processes (in this case, university admissions exercises designed to improve access to programs for "non-traditional students") actually (re)produce the very social relations they hope to dismantle. Of course, no one in the department *intends* to limit entry to middle- and upper-class young people. This particular program – like many programs in universities across Canada – explicitly invites "applications from qualified students from a diverse range of backgrounds *and refrains from systematically excluding* students on the basis of personal factors not relevant to probability of success in graduate school, including race, ethnic origin, gender, age, sexual orientation, religion, or physical disability" (UBC, 2018c). Since the problem in this particular example is not overt classism and racism, "refraining from systematically excluding students" will not engender more diversity within the field. To "refrain" from doing something implies intentionality. Here, and elsewhere across the public sphere, the problem is the ubiquity of institutional processes, programs, and policies that subtly or explicitly include, privilege, protect, or enable some people while simultaneously excluding, punishing, and blocking others.

In the context of education, an institutional landscape saturated in the language of inclusion, diversity, opportunity, and equality, one is unlikely to find evidence of overtly racist curricula, pedagogical structures, and institutional discourse. But the popular educational policy mantra of "Success for All" is undermined by an education system and capitalist social organization that produces and depends on competition and inequality. The education system grooms and sorts people for participation in a capitalist labour market, and it employs – and naturalizes – objectified systems of classifications, rankings, rewards, and punishments to accomplish this task. The functional outcomes of public schooling are at odds with the discursive organization of the space. This chapter shows how policy narratives about success for all, inclusion, diversity, and equity are incompatible with – but effectively obscure – the actual project of education as it articulates with the economic organization of the nation-state.

Comparing Educational Contexts: Toronto and Montreal

Despite differences in the provision and management of public education in Montreal and Toronto, in both cities educational opportunities are unequally distributed along race, class, and gender lines. Processes of institutional organization that cut across both provincial contexts include: (1) A policy and institutional focus on Safe Schools, regulated locally through board and school-level Codes of Conduct; (2) The use of standardized academic performance measures (test scores, credit accrual rates, and graduation rates) to compare and rank students and schools; and (3) Ubiquitous processes of race, class, and gender segregation built into the delivery and management of access to specialized programming and the dispersal of educational exclusions and punishments. Young people in both provinces may be moved out of mainstream programs for issues related to identified educational needs, discipline, school attendance, and credit accumulation. Differences between the provincial contexts reflect the distinctive social, political, and economic organization of these two provinces. In chapter 5, I will explore the institutional and policy context of the two provinces more fully. For now, it is simply important to note a few key differences in the institutional practices through which educational segregation is accomplished in the two provinces.

Where Ontario has integrated provincial and board- and school-level Safe Schools policies, procedures, and programs, in Quebec the approach to school discipline is much less centralized. Schools develop and implement local codes of conduct and disciplinary cultures that reflect a less centralized policy and legislative infrastructure (e.g., a single document – the English Montreal school board's Safe Schools and Centres Policy – governs the board's youth, adult, and vocational sectors and there is no network of alternative programs in the English Montreal school boards that is comparable to the Caring and Safe Schools programs in Toronto). Another factor, which shapes different educational processes and outcomes in the two provinces, is the legal age of compulsory school attendance – eighteen years of age in Ontario and sixteen years in Quebec. Once young people reach sixteen years of age in Quebec, some choose or are directed to finish their schooling in the adult and vocational system.

Further differentiating Montreal's educational landscape from Toronto's is the Montreal's "libre choix" or free choice, open-market model. Within this market-based approach to the provision of public schooling, some public schools have obtained a special project status that enables them to create highly competitive admissions criteria (e.g., standardized testing, grades, interviews with children and parents, and community service requirements). An additional aspect of the open-market approach to education in Quebec, and one that I explore in more detail in chapter 5, is the public investment in private education. Private schools that agree to deliver the provincial curriculum, impose provincially mandated tuition caps, and operate in compliance with the Charter of the French Language (regarding eligibility for English instruction) are qualified to receive public funds. Public funding allows Quebec private schools to offer tuition rates that are a quarter of the cost of tuition for similar schools in Ontario.

In Montreal, this has resulted in a large number of middle- and upper-class parents opting for the private system, exacerbating severe underfunding of the public system (as a result of the enrolment-based or per-capita funding models, which are used in both Quebec and Ontario); it has also polarized the have/have-not schools across the public boards serving Montreal and the surrounding areas. Finally, as

Quebec language laws intersect with education law in the province, young people arriving as immigrants are legally obliged to enter the French language school system, no matter their age and regardless of their language proficiencies. This legislation severely disadvantages English-speaking young people arriving during middle childhood or adolescence, who must acquire content knowledge and participate in standardized testing regimes in French. Unsurprisingly given these context factors, the distribution of educational opportunities and exclusions is highly gendered, classed, and racialized across the city of Montreal. Many racialized youth and youth living in poverty are seeking to complete their education in one of the city's outreach schools or within its severely underfunded adult education system, often with thousands on waiting lists (Fédération des Cégeps, 2006).

Similar raceclassgender patterns are evident in Toronto, where Black and other racialized young people live disproportionately in the city's designated NIAs and attend the city's most vulnerable schools as measured through the school board's Learning Opportunities Index. Teachers, youth workers, and administrators in Toronto refer to the city's most vulnerable schools as "bucket schools" or "sink-hole schools." One young man named Kai observed that schools are "procrastinator schools" or schools with fewer expectations for student success. By paying attention to the institutional and policy contexts that produce these disproportionalities, it is clear that in both provinces the education systems are organized to produce the unbalanced outcomes that they do.

Educational Exclusions and the Evidential Turn in Education

The first interviews conducted with young people for Schools and Safety were held with students in Rosewood's School Away from School program. Based on my earlier research on youth homelessness (Nichols, 2008, 2014), I knew that a single staged question could be effectively leveraged to generate rich and useful data. In my earlier research, when I interviewed young people staying at a youth shelter, I simply asked them to tell me the story about how this came to happen – that is, how they came to be living at the shelter. In this subsequent project, the first interviews I did were with young people who were learning at Rosewood. After giving young people a chance to tell us about themselves, a research assistant or I would ask: How did you end up learning here at Rosewood? This starting place works because the interviewer and the interviewee begin their conversation speaking about the very context that brought them together. Because the School Away from School program was (at the time of this research) an official assessment and support program, situated within the school board's Caring and Safe Schools initiatives,[1] I also knew that this question would invite young people to talk about their experiences with institutional responses to school safety. The institutionally derived reasons for moving young people out of the mainstream system and into Rosewood pertained to – often interrelated – issues of attendance, school discipline, and academic progress. But these institutional explanations only superficially explain how and why it happens that some young people are moved out of mainstream programs to be educated on the margins of the system. To fully understand how these educational moves are coordinated and justified, institutionally, one needs to pay attention to the evidential practices used to manage public education at this moment in history.

Across Ontario and Quebec public schools, administrators are under considerable pressure to demonstrate empirical improvements in academic performance, largely based on shared metrics (e.g., graduation and credit accumulation rates, attendance and expulsion rates). The aggregation and monitoring of administrative and other institutional data to assess school performance enables policy and other decision makers, who are not on-site in schools, to make and implement managerial, policy, and resource allocation decisions at the provincial or board level, which influence how schools operate. But these data can obscure as much as they reveal. For example, decontextualized data tells us very little about what it is like to teach and learn in a particular school, or about the contexts shaping the variables that are tracked and the trends they reveal. Furthermore, where school performance is linked to graduation, attendance, and credit accrual rates, educational transfers and other administrative relocations are incentivized. Particularly in struggling schools, with student success programs (for "at-risk" youth) that are already stretched, there is little remaining capacity/ incentive to retain students who are really floundering.

When asked why she was going to school at Rosewood, Marianna explained that she'd arrived at her mainstream school in

---

1 The School Away from School program falls under the school board's Safe Schools services (that is, it is one of the programs overseen by Safe Schools principals, placement coordinators, and superintendents), but it is not a Long-Term Suspension and Expulsion Program, which I describe in more detail in the next section. Officially, Rosewood could not receive expelled students; instead, it tended to receive students who have been "excluded" formally from school, but not expelled.

September (three days after the start of classes) to discover she'd been de-enroled:

> Well, I started skipping a lot of school. That's a really bad habit of mine, which I'm trying to fix. I came back this year to J-school. (I used to go to M-School.) Then they asked me like why am I here, and I'm like, "What do you mean?" They're like, "You're not supposed to be in the school." I'm like, "But I got a timetable. I got the 'Welcome back to J-school,' and all this stuff." So I'm kind of confused. I got my schedule and everything. I even got my locker number. I'm just like explaining to them, "Why wouldn't I be here? You gave me my stuff" … [The principal] started to explain, "Because you failed." We [my sister and I] failed grade 9. We didn't pass – well, I only passed half the year of grade 10. So that's not enough credits to continue to grade 11. Then they started to explain it, and I'm like, "Oh, well, that makes sense."

With patchy attendance records, and slower-than-grade-level credit accumulation rates, Marianna and her twin sister, Monika, were unceremoniously de-enroled from their mainstream school and enroled at Rosewood. Marianna describes the move as understandable, given her "bad habit" of skipping school and her subsequent failure to accumulate credits. Relying on the use of student success data (e.g., the proportion of students achieving twenty-four credits by grade 11) as indicators of school performance perversely incentivizes the removal of those students whose credit scores diminish the school's progress towards the twenty-four-credit target. It is not coincidental that Marianna and Monika were moved out of their mainstream school before grade 11.

Furthermore, Marianna's individualized explanation for – and acquiescence to the futility of resisting – the exclusionary relations she describes reflects her experiences with educational and other human service professionals to date. A history of intersecting and invasive child protection and educational interventions shape her response. For example, like other young people I interviewed in Toronto and in Montreal, Marianna was repeated threatened with suspensions by school administrators for arriving late and missing school. Ultimately, she and her sister were both suspended for having too many "lates." In addition, she describes a long-term and negative relationship with child protective services throughout her childhood and adolescence, including a social worker named Rosana, who she says works for "the Catholic School Board or something," and whom she describes in the interview as "worse than the vice-principal." Marianna explains,

> She's always suspecting and she's always threatening my mom and saying these things, just barging into our house whenever she wants to and is really disrespectful. Like there's a certain amount of respect that she needs to follow, but then again, what can we do, right? She's a social worker ... [She's always threatening] to take us away, take my little sister away, everyone, everyone under sixteen years. And then they threatened to take me and my sister away until we turned sixteen. It was really just the way she would always invade our lives, just ask too many personal questions.

Relations of gender are visible in young people's accounts of their connections with their mothers. Marianna and Monika were frequently late for school because they were often responsible for taking their younger siblings to school first. Marianna's frustration with the school social worker, Rosana, reflects a history of interactions between social workers and her mother, which Marianna found disrespectful: "threatening my mom and saying these things, just barging into our house whenever she wants to." While young men sought to protect their mothers by earning money, young women protected their families by engaging in caregiving work at home and keeping silent in public. Rosana's relentless questions and surveillance add to Marianna's work to protect her mother and her siblings from further child welfare interventions. A history of punitive, intrusive, and threatening relations with the education and child protection systems, as well as other institutional relations that are not visible in this particular passage, shape what appears like passive acceptance on the parts of Marianna and her sister Monika. Over the years, I've come to see young people's quiet passivity and even absenteeism as measured acts of resistance. Efforts to try to explain your life and experiences to adults who are unlikely to believe you and neither understand nor empathize are futile. It's more effective not to come (to school), not to talk, and not to answer their persistent questions. Young people require extraordinary fortitude to spend their days participating in public sector institutions that were not designed for them, are populated by authorities they cannot relate to, and who do not (and do not try hard enough to) understand them.

Like Marianna and Monika, Jerome, another young man interviewed by one of our youth researchers, said he stopped going to school when he was one credit shy of graduation, having arrived on the first day to find he'd been de-enroled:

INTERVIEWER: So you do intend on finishing that one credit?

JEROME: Yeah. I was supposed to finish it last year, but I went to school. And I went to the office like, "I need my timetable." And they were like, "There's no timetable for you." I'm like, "What do you mean?" She's like, "Go see the guidance counsellor." [So I went to see the guidance counsellor] and she's like, "Oh, the school's too full, so I don't know what I can do for you." I'm like, "What do you mean the school's too full?" And she's like, "Yeah."

INTERVIEWER: Even for one class – just to get into one class?

JEROME: Yeah. And from there, I was like, "All right, whatever." It was September, and then I ended up getting arrested.

Many of the young people we interviewed describe non-disciplinary relocations based on below-grade-level performance, like the ones Marianna and her sister experienced or ambiguous exclusions like the one Jerome describes. Few young people actively resisted these moves; for many they reflected entrenched patterns of systemic exclusion that had forcefully shaped their lives since they were young children.

On the other side of the spectrum, one of the youth research assistants I worked with for two years in Ontario explained that his secondary school principal "fixed" his final grades during his last year at school, giving him passing grades for classes he had failed and allowing him to graduate and go on to participate in post-secondary schooling. This young man's experience is a reminder that the same complex of institutional relations can produce vastly different outcomes at the individual level. At that time, he'd been attending one of the Toronto high schools in the neighbourhood with the lowest graduation rates in the city. Backgrounding all three stories, one catches glimpses of the institutional pressures to demonstrate school improvement, particularly in historically underperforming schools. As much as these pressures influence the educational trajectories of young people, they also undermine educators' efforts to work with students living complex and varied lives.

In the following passage, a student success teacher – a teacher tasked with working with youth "at risk" in a mainstream school – describes an encounter with a school board representative who was concerned about the rates of credit accumulation documented by the school:

K: She's concerned because the graduation rate was low. Like they look at how many credits per [student] – so sixteen by sixteen, right, and then how many [students] make twenty-four by Grade 11. And so we're below every time … So she wanted to know why that's happening. I was pissed. Like why is that happening? Because Christina's got a tumor and Cindy's pregnant and Thomas is depressed, and so-and-so's up on murder charges, and – like you can't put a blanket over all those things, and say why that is … [But] if you want to know the thing that I think that all the kids have in common and maybe this is not a very good perspective because I only see the kids that are "at risk," but I would say the one thing that these kids have in common is poverty. Because the kids who have health problems and money, they can get tutors … The kids who have depression problems [and money], they can afford outside counsellors. They have parents who can like dote on them. These kids are on their own.

AF: So when the board person said, "Why are the kids not accumulating credits?"

STUDENT SUCCESS TEACHER: You can't say, "Because they're poor."

Here, Kayla conveys her frustrations with the institutional preoccupation with educational metrics (e.g., credit accumulation and graduation rates) that suggest that she, her colleagues, and their students are failing. Despite the important critical class analysis Kayla offers above, the social relations of race and gender are submerged by speaking about poverty as though it isn't racialized and gendered. Indeed, despite well-documented statistics on the racialization of poverty *and* race- and class-based disproportionalities in academic achievement in Toronto (Brown & Parekh, 2013; Galabuzi, 2014; Zheng & De Jesus, 2017), the school board consistently argues that the best predictors of academic performance are socio-economic ones (Toronto District School Board, 2014). Racial inequality is only imperceptible to those it benefits – rarely to those it burdens (Lawrence & Williams, 2006).

Given that educational performance data remains an important indicator of national economic success (OECD, 2010; World Bank, 2007), the pressure to demonstrate improvements in graduation rates cuts across Canadian provinces and territories. Like it has in Ontario, this pressure materializes in Quebec as exclusionary practices in schools. When I moved to Montreal and started working with the young people at Chalet Parc, I invited young people to talk about their lives and experiences. One young man referenced an experience much like those youth described in Toronto:

Okay, so, starting of sec 5 [grade 11], I went to my normal high school – Y High School. I went to the auditorium to pick up my schedule, and I couldn't find it. So, they said, "Go to the office." So, I went to the office, and they were like, "We don't have it. Go to the guidance counsellor." So, I went to the guidance counsellor, and she said, "You're not even in the school anymore." And I asked, "What? Like, I got the letter in the mail in the summer." She said, "Oh, really? What? I don't know." So, yeah, she looked in the computer [database], and I was completely wiped for good. My picture wasn't even there anymore. I was nobody to them. (David)

Without any prior warning, and just like youth in Toronto, youth in Montreal are being de-enroled from mainstream schools and moved into alternative programs. The institutional orientation to school improvement and performance – evidenced by attendance rates, credit accrual rates, and graduation rates as proxies for "school success" – is representative of the types of reductive performance management regimes implemented in education and elsewhere across the public sector (Nichols, 2014).

Such data collection and analytic practices – exemplary of the managerial turn in public sector work organization – may well incentivize educational transfers in order to consistently demonstrate indications of school improvement and/or performance. At first glance, none of this is about race, class, and gender. But it is important to note that Marianna and Monika are Latina, my research assistant is Asian, and David is Black, and none of these young people come from economically privileged households. They were not de-enroled *because* they are economically precarious youth of colour; but the institutional relations of accountability linking educational performance to economic productivity play out differently for young people, depending on the range of ways that they participate in the social relations of race, class, and gender. The experiences of individual youth and educators reflect broader political-economic relations, connecting processes of racialization, gender, and class in individual schools to the prevailing discourses of meritocracy and the larger interrelated historically situated projects of capitalism, imperialism, and colonialism (Galabuzi, 2014; Maynard, 2017).

Teachers: "Most of Them Mean Very Well"

Between 2012 and 2018, Rosewood was home to a number of teachers – employed by the Toronto public and Toronto Catholic school boards – who had competencies in the generalities of lesson planning, tailoring curricula to student needs/strengths, and classroom management but variable degrees of knowledge about the neighbourhood and the experiences of the young people who grow up there. None of the teachers at Rosewood were from the neighbourhood, and many were early career teachers in their first full-time position. Towards the latter years I was there, due to declining employment opportunities in the two boards, newer teachers were replaced by more seasoned educators. Only a single teacher (Fern) spent more than a single year at Rosewood between 2011/2012 and the closure of the school in 2016/2017, having accepted the position because it was the only full-time job on offer at the time. While they were not always White, none of the teachers were Black. In contrast, all of the youth workers, wraparound workers, and outreach workers at Rosewood are, and have historically been, Black. Kim, Odinegbo, and Warren – the three youth workers with whom I worked most closely at Rosewood over the years – all talked about how race mattered in their work with youth and in the disconnect young people experienced with their teachers. I am a White woman who didn't even live in Toronto at the time of this research. It would be hypocritical for *me* to hang my critique on this particular dynamic; but it definitely matters. There is a reason why this project was conducted using participatory methods and in collaboration with the organization.

Over the years, Warren and I have had many conversations about this, but the first time he commented on the racialized, classed, and gendered disconnect between the teachers and the students in the neighbourhood was during an interview in 2014. During the first part of the conversation, Warren relied on racialized euphemisms (inner-city kid and the hood) rather than naming race and anti-Blackness in particular, but as the interview develops, he is much more explicit about how he understands the roots of problems he uncovers in our conversation:

> I work in the high schools around here, three of them, right? You got good teachers. Not knocking the teachers. Beautiful teachers. Most of them mean very well. You understand? They try hard. The thing is our kids have a lot of issues, so it's hard for a teacher to come to school, "I'm here to teach. I'm not here to be a social worker, a CYW, a nurse, a parent." You understand? So, a lot of the teachers find themselves in that situation, and it's overwhelming … And then *again* the problem comes when you have a lot of teachers that come from – they don't know how to relate to inner-city kids. Then you have the school resource [police] officers who are just sitting down there *waiting* for somebody to call. So, a kid will come to school with a problem, and be like, "Miss, I don't need someone to F-n

talk to me!" And they flip out. Teachers here, they get nervous. They're from Hamilton, Owen Sound. It's the truth. I'm not knocking nobody. I'm just saying the truth. Well, all they see of inner-city kids, "Oh, they just shoot 'em up, bang bang," you know, they watch City-Pulse 24 out where they're from. So, they come in – it's that same attitude. You understand? The first time the kid flips out, they get scared. They run, they say to the officer, "I'm intimidated. I feel I was threatened," and the officer is going to come, "You're under arrest."

Without ever referencing anti-Black racism in this passage, Warren shows us how it is able to structure what happens in schools. "Beautiful teachers" who mostly "mean very well" do a lot of damage in a school with "school resources [police] officers who are just sitting down there waiting" and classrooms full of children whose actions they interpret through schema derived, not via direct experience, but through their engagement with common textual and discursive representations of the neighbourhood. I am not suggesting *all* White teachers fear their Black students, but some do, and I am interested in how people's interpretive practices are conditioned by their participation in textually and institutionally mediated relations, including discursive relations. If a teacher's prior knowledge of the neighbourhood in question is based largely on decontextualized and sensational representations of the neighbourhood disseminated through popular media outlets like CP-24 (the "breaking news" station for the Greater Toronto Area) and the racist and racially coded comments of friends and family in the suburbs who learn that this is where one is teaching (e.g., "you better wear a bullet proof vest"[2]), teachers are likely to draw on these readily available discursive resources in their interpretations of young people's actions and words.

Towards the end of the interview with Warren, I bring aspects of my own analysis into our conversation to see what we understand about education when we view it from our two distinctive standpoints. While not an interviewing convention that typifies traditional qualitative methods, in institutional ethnography (where the focus is not on the person a researcher is interviewing but on a complex of institutional relations you and the interviewee both know and have experienced) it is not abnormal to proceed in this way. By doing so, I demonstrate

---

2 This was actually a warning I received when I announced to White friends and family that I was going to attend the university, which is located in the same neighbourhood.

transparency in my own analytic process and commitment to a shared mechanism of discovery as we try to figure out how it happens that "beautiful," well-meaning teachers and other youth-serving professionals produce such disastrously racist outcomes. Only after I lay my own cards on the table does Warren explicitly address the role that he sees race playing in the social relations I begin to describe:

NAOMI: Growing up, I always I believed all the stories [that institutions offer youth] because they worked for people like me. Like: go to school, then you go to college, then you get a job, and life is good. And I would say I've struggled on the getting a job part, but life has been really easy for me, and that narrative was true for me. But I think if you haven't seen it be true for [you and] others [like you] and as you get older, you realize, "That's a story that's not mine. Like that story is other people's story and you fed it to me for my whole life," and –

WARREN: – And it doesn't apply to a lot of people. It doesn't apply to a lot of people. Because I go to school. And I've been going to school. I went to Ryerson, I did the Child and Youth Work program at Centennial. And I'll tell you, even as a big man, I had to, a lot of times, walk out and take a deep breath and people were saying, "Just chill." Because I was ready to snap on teachers because racism is institutionalized. True racism is institutionalized, right? Whether it be the police force, educational system, the medical, it's there, it happens. And I've encountered it. And for me to jump and say, and pull the Black card, it's going to be like, "What the hell are you talking about?" But it is what it is, you understand? So being patient, for me, and understanding and laughing a lot of time, and it's "Oh God. I can't believe this exists here," and I'm a grown-ass man. I'm a grown-ass man, "I can't believe this exists here." It's crazy. So, you face it. I'm facing it at this age trying to get my shit together. Imagine what these kids face. You understand what I'm saying? And it happens. They face it. I know a friend of a friend who was in school, got in some trouble, the cops came to the class, for something, he didn't say. And finally, when I got to talk to him, because I like to document things, like, "What happened?" He's like, "Yo, I got in an argument with security at the school. I had an argument with them, and I went to my class. Four days later–" This was just after the Danzig shooting in Scarborough. Remember that shooting?

NN: Yeah, yeah.

WARREN: "Four days later, they came, TAVIS [Toronto Anti-Violence Intervention Strategy unit] came, arrested me in class, and told me I threatened security with a gun." So why would you come four days later after Danzig shooting in Scarborough? You would have come right away.

You understand? They arrested him. He dropped out of school. He said, "Eff the system. I'm done with this. I'll do what I do." And he's smart. A smart guy. He had one year to go. One year to get a diploma, with plans of going to university. Because the way we look at it, "I'm a Black man in this system, and it's not meant for me," you know what I mean? Like say what you want to say, it's just not.

The sense that "I'm a Black man [boy, girl, woman, child] in this system and it's not meant for me" reflects a way of knowing that is shared by young people and adults working in relation to the very same public and private sector institutions that background my own life and against which I grew up believing that as long as I tried hard and followed the rules, anything I wanted was possible for me. A small group of young Black men are implicated in a neighbourhood shooting, and suddenly all young Black men are suspects, and antiviolence prevention warrants pulling them out of class after an altercation with campus security. The work Warren has to do – to be patient, not to snap, to "just chill" – in institutional spaces, saturated by racism that is inescapable for him and not even remotely evident to others, is exhausting. He is a "grown-ass man" incredulous about – and resigned to – the racism he experiences; he knows it is likely his experiences will be denied if he "jumps up and plays the Black card."

The youth research team and I had a long conversation about this same topic the following summer in a university classroom, using whiteboards to document and critically analyse the relations that link their drug consumption with their efforts to "not snap" on teachers and other well-meaning, but completely out of touch adults in their lives. Warren reflects on how young people coming to terms with similar realizations end up saying, "Eff the system." Where policing meets education, schools exacerbate rather than ameliorate racialized, classed, and gendered inequalities:

I've seen this a lot of times. I'm in the school, I'm like, "Officer, what did he do?" [And the officer responds:] "Stay away. This is of no concern to you, sir." I'm like, "Officer, I work with him." [And the officer responds:] "You're going to get an obstruction of justice [charge]." So, you can't even advocate, because you've just been warned. The minute a cop does this to a kid, it's police business. You've got to stay away because you'll get stuck with an obstruction of justice charge … You're trying to tell them, "He has problems at home. He didn't eat last night. He had to walk here from ten miles to come to school." There's a lot of issues these kids face. They don't want to hear that. So you lock the kid up.

Once teachers frame an interaction with a young person as a threat to their own or other's safety, they establish conditions, institutionally, for a transfer of disciplinary power from the school to the youth criminal justice system. Only at this point can questions and/or efforts to de-escalate on Warren's part be framed as interference with a criminal justice proceeding. Young people describe being charged by police in schools for speaking back aggressively to teachers or, in one young woman's case, wearing strong perfume in the presence of a teacher with an allergy. In all instances, the necessary institutional switch, activating a criminal justice response, is the declaration on the part of the teacher that they felt threatened. The problem is that fear – and the range of institutional security efforts it inspires – are racialized, through and through (Hines-Datiri, 2015; Mbembe, 2017). When I ask Warren whether the educative and policing practices he describes above are characteristic of all schools, he is clear:

> You can't do this at – let's take a school for instance right now, like, Richmond Hill. You can go up there and grab, slam the kid on the floor in front of the whole school, cuff him. Are you kidding me? You could never get away with that up there. But you do it in the hood all the time. You can't go in those [Richmond Hill] schools and intimidate those kids and talk to them hard. No, because their fathers are judges and lawyers and this and that. They'll be breathing down your back faster than you can blink.

Warren's insistence that police practices in the schools near Rosewood differ from those in schools in Richmond Hill reminds me of Nadia and Kaneesha's differential descriptions of the policing conventions in their neighbourhoods. The state's divergent deployment of policing resources and the contrastive use of force represents a fundamental site of social action through which raceclassgender inequalities are visible and become entrenched. Where these relations play out in schools, they are magnified.

Police in Schools

One of the reasons the School Resource (Police) Officer (SRO) program was recently disbanded in Toronto is because the deployment of SROs disproportionately impacted young people living in economically struggling and racialized communities (Gordon, 2017; Toronto District School Board, 2017b). Where some SROs were assigned to up to eight schools across the city, and some schools had none, still other schools had officers present on a full-time basis. During the course of the project, I interviewed an SRO named Chad who worked in another of Toronto's NIAs. White, not very tall, in his mid- to late thirties, and sporting a shaved head, Chad came to the interview at Rosewood in his street clothes – a sign that he is aware of and is sensitive to young people's trepidation about police. He was generous in his descriptions of the young people he worked with, reasonably frank with Chantel and me, and seemingly committed to delivering recreational programming at the school where he worked. He also recognized, however, that his approach to the position was not shared by others.

Without a clear job description, the work of SROs differed from school to school. Furthermore, as Warren notes above, even people who are kind and well meaning participate in – and contribute to – the institutional relations that produce the racialized outcomes research continues to document. The young people we interviewed witnessed and suffered relentlessly violent and disrespectful interactions with the police in their neighbourhood, as they walked to the bus, hung out in the park, and/or travelled to and from school each day. Even where they have the good fortune to encounter a benevolent SRO like Chad, this single interaction does not undo the impacts of police violence in other aspects of their lives. Towards the end of the interview, reflecting on how young people grow up to hate the police, Warren observes:

> [X] Division is like a training ground [for the police]. If you can do your policing here successfully, you can do it anywhere in the city. It's been like that from the '80s. Sorry to say it's the truth. That's how it is. And our kids pay the price. They do, they do. They pay the price. Thirteen years old. Even twelve years old. You talk to Daniel, and you ask him what he thinks of cops. He'll tell you that they're the worst thing that ever happened. He hates them and he's thirteen. Why? "Because they shout at me, they threaten me, they talk back to my mom." I had that conversation with him. Yeah, thirteen.

In addition to higher numbers of school exclusions and criminalizing interventions, paying the price means young people grow up hating the police, mistrusting all other institutional authorities, and resigned to the realization that the meritocratic narratives of the neo-liberal age are written for others and do not apply to them. In Warren's observations about the experiences of Black youth going to mainstream schools in "the hood," the complexity of the problematic I am seeking to reveal in this book comes more clearly into focus.

Institutional structures are created at particular moments in history by and for those in positions of power tasked with overseeing their development. As these structures are operationalized, they create vastly disparate effects when engaged by actual people living at other points in time and under different conditions than those the institutions were made by and for. Those young people and families who are unable to merge the evolving conditions of their actual lives with the normative relations, priorities, interventions, and policies that comprise public systems are framed within this system as non-normative, delayed, pre-cocious, or in other ways out of sync with the system's normative ideals (Griffith & Smith, 2005; Nichols, 2018).

Conclusion: The Affirmation of Race, Class, and Gender Categories in Post-race, Post-class, and Post-gender Times

Forty years ago, Bourdieu and Passeron proposed that schools and school-based processes (e.g., entrance examinations) are neither objective nor fair. Their careful research revealed just how school processes, communicative practices, and policies privilege and reward the speech mannerisms, cultural practices, epistemological frames, and methods of comportment of the dominant classes. Since then, the public sector has produced – and been reorganized by – a proliferation of discourse proclaiming the objectivity of public sector processes and institutions (e.g., evidence-based and data-led policy-making, programming and practices). Against this discursive stronghold, public sector institutions remain shaped by and continue to produce race, class, and gender inequalities.

In 2017, Robyn Maynard published an historical account of the classed, gendered, and racial disparities in terms of academic progress, suspension and expulsion rates, streaming and special education rates, incarceration rates, labour market, and health outcomes produced by Canadian institutions, shaped by historical and present-day state policies and programs steeped in and reflecting a constellation of racial bias (i.e., anti-Black racism, White supremacy, and settler colonialism). One of the most devastating outcomes of the post-racial, post-class, and post-gendered neo-liberal turn (Howard, 2006) is the discursive coupling of evidence-based policy and practice with the documented racial-ethnic and class-based disparities resulting from these same purportedly "neutral" policies.

Of course, state policies are not neutral. But this theoretical assumption – which comprises the foundation of critical legal and critical race feminist scholarship (Alexander, 2012; Bannerji, 1995;

Crenshaw, Gotanda, Peller, & Thomas, 1995; Lawrence & Williams, 2006; Razack, Smith, & Thobani, 2010) – must be cultivated against the grain of increasingly dominant tropes about uses of evidence and objectivity in the policy-making process. As Zellars (2017) notes: "Historically, de facto anti-Black discrimination throughout Canada has been practiced in two primary trends: first, through the implementation and sustenance of colourblind codes, laws, and policies that yielded racially discriminatory impacts, and secondly, through the discriminatory behaviours of its citizens and state actors – mayors, prime ministers, and judges – that the law permitted. Public schooling served as a meeting place for these dual practices." In light of recent moves towards the use of technology in the collection and use of data across the public sphere (enabling more pronounced claims about the neutrality of public sector processes), the imperative to demonstrate where and how human subjectivity and bias shapes data collection increases sharply. In schools and in their neighbourhoods, racial minority young people describe experiences of targeting, harassment, reduced access to programs and resources, and physical and epistemic violence (e.g., begin "roughed up" by the police and not believed by anyone). Against the fortress of evidence avowing to the race, class, and gender neutrality of institutional decision-making processes, youth are told that their school failures, attendance issues, involvement with the youth justice system, and endlessly negative experiences with the police in their neighbourhoods are a reflection of their individual deficits.

Chapter Five

Risk, Safety, Inclusion, and the Inter-institutional Organization of Educational Interventions

Links between adolescence and risk have structured common-sense understandings of youth since the concept of adolescence emerged in the Western world as a salient developmental category (Lesko, 2001; Raby, 2002). While the specificities of language have shifted across time and space – from delinquency and deviance to risk and vulnerability (Vasudevan & Campano, 2009) – practices associated with the classification and treatment of adolescent risk have remained central to dominant understandings of adolescence and subsequently the governance of youth-serving institutions (Nichols, 2014). Contemporary youth-serving institutions (e.g., child welfare, youth criminal justice, education) produce and rely on risk or vulnerability assessment measures to guide policy-making and the implementation of various social, criminological, and educational interventions (Goddard & Myers, 2016; James, 2012; Nichols, 2014). The use of actuarial discourses and technologies to guide policy and practice suggests a rational post-racial, post-class, and post-gendered objectivity; yet, the racialized, classed, and gendered outcomes of the policies and practices calls any neutrality into question (Clandfield, 2014; James, 2012; Raby, 2002).

This chapter begins with people's experiences learning in neighbourhood schools, private schools, universities, jails, "Safe Schools" programs, colleges d'enseignement general et professionnel (CEGEP), and a range of alternative education programs (e.g., outreach and adult education sites). To a lesser degree, the chapter also draws on the experiential insights of educators and social workers in various educational programs in Toronto, illuminating how their work is co-ordered with the work of young people, as well as with the work of those acting in a professional capacity across the youth sector (broadly conceived). Beginning with the embodied knowledge people have of their own lives and experiences – particularly their experiences being moved or coordinating moves for young people across a range of educational environments – this chapter seeks to produce an empirical analysis of interinstitutional risk-management efforts, which shape raced, classed, and gendered patterns of educational exclusion.

In Schools and Safety, these experiences anchor a mapping of the educational terrain upon which youth designated as "at risk" travel once they have been removed from mainstream educational environments. In this first project, the research presupposed that the very young people who get coded, institutionally, as at risk or unsafe, have important knowledge about how their worlds are organized to produce the conditions of unsafety the system seeks to mediate. In Sampling Youth Development young people's experiences reveal other aspects of social organization (or sections of the map) that were not as evident from the grounds of the first project (e.g., the intersections of immigration, education, and linguistic policy). Grounded in two provincial contexts, this chapter reveals the policies, assessment procedures, and programs through which young people come to be known as successful and/or "at risk" academically – and then how these risks/successes are mediated institutionally. I highlight how particular interventions (e.g., Student Success programs, Welcome Classes) and educational disciplinary strategies (e.g., the movement of young people into alternative programs) organize young people's lives and the degree to which they experience what is categorically understood as "academic achievement."

Like Moves on a Chessboard

As well as conveying a sense that young people are – as David remarked in chapter 4 – "nobody to [educators]," the coordination of educational interventions (typically moves) requires extensive work on the part of youth themselves, school staff, caregivers, and other adults involved in young people's lives (e.g., youth workers and probation officers). The moves can take weeks or months to coordinate – time when young people are typically not involved in educational programming at all. Furthermore, there is little indication that the moves themselves lead to improved educational or social outcomes for most young people (Nichols, 2014, 2017b; Nichols & Braimoh, 2016; Rankin & Contenta, 2009). The cynical observation from a former employee at Rosewood that young people are simply being "moved around like pieces on a chessboard" (Rosewood Unpublished Social Impacts Evaluation, 2012) resonates with my own research findings, across various institutional contexts ostensibly designed to serve the needs of "at-risk" youth

(Nichols, 2014, 2016). Under the pretense of providing a more suitable learning environment for young people, they are being moved out of mainstream programs and into a range of different off-site alternative environments, where indeed many are more likely to receive one-on-one attention and a holistic response to their educational, social, *and* material needs (Nichols, 2014, 2018 Nichols, Griffith, & Fisher, in press). Unfortunately, for some young people, the educational moves they experience in adolescence reflect a complicated history of educational exclusions and interventions, which have disrupted the continuity of their learning, ruptured their relationships with teachers and neighbourhood schools, failed to enable adequate assessment and support interventions, and shaped a profound sense of otherness – framed around educational deficits but marked by obvious race, class, and gender disparities.

When she wrote the following field note, Chantel was a post-secondary-school-aged youth research assistant from the neighbourhood, spending one full day per week at Rosewood as a mentor-tutor and participant-observer for eight months. After a particularly difficult day, Chantel stayed around to chat with the youth worker, Kim, and two of the on-site teachers about some of the students who were clearly having challenges in school. In their framing of the students' difficulties, the educators and youth worker identify the locus of the problem within each of the students experiencing difficulty. Chantel, in contrast, clearly sees an institutional basis to the young people's struggles. I've left all field notes entries largely unedited (except for minor copy edits and my own additions in square brackets), so that people's distinctive voices are maintained. On our team field note blog, Chantel writes:

> I stayed around for a while when school ended and spoke with [youth worker,] Kim and the teachers for a bit. I asked if there was any insight as to why Jani is so hostile, and Kim stated that she is going through a lot. Jani came to her yesterday and told her that she felt like no one loves her. Jani has been told that she is ugly and stupid, and she has started to internalize these feelings. She is depressed and questions living. I asked if she has a counsellor and I was told she has a social worker. I asked if there was any access to therapy/counseling services and [the teacher,] Giuliana said they are looking into it. I mentioned that although Jani and I had gotten through her homework she had a lot of trouble reading and spelling. Giuliana informed me that Jani has zero credits and does have a difficult time reading. Jani is supposed to be in grade 10. She was previously taking applied courses but has been moved into a stream called "locally developed." These courses provide a student with the most basic skills. I

told Giuliana that when Jani was given the work she complained that the work was too easy. Giuliana stated that Jani is not able to handle the work for the applied stream. I asked her if there was no place in the middle of applied and locally developed where the curriculum could match her needs. Giuliana had no reply. [In a subsequent field note, Chantel observes that the teachers are afraid to tell Jani that they've been having her work on locally developed English courses because she will be angry.]

Much of Chantel's and Andy's work at Rosewood in the first year of the project involved the provision of one-on-one educational and social supports to young people like Jani. They also produced field notes, which capture the day-to-day work of teaching and learning at Rosewood. In the excerpt above, Chantel offers insight into the magnitude of the interconnected challenges facing students like Jani and the adults with whom she works in and outside of Rosewood.

According to Rosewood youth worker Kim, Jani believes she is ugly and stupid. She is in her second year of high school and has received no credits to date. Because of reading and spelling difficulties, the teachers have started giving her locally developed coursework; that is, courses that are compulsory for the completion of a secondary school diploma (thirty credits), certificate (fourteen credits), or certificate of accomplishment (less than fourteen credits). Ontario schools use locally developed courses to accommodate students who are working below grade level. They enable students to complete a secondary school diploma or certificate, but they do not enable subsequent participation in post-secondary education programs as most colleges and universities require the completion of a certain number of "university," "college," or "university/college mixed" credits. Furthermore, according to Jani – who does not yet know at the time of this field note that she has been given coursework for a locally developed course – the content of the work is too simple.

While a few field notes obviously do not provide enough information to make a diagnosis, I immediately question whether Jani has a learning disability, which would make reading and spelling difficult *and* would explain her sense that the content of the locally developed course is too easy. If her capacity for reasoning is average or above-average, but she has significant decoding issues, then the appropriate response is to address the decoding issues, so that she can participate in grade-level content knowledge acquisition. Chantel similarly notices a misalignment between Jani's learning needs and the options that are made available to her, questioning whether "there was no place in the middle of applied and locally developed where the curriculum could match her needs"? Chantel's question is met with silence on the part of the teacher. It's not my intention to produce a speculative account of Jani's learning needs here; rather, I seek to bring into view the ways that Jani's social and educational needs – like every other young person I met at Rosewood and all the youth I worked with at the Loft school for homeless youth – are misaligned with what the system offers (Nichols, 2016, 2017b, 2018). Like others, Jani vacillates between internalizing this lack of fit as an affirmation that she is ugly and stupid and a concerted resistance (hostility, in Chantel's words) towards the intervening institutions in her life. Although it is framed as such, the problem isn't simply that Jani has poor self-concept and a reading difficulty; instead, problems result for Jani as the particularities of her life and experiences intersect with generalized public-sector interventions that position her as their target.

Towards the end of the field note, Chantel describes some of her own reactions to the things she's been observing at Rosewood and, like she's been trained to do, she begins to pose questions about the experiences she's been having: "Today I felt really troubled; it's blatantly obvious that Jani and Ahmed [a student transitioning from an inpatient mental health facility back into community] are not getting the services they need. I feel like Rosewood is some type of dumping ground for undesirable students. How is it possible that Jani has zero credits? Didn't any of her teachers ever notice that she was not reading at the right level? Why do some of the teachers at Rosewood spend more time on their phones instead of teaching Jani how to read?"

Chantel is surprised and dismayed to discover how little is being done for Ahmed and Jani. She is flabbergasted that both students ended up at Rosewood during adolescence, having had so few of their needs addressed, and disappointed that she seems to be the only one asking how this could have happened.

I remember asking similar questions when I was a student teacher (almost twenty years ago), teaching applied grade 9 English classes at my own former secondary school. I taught two sections of this class and both had a number of students taking the course for the second or third time. Shocked to discover how little some of my students could read and write, I followed up with the guidance department to check out how they'd been doing in their other classes. I learned that despite having failed almost all of their grade 9 classes the year prior, they had not been identified as "at risk" not to graduate and no additional educational resources were being pulled into place to address their apparent academic difficulties. Despite phone calls home and visits to the guidance department, I was unable to mobilize supports and was left with the cynical impression that everyone was simply waiting until these young, White, poor, working class men dropped out at sixteen years of age. This was before the introduction of Learning to Age 18 legislation in Ontario, which required that young people attend school until they were eighteen years of age or had completed the requirements for a secondary school diploma (An Act to Amend the Education Act Respecting Pupil Learning to the Age of 18 and Equivalent Learning, 2006). Coupled with other systemic changes during the last twenty years regarding the inclusion of students with exceptionalities and the use of exclusionary discipline practices, the mandate to provide access to education for all young people until eighteen years of age has reshaped the educational landscape.

One consequence of these reforms has been the creation of new alternative learning environments within the K–12 (that is, not the adult education) system for young people like Jani and Ahmed. But just because these programs now exist, it doesn't mean we are any closer to addressing the complex issues underpinning the inequalities that necessitated them in the first place. Rather, the lack of substantive resources and continued low levels of credit accumulation (Directions Evidence and Policy Research Group, LLP, 2014; King, Warren, King, Brook, & Kocher, 2009) in these sites suggest that the moves are intended to serve a bureaucratic purpose (i.e., demonstrating compliance with the Education Act) instead of actually addressing the needs of the young people who are placed here. Chantel's sense that Rosewood is a "dumping ground" for young people the school board doesn't want echoes my own youthful observations that my former high school was simply waiting for its lowest achieving students to drop out.

But there are important differences. Unlike the young people cycling repeatedly through the grade 9 program in my own hometown, none of the young people attending school at Rosewood were White. Growing up in similarly working class and/or poor families – albeit in urban rather than rural settings – young people at Rosewood represented a range of races and ethnicities (other than White), with Black youth who cited Caribbean heritage being dominant. Chantel, Jani, and Ahmed are Black. So is Kim. Until the school closed, there was not a single Black teacher at Rosewood.

Race, class, and gender relations are salient in every social setting, but they are particularly visible to those who suspect an exclusion is a function of the colour of their skin, the money in their pocket, and/or their embodied mannerisms. The student body in the public high schools surrounding Rosewood – and the make-up of the student body at Rosewood itself – reflect the racial and class-based organization of the city of Toronto more broadly. Although racially segregated education in Canada officially ended in 1996, with the closing of the last residential school (CBC News, 2008), de facto school segregation – a function of residential segregation (e.g., by race and class) – allows school systems to act as colour- and class-blind institutions. But they maintain race and class inequalities through a range of other educational relations – fundraising, school discipline, special education, and so forth (Allen & White-Smith, 2014).

As noted in chapter 3, the racialized distribution of poverty in Toronto mirrors the distribution of the city's most vulnerable schools[1] (Toronto District School Board, 2017a). Nine of the twenty most vulnerable schools in the TDSB, as indicated in the most recent Learning Opportunities Index (LOI) results (Toronto District School Board, 2017a), are in the two wards closest to Rosewood, and a tenth school is geographically close – although officially it falls in an adjacent ward. According to the 2011/2012 TDSB student census, the TDSB wards with the highest concentration of vulnerable schools also have the highest numbers of Black students. A further distinction between the local contexts shaping Chantel's observations and my own is the prevalence of police in the neighbourhoods surrounding Rosewood. In data-led or evidence-based policing, decisions regarding the deployment of policing resources are guided by policing data (e.g., calls for service). The stationing of police on the streets reflects a history of racially biased policing in the city, from which today's evidence-based policing practices have been built (Lorinc, 2018). The Ontario Human Rights Commission has documented a history of anti-Black policing in Toronto (OHRC, 2018). In

---

1 The Toronto Board of Education and later the Toronto District School Board have historically sought to offset educational and social inequalities using equity-based funding formulas, in addition to those set formulas set provincially. From the Inner City School Index of the 1970s (Griffith, 1992) to the Learning Opportunities Index (LOI) of today, Toronto school boards have used a range of socio-economic and demographic indicators to equitably redistribute educational resources. The most current LOI is based on a range of variables in students' neighbourhoods, which have been shown to consistently correlate with academic achievement, as measured through credit accumulation rates, graduation rates, and standardized test scores: (1) Medium neighbourhood income; (2) Percentage of households in neighbourhood below the low-income measure; (3) Percentage of households receiving social assistance; (4) Percentage of adults in neighbourhood without secondary school diploma; (5) Percentage of adults in neighbourhood with one or more university degree(s); and (6) The proportion of lone-parent households in the neighbourhood (TDSB, 2017).

addition, a number of legislative and policy-level alignments between schools and police departments in the wake of changes associated with the Safe Schools amendments to the Education Act (An Act to Amend the Education Act in Respect of Behaviour, Discipline and Safety, 2007; Bhattacharjee, 2003), as well as similar alignments between Toronto Community Housing Properties and Toronto Police Services (Nichols & Braimoh, 2016), shape the high numbers of police in young people's homes and schools in the neighbourhood where this research occurred. In order to grasp the significance of racially biased school discipline practices (Galabuzi, 2014; Gregory, Skiba, & Noguera, 2010), one must also engage with evidence of racial disparities in other institutional sites (e.g., social housing, policing, and immigration). As I proceed with this chapter, I continue to demonstrate how the coordination of educational interventions (e.g., moves into various kinds of special programs) for youth "at risk" is shaped by crosscutting policies and programs, linking education with corrections, policing, child welfare, mental health, and immigration systems.

Not long after starting at Rosewood, Jani was suspended from school for threatening another young person with a knife she grabbed from an open drawer in Rosewood's kitchen. Jani was helping to make lunch at the time and picked up the knife amid an escalating conflict between herself and a young man, who was antagonizing her. Having threatened to hurt this young man with the knife, one teacher sought to separate the two students while another phoned the police. Unsurprisingly for anyone who spends any length of time in the neighbourhood, the involvement of the police escalated Jani's state of agitation. The arrival of the police had a very different effect on the young man (Jason), who unlike Jani was Asian and also not from the neighbourhood – although he had originally intimated to the other students that he was, provoking their disdain when it was revealed he was from a nearby (and more affluent) suburb. Further, while both students were clearly implicated in the conflict (and both were suspended as a result), only Jani was taken away by the police and charged. Chantel describes arriving at Rosewood, just as Jani was being "dragged" into the police car:

As I walked up the driveway towards Rosewood I saw a police car parked a few doors down. As I walked up closer I saw that Jani was in handcuffs and Giuliana, Fern, and [the executive director] Shaheen were standing outside close to the police car … As I turned to go inside Jani began screaming and crying hysterically. Yelling at the officer to let her go, "call my worker right now," "I don't want to be searched by a male officer I want a female officer." She yelled "you're only treating me like this because I'm Black." When she said this the officer turned to a group of guys [who are also Black] on the other side of the fence and asked them if they were recording this as well. I stood outside watching as this all took place ... As she was screaming, two additional cop cars pulled up and out came four more officers. One officer came and put his hands on Jani's arm as she was yelling and she jerked her hand away from him screaming at him not to touch her. The first officer on the scene decided she should sit in the back seat. Again, she screamed she can't go in the car because she needs fresh air. The officers basically dragged her to the back doors and shoved her in the backseat and shut the door.

Later that day, Ahmed softly – and incredulously – asked Giuliana why the teachers had to call the police. She responded that the presence of the weapon meant she *had* to call the police. When Ahmed asks the question again, she tells him she had no choice. Indeed, according to the Police/ School Board Protocol for all Toronto school boards, under the Mandatory Notification of Police section "the police must be notified for ... possessing a weapon ... [or] using a weapon to cause or to threaten bodily harm to another person" (Ontario Ministry of Education, 2015; Toronto Police Service, Toronto District School Board, Toronto Catholic District School Board, Conseil scolaire de district catholique Centre-Sud, & Conseil scolaire Viamonde, 2011). While Jani will go on to explain that she picked up the knife in self-defence, it was this move (picking up the knife) – rather than Jason's original antagonisms – that led the teachers to call the police. Jani's move to pick up the knife triggers an institutionally mandated sequence of action (Griffith & Smith, 2014), which legitimates the teachers' move to transfer control to the police.

Research suggests that the actions of young Black men and women are more likely to be interpreted as aggressive or dangerous than their White peers and that they are more likely to be exceedingly disciplined, including through the use of criminal-legal sanctions (Alexander, 2012; Buckingham, 2016; Rios, 2011). Although less research has attended to school discipline disproportionalities impacting the lives of young women, recent research finds that young Black women receive higher percentages of out-of-school suspensions than White or Hispanic girls (Slate, Gray, & Jones, 2016); they are three times more likely to be called to the office or receive an office referral than White girls (Morris & Perry, 2017); and they experience surveillance in schools (Wun, 2015). Fifteen years old and unable to read and write at grade level, Jani gets streamed into locally developed courses and, later that same month, hauled off to the divisional police station in the back of a police car after trying to "defend [herself]" against another student. Peppered with exclusions, framed as the consequences of her own naturally occurring deficiencies, Kim's earlier observation that Jani questions her self-worth should not shock us.

Despite police assurances to staff that Jani would simply be taken to the hospital for an assessment, she ends up being detained by the police and receiving a criminal charge, which leads to subsequent interactions with the court system. When Shaheen, Rosewood's executive director (at this time), phoned the police to make a formal complaint about the police intervention, she was advised by the duty officer that her concern (i.e., that the police intervention was unnecessarily aggressive and served to escalate the conflict) did not match the standardized list of complaints that could be processed. Elsewhere, I have written about the way that evidence is generated and used as part of institutionally organized processes through which other forms of evidence can be dismissed as anecdotal or non-factual (Nichols, 2017a). Shaheen's efforts to lodge a complaint against the police is exemplary of the relations that I pointed to in this other article.

In my field notes, I summarized Shaheen's descriptions of her efforts. When she phoned the police station to make a complaint, she was advised by the officer she spoke with in the Community Relations Office that unless the complaint was one of racism, sexism, assault et cetera (i.e., it needed to be part of an existing list of complaints), there was nothing the officer could do about it. Shaheen's observation that the officer responding to Rosewood's call for service unnecessarily personalized and escalated the situation with Jani was unactionable from the point of view of the Community Relations Office. All she could do, the officer explained, was informally pass on Shaheen's complaint to the responding officer when she next saw him. Shaheen's experience offers insight into the disconnect between the actual conditions of oppression and marginalization, which people witness and participate in every day, and institutional courses of action (in this case, ostensibly designed to increase public transparency and accountability), which require the use of predetermined frames and categories that cannot attend to the range of experiences people might wish to convey.

Additionally, because Jani was immediately detained and charged, there was no opportunity for any Rosewood staff to debrief with her prior to her eventual return to the organization after completing her twenty-day suspension. My field notes reveal that Odinegbo, another Black Rosewood outreach worker whose caseload was largely made up of youth navigating the youth criminal justice system, had reached out to Jani but no formal discussion of the events leading to her charge had occurred between Jani and any Rosewood staff. Having already participated in an intake meeting when she arrived at Rosewood the first time, more than a month after her suspension, Jani is required to participate in a "re-intake" meeting as part of the readmission process after having been suspended from Rosewood.

It is during this re-intake meeting – months after Jani began attending school at Rosewood – that Chantel learns Jani has a documented learning exceptionality (although the precise nature of the exceptionality is not shared). Because she has been previously identified as having an exceptionality, the teachers' preparation for Jani's readmission was guided by the province's Caring and Safe Schools in Ontario policy for supporting students with special education needs. The meeting began with a pre-meeting of the three teachers at Rosewood at this time (Fern, Giuliana, and Paul), the youth worker (Kim), and Rosewood's operational director (Michelle). The meeting was structured by an exemplar for a Behaviour Support Plan (also called a Behaviour Management Plan). A Behaviour Support Plan is meant "to target the under-lying reason for behaviour, replace the inappropriate behaviour with an appropriate behaviour that serves the same function, and reduce or eliminate the challenging behaviour" (Ontario Ministry of Education, 2010, p. 39). Behaviour Support Plans are used across North America, the United Kingdom, and Australia in educational and social service contexts, with children, youth, and adults. They are often guided by templates that frame how the plans are produced and used. In Jani's case, the teachers went online and found an exemplar that guided their own efforts to produce this document. Based on the template, they sought to identify "the behaviours" that suggest Jani is agitated or anxious, the things that trigger her anxiety, and strategies for modifying these behaviours. During the meeting, Chantel observes:

> Fern went over each section of the form. Kim and the teachers highlighted areas that they believe apply to Jani. For example, under signs of increased anxiety or agitation they all agreed that restlessness, doesn't do work, gets out of seat, withdrawn and teary eyes are all signs that Jani is agitated. Kim added that Jani threatens to hurt herself on a regular basis according to her worker. [The team decides that] keeping Jani busy with either academic or non-academic work is the best way to keep her from being agitated … Kim and the teachers all agreed that Jani requires an individual learning plan because she is learning disabled (her learning disability was not disclosed).

Although Chantel's description of the meeting continues, it's important to stop here and point to one of many structural barriers that impede educational progress in sites like Rosewood. There should be no need to create an Individualized Education Plan (IEP) for Jani; if she has a diagnosed learning disability, then the teachers should have received her IEP when she was transferred into the program. At this stage, Jani has been learning at Rosewood for months – long enough to be suspended from the program for threatening another student. The fact they still have not received her IEP and are unsure of the precise nature of her specific diagnosis and the supports she needs to be successful goes some way towards explaining why the teachers decided to stream Jani into locally developed courses, rather than ensuring she has the additional supports she needs to complete the applied-level courses she had been working on. Teachers at Rosewood complained to me over the years that they often did not receive a student's educational records (the Ontario Student Record or OSR), progress reports detailing completed work towards a credit, or much information about the students they teach at all. Safe Schools administrators in Long-Term Suspension and Expulsion programs, in contrast, described receiving OSRs, which they metaphorically described as having to be "rolled in on a dolly" because the students' educational histories had been so tumultuous. Where young people have experienced large numbers of educational relocations and/or are moved less formally (that is, outside the formal expulsion process), it becomes less and less likely that pertinent educational information accompanies each of the moves a young person makes.

Instead, the coordination of the transfer (or re-entry) of a student like Jani is often done in the form of a written referral and a face-to-face case conference, like the one that Chantel goes on to describe. As the teachers and the board administrators are about to conclude their private meeting, Jani arrives, followed shortly after by her mother. Chantel's description captures the dynamics between Jani, her mother, Kim (the youth worker), and the teachers at Rosewood. She also captures something of the energy of the space, noting other students who pop in and out of the room. For example, Jani's arrival is announced by Ahmed, who pops his head into the classroom to enthusiastically alert the group that Jani has entered the building, and then later Jani reconnects with an old friend (Shanae) from a previous school. Having spent a lot of time at Rosewood – and knowing most of the people Chantel describes – I can feel the energy in the space and vividly picture and hear the communicative interactions she describes. I have included large sections of the field note in the hopes that some of this dynamism also comes through for the reader. The passage begins with Jani's entry into the room:

> Jani walked in and the teachers said hello to her. She didn't respond. As soon as she saw Kim [however] she completely brightened up and jumped in for a great big hug … She stayed cuddled up to Kim for a

few minutes and when she finally looked up and saw me she said hi and I said hi back. The teachers tried to encourage the [other] students to leave so that the meeting could start. Shanae came into the classroom and struck up a conversation with Jani. Apparently they were friends at [C-School]. Shanae mostly talked about herself and what she planned to do for her birthday. What was interesting about this [interaction] is how completely engaged Jani was when she was speaking to her friend. I have never seen her that engaged by anything. We all left the classroom because the meeting was going to take place at the table in front of the kitchen where the students eat lunch. Fern, Giuliana, Kim, Christopher, the Safe Schools principal, Jani, her mother, and Michelle [the operations director] all gathered around the table ... I noticed that as Jani sat waiting for the meeting to begin, she sat on the other side of the table away from her mother. She kept a seat open beside her that she had designated for Kim. Realizing that this location was not ideal [for the meeting] because it was noisy and too open, we moved to the classroom where the initial meeting had taken place. When we moved to the classroom the meeting began. [Principal] Christopher started by having all of the staff introduce themselves. From here, he said that he spoke with Jani's mother when the incident [with the kitchen knife] happened. He said that Jani is being [criminally] charged for this incident, and [the criminal legal process] is something ongoing that she and her mother will have to handle ... [He turns to Jani.]

CHRISTOPHER: How do you feel about what happened?
JANI: [I] feel normal. It was self-defence. He was physically assaulting me, so it's ok that I did what I did.
CHRISTOPHER: How do you feel about being in trouble with the police?
JANI: Not good
CHRISTOPHER: Would you do the same thing again?
JANI: No. I would use my fists. If someone touches me, I'm not gonna walk away.
CHRISTOPHER: What else can you do?
JANI: Go talk to Kim.
CHRISTOPHER: Can Kim be substituted for anyone else? Kim may not always be here. If Kim's not here what can you do?
JANI: Tell a teacher.
CHRISTOPHER: Mom how do you feel?

Mom immediately bursts into tears. Speaking through her tears, she says: "I'm ashamed. This has been a painful experience. I'm a single mom. I don't have nobody. I pray to God to help change my daughter. I beg for help from everyone to help change Jani. I need help disciplining her. I don't know. At home she is ok. Outside she's ok. But at school she is a problem."

While her mother cried and spoke about her struggles Jani smiles and rolls her eyes. There was no [demonstration of] compassion or even a hint of sadness over how hurt her mother is.

FERN: Jani has a learning disability.

This is said, as if to explain why Jani has problems at school and not at home. When Fern mentioned Jani having a learning disability, Jani's demeanour changed. She kind of scoffed at Fern and indicated she was annoyed by her statement.

CHRISTOPHER: What makes you mad?
JANI: People just piss me off. Everything pisses me off.
CHRISTOPHER: What do people do that pisses you off?

Jani shrugs her shoulders.

CHRISTOPHER: Many of us in here haven gotten pissed off and maybe want to hit someone or do something drastic but we don't act on it because there are consequences. You have to understand that actions may have consequences.

[At this point,] Fern passed out copies of the Behaviour Support Plan. As she started going over it with the group, Christopher interjected and suggested that Jani and her mother take it home to read in order to really digest the information on the form. Jani's mother immediately told her to give the forms to Deanna, her worker.

Christopher ended the meeting by saying, "we are not afraid, and we are not giving up on you. You will start on Monday with a clean slate."

JANI'S MOM: Thank you to everyone. I wish this never happened again. Jani please change these ways. Please. (pleading with Jani)

Mom gets up and shakes everyone's hand. We all leave for the day.

Several things are worth noting in this passage that contextualize Jani's experiences in schools and the efficacy of an intervention like the School Away from School at Rosewood. The meeting begins with Christopher stating that Jani has been charged by the police, specifying that Jani and her mother will have to navigate the youth criminal justice interactions on their own. Although school board staff were responsible for placing the call to the police, which led to her charge, with one swift comment Christopher abdicates any responsibility for Jani's subsequent interactions with the criminal legal system.

From here, Jani is asked how she *feels* about what she did (which comes across as an invitation to show remorse for her actions). She responds by stating that she feels nothing and would use her fists to defend herself in the future. She is prompted about what else she could do and responds that she could speak to Kim or one of her teachers. Reminiscent of what young people serving sentences or being detained told me about their community reintegration plans (i.e., that they would make better choices), the onus for change is placed squarely on Jani's shoulders. At no time does the conversation address things others could do to de-escalate conflicts among students or ensure Jani feels safe, nor does anyone at the table acknowledge her claim that she picked up the knife because *she* was being threatened by the other young man, Jason. Jani's mother similarly individualizes responsibility for Jani's outburst, explaining that she is a single parent and noting through her tears that she needs help disciplining Jani – she pleads with Jani to "please change [her] ways." The focus on the family and the young person as the locus of change reflects the dominance of psychological explanations and interventions in school (e.g., that individual or family-level deficits predict negative outcomes), as well as the ways program efficacy is tracked in educational and other social settings (i.e., through measurable changes in individual performance, behaviour, attitudes, etc.). There is no effort made to learn from Jani about the conditions of her life and why "everything just pisses [her] off," nor do people seem willing to think about Jani's mother's observations that "At home [Jani] is ok. Outside she's ok. But at school she is a problem."

Instead, Fern jumps quickly to explain that Jani has a learning disability. In the end then it appears as though the problem is single parenting, a learning disability, and poor anger management (or oppositional defiance disorder as the teachers claim earlier), rather than the myriad other intersecting social, economic, and political factors that shape what people are able to do and be at any given moment. No clear strategy for how to collectively move forward is discussed. Even the Behaviour Support Plan prepared by Fern is simply sent home for Jani to discuss with her social worker, Deanna. In the end, the meeting comes across as hurried, lacking focus, and as though it doesn't appear to accomplish anything. Overall, this gives the impression that the entire purpose is performative, simply a demonstration that all of the key stakeholders met to discuss Jani's return to school.

Having made these critical observations, it is important for me to point out that problems we see in this passage are not simply deficiencies on the parts of any of the individuals involved – Jani, her mother, or the school board staff. Rather, these material relations among individuals at the table point us to a broader system of social relations and complexes of bureaucratic activity, through which Jani's needs are not met. Declining enrolment and union seniority policies meant that teachers were often getting bumped into and out of Rosewood, which limited relationship building, shaped historical discontinuity, and prevented the hiring of teachers who better reflected the student population and had skills/dispositions that the work required (e.g., strategies for de-escalating conflicts). Further, Christopher was one of a minority of Black school administrators and *the* principal for a number of Safe Schools alternative education sites in this quadrant. Despite good intentions, he was being pulled in a number of different directions, and the reality is that for Jani – like many of the young people who ended up at Rosewood and other sites like it – the school board simply doesn't offer what she needs. Unsurprisingly within the same school year, Jani is moved out of Rosewood for good. There is another violent altercation between her and another young man – he is later observed trying to aggressively kiss another student (Shanae) without her consent as well as charged with abusing his partner. Jani is eventually suspended and moved to another school, while the young man remains at Rosewood.

In addition to the performative and psychologizing tenor of the meeting, Chantel's notes suggest important relational elements. Like most of the young people learning at Rosewood, Jani has a stronger connection with Kim, the youth worker on-site, than she does with the teachers or administrators. Later during this same school year, Kim is actually "let go" from the Rosewood staff because she is seen – particularly by the teachers – to be too close to the students. Kim, like Jani and Chantel, is a Black woman with Caribbean ethnicity. Of anyone else at Rosewood at that time, she'd been involved in the organization for longest and had historically significant and personally rich relationships with many of the young people who'd come through the school and the wrap-around or outreach programs over the years. After the altercation between Jani and Jason, Andy questioned in his field notes whether "any of this" (meaning both the escalation of the conflict between Jani and Jason and Jani's subsequent charges) would have happened had Kim been on-site that day.

While neither Chantel nor Andy were trained as teachers, they had both grown up in the neighbourhood and brought other kinds of knowledge that helped them establish connections with the young people at Rosewood; they saw the problems that young people experienced in school very differently than the teachers. These differences are evident in their field notes and in my observations of their interactions with the youth at Rosewood over a year (Chantel and me) and three years (Andy and me) of working together. Here, I encourage the reader to circle back to Warren's observations about the experiences of Black youth going to mainstream schools with White suburban teachers in "the hood," and connect these observations to Chantel's notes about Jani, and her sense that Jani's needs are not being met effectively at Rosewood. The institutionalized structures, processes, and knowledges through which Canada's public sector operates, creates, and entrenches inequalities through the use of race-, class-, and gender-neutral terms (risk, vulnerability, exceptionality, criminology, and pathology) legitimizes racialized, classed, and gendered patterns of exclusion.

"Special" Education – Assessment, Identification, and Segregation

In Ontario and Quebec, the practice of segregating non-normative children and youth into special programs has a long history and continues to this day in the context of Identification, Placement, and Review Committee (IPRC) processes (in Ontario), clinical diagnosis and coding processes (in Quebec), and, in both provinces, the development and implementation of Individualized Education Plans (IEPs) and the classification of students as "at risk" (Advisory Board on English Education, 2016; Clandfield, 2014). Teachers and educational psychologists draw on academic, psychometric, and/or observational evidence in order to make determinations about young people's educational and social-behavioural needs. Although test results are often presented as reliable and unbiased accounts of a child's abilities, decisions about when and why to embark on testing, which tests to employ, and their foci all influence the generation, interpretation, and use of results.

For example, research has long tracked racial and gender bias in language (Freedle, 2003; Green & Griffore, 1980), content (Zoref & Williams, 1980), and results (Donlon, Ekstrom, Lockheed, & Harris, 1977) of intelligent quotient (IQ) testing. Beyond the content, standards, and results of psychometric testing (of which an IQ test is only one type), the decision to initiate a testing and review process for a particular young person begins with someone's subjective construction of a child's behaviour and ability as non-normative. Where parents launch an assessment process to enable increased access to assistive technologies, for instance, the outcomes are markedly different than when teachers decide to begin a review process to have a student removed from their class.

Most of the youth we interviewed in Toronto, and who were involved in Safe Schools initiatives there, had first been moved out of mainstream programs during elementary or middle school. Reflective of documented trends in the city suggesting that economically disadvantaged and racialized children are disproportionately represented in special education programs in Ontario and Quebec (Maynard, 2017; Smaller, 2014), they describe being moved into special education programs. The (2011) Commission des droits de la personne et des droits de la jeunesse found that youth from immigrant families and certain minority groups – that is, particularly youth with Caribbean backgrounds – are more likely to be diagnosed as special needs (17.7 per cent) and sent to special classes than the general rate of identification for all students (8.9 per cent). Abilities streaming is associated with class- and race-based disparities in graduation and post-secondary participation rates (Smaller, 2014). Brown and Parekh (2013) observe that students from economically disadvantaged households are over-represented in Toronto's special education and workplace-oriented programs, leading to reduced access to post-secondary education opportunities for students in poor neighbourhoods. Given the racialized distribution of poverty in large urban centres, the lowest income neighbourhoods are also the least White.

Among the young people I've interviewed in Montreal and Toronto, many were unsure of the precise nature of these moves. Instead, they provided general explanations that suggest the interventions resulted from behavioural issues or learning challenges. Kenneth, a young Black man who we interviewed and then later hired as a youth researcher, offers an explanation for his removal from the mainstream school system that is typical of the stories we heard: "In grade 7 they had me in, like, a behavioural class. But it wasn't because of my behaviour – [it was] just because I had too much suspensions, and they thought that I wasn't suitable enough to be in a regular classroom." Another Black youth, Tyrone, told us he'd been streamed into behavioural programs starting in grade 1, even though his mother had refused to give her consent to the school's request for psychoeducational assessments. He went on to explain why he thinks was he was unable to find success in mainstream programs: "I don't have the same mentality. I ask other students, like normal kids, 'What do you do after school?' They go home, they sit at home, their parents buy them food, their parents take them, buy them shoes." Young people's beliefs that they are "not suitable" for mainstream programming – or that they are not "normal" – arises in the context of streaming practices and other educational interventions for addressing "non-normative" intellectual and social development and behaviour. It is not coincidental that Tyrone and Kenneth employ race-, class-, and gender-neutral language to describe their segregation into special education programs, despite their astute analysis of race and class politics to describe other institutional phenomena (e.g., policing practices and access to labour market opportunities).

Increasingly in educational settings, psychoeducational procedures are used to make decisions about resource distribution and access to particular educational interventions. Streaming requires *and* reproduces naturalized developmental norms and standards, whereby children and youth can be compared and categorized. These standards and procedures are framed as important tools for enabling objective decision-making and the equitable distribution of resources. But the normative standards within which the education system operates, and the institutional procedures that segregate young people into specialized programs and/ or provide them with access to specialized supports, are determined by and reflect the interests of those in power – those by whom and for whom the system has been developed. The very same institutional processes teachers and principals use to have a child removed from their classrooms or schools can be used by parents to ensure their child gets access to additional resources to enable their ongoing participation in a mainstream program.

For example, two years ago, we initiated the process of seeking additional educational supports for my oldest child – who was eight years old at the time. While the school had not signalled any issues with her academic performance or behaviour in class, I had noticed some issues with reading fluency, which I wanted to understand a little better. I reached out to a colleague in another department and received an informal referral to a neuropsychology clinic where she maintained a clinical practice. After close to $3,000, hundreds of pages of paperwork (family and educator assessments of my daughter), and four half-days of testing, we received the neuropsychological results. The results suggest high average results in cognitive ability and low average results in cognitive efficiency (i.e., processing speed). Significantly, in all areas where socialization would (dis)advantage a child, my daughter did very well – for instance, she scored in the ninety-fifth percentile for "knowledge of word meaning" and "expressive language skills."

Communicative practices are steeped in and reflect historically entrenched patterns of privilege and dispossession – as Bourdieu and Passeron's (1977) work illuminates. In my daughter's case, the tests effectively mapped on to the language practices of our home and social life, as well as the cultural activities she regularly participates in (e.g., philosophy camp and creative arts programs). Further, the established discrepancy between her intellectual capacity and her performative efficiency ensures that my daughter is diagnosed as learning disabled. This classification allows me to advocate for access to educational accommodations, which have been designed to improve her performative capacities in school-based assessments. I can use the results of the test to acquire resources for my child because it is easy to navigate institutional contexts with which I am familiar and where I still hold professional clout as a professor of education. These tests, and the institutional processes whereby they become useful to achieve things in schools and in other institutional settings (e.g., jails), have been designed by and for people like me, and as such, I can use them to my own advantage.

My experiences navigating psychoeducational testing and special education processes offers a glimpse into some of the ways that assessments of cognitive ability reflect and entrench a particular set of normative standards, which are, as Bourdieu and Passeron note, arbitrary. They reflect the cultural and communicative norms of the dominant classes. My experiences also serve as an important counterpoint to the experiences of most of the young people I interviewed – revealing how the same set of testing procedures and results can be used to create vastly differential outcomes. When psychoeducational tests results are actively sought by parents who have the financial means to access them through the private system, they are typically used to negotiate a further scope of access to resources, time, accommodations, and support, which are all designed to ensure a child experiences increased success within the mainstream program. Where formal psychoeducational assessment procedures and/or informal observational assessment practices are pursued by educators, they are more often used to recommend or substantiate part- or full-time segregation into resource programs (Green, Mcintosh, Cook-Morales, & Robinson-Zanartu, 2005). Combined with my own professional credentials and institutional knowledge, the assessment results open doors for my child. The assessment requires that the school create and abide by an IEP for my daughter and has allowed me to ensure she receives all of the resources and supports that the school can offer.

Think back to Nadia's efforts to pull the police into her world. White, middle class, professionally privileged, knowledgeable about education, and confident in my rights – I sought out and paid for the very intervention that Tyrone's mother refused. By bringing my own mothering work into view here, I show how it happens that the same complex of institutional relations – and the vast array of texts that coordinate them – produce the raceclassgender dynamics that shape my child's and Tyrone's distinctive experiences. Just as I suspected that the results of these tests would serve as resources for my child's education, Tyrone's mother suspected that they would be used to substantiate further exclusions for her son. Indeed, young Black men and women are disproportionately streamed into special education programs in the US (Skiba et al., 2008), in Ontario (Clandfield, 2014), and in Quebec (Commission des droits de la personne et les droits de la jeunesse [CDPDJ], 2011). But neither Tyrone's mother nor I need to have engaged with these studies to know this truth; we know it because we are active participants in our lives, and we are experienced in/knowledgable about the raceclassgendered outcomes school systems continue to produce.

"Welcome Schools," Language Laws, and Intercultural Policies

In addition to their disproportionate representation in special education programs and workplace learning streams, young Black men and women are frequently streamed into linguistically focused Welcome Classes (Classe d'accueil) in Quebec (CDPDJ, 2011). Institutions shaped by federal legislation – like policing, criminal justice, and immigration systems – produce clear and documented disproportionately negative outcomes for young Black men and women in both Montreal and Toronto. Training, institutional discourse, and local practices differ in important ways, though, between Montreal and Toronto, as the two contexts are shaped by differences in provincial policies (e.g., language policies and cultural policies), public discourse, and other historically situated social relations (Maynard, 2017).

As a newcomer to Quebec, three things strike me as particularly surprising about the policy context here: (1) the free-market approach to the provision and management of the public education system; (2) a policy and legislative context that has addressed one form of oppression, while simultaneously sustaining and denying others; and (3) the lack of public will to entertain a conversation – let alone a provincial inquiry[2] – into systemic racism in the province's institutions. Of course, there are a range of other progressive policy and institutional initiatives within the province (e.g., the maintenance of low post-secondary tuition rates and greater investment in the provision of subsidized childcare than Ontario), but the effects of these moves are deeply diminished by the ones highlighted here. In what follows, I focus on points one and two above, elaborating on the policy relations I began to bring into view in chapter 4.

Since the passing of the Private School Act of 1968, the province of Quebec has publicly funded its private schools (Magnuson, 1993). As of 2008/2009, the main source of funding for private schools comes in the form of government grants from the Government of Quebec (at 44.2 per cent of the total budget) (Government of Quebec, 2009). Because of the government subsidies, tuition rates are much lower than they would be for comparable schools in other provinces. Additionally, since the passing of the Charter of the French Language, or Bill 101, in 1977, French is the legally mandated language of instruction in publicly funded private and public schools for French Canadian and all newcomer children and youth. According to the Charter of the French Language, all educational instruction in publicly funded schools must be given in French, except to those with a legal certificate of eligibility for English instruction. Access to English language education in Quebec is limited to those who can provide verifiable evidence of the following:

(1) [...] whose father or mother is a Canadian citizen and received elementary instruction in English in Canada, provided that that instruction constitutes the major part of the elementary instruction he or she received in Canada;

(2) [...] whose father or mother is a Canadian citizen and who has received or is receiving elementary or secondary instruction in English in Canada, and the brothers and sisters of that child, provided that that instruction constitutes the major part of the

---

2 A 2017 move on the part of the provincial Liberal government to task a commission to investigate systemic racism throughout the province was met with vehement opposition from groups who maintain the position that multiculturalism is "collective suicide" for White francophone Quebeqois (CBC News, 2017). As a result of this (and presumably additional) pushback, the province shifted the focus of the commission to the improvement of labour market opportunities for immigrants and visible minorities. Some community organizations proceeded to conduct an inquiry of their own accord (Shingler, 2018).

elementary or secondary instruction received by the child in Canada. (*Charter of the French Language*, 1977, Section 23[1][b] and Section 23[2])

As language laws intersect with education law in the province, young people arriving in Quebec from somewhere else or whose parents were educated outside of Canada are legally obliged to enter the French language school system, no matter their age and regardless of their language proficiencies.

After refusing to adopt the Canadian Multicultural Act in the 1970s or sign the amended Canadian Constitution in 1982, Quebec formally rejected multiculturalism in favour of an intercultural model, which aims to integrate all minority languages and cultures into a common Franco-Quebecois culture (Courtemanche, 2017). Canadian multicultural discourses and the Canadian Multicultural Act are themselves highly problematic – for example, for Indigenous peoples whose distinctive national identities, cultures, and languages are unrecognized (Bannerji, 1991; Dhillon, 2017; Thobani, 2007) and for the ways they ignore systemic racism and contribute to post-racial, colour-blind national discourses (Bannerji, 1991). Just as problematically, Quebec's intercultural model is explicitly oriented toward the assimilation of newcomers into Francophone Quebecois culture. Although the intercultural model has no significant legislative weight, it is a conceptual anchor for a range of policy and other government documents in the province (Courtmanche, 2017) oriented to the promotion of national cohesion through the advancement of a common public language and culture. It presupposes the importance, rightness, and preservation of the existing common public culture, enabling integrative state policies and programs and destabilizing public inquiry and discourse regarding systemic racism in the province ("A minority within a minority," 2018).

Bill 101 was meant to encourage the integration of newcomer youth into the dominant French culture and language, but according to Claude Lessard – a professor emeritus of education at L'Universite du Montréal and the chairperson of the Conseil Súperier de l'éducation – the introduction of Bill 101 also shaped an exodus of French Canadian children from the public system and their subsequent enrolment in private high schools (as cited in Gutnick, 2017). In Montreal, close to 33 per cent of high school students attend private school, compared to less than 5 per cent in the rest of Canada. Another result of the aforementioned legislative moves is the movement of immigrant students into Welcome Classes (Classe d'accueil) meant to support intensive language immersion for newcomers to Quebec. After graduating from one of the Welcome Classes, the young person can enrol in the public

French school of their choice, with priority given to those able to demonstrate close residential proximity to a school. This "libre choix" or free-choice aspect to school participation is the final contextual factor, influencing educational moves in this city.

Each autumn, across the city of Montreal, parents can be seen shepherding their eleven-year-old children into school gymnasiums to sit the high-stakes entrance exams at top-ranking schools. Parents pay a fee for their child to take each of these exams and where they can afford to do so, they also purchase private test-preparation supports. As well as creating a culture of competition among students, the market-based approach to education (and a per student or per capita funding model like that employed in Ontario) shapes competitiveness between schools. Particularly in the English language boards, where enrolment has been stagnating because their schools are inaccessible to immigrant families, secular "special project" public secondary schools significantly destabilize any potentially equitable outcome associated with public education by selecting for the city's top students using highly competitive entrance criteria (e.g., standardized testing, grades, interviews with children and parents, and community service requirements); they also reserve the right to deny entry to students simply on the basis of "fit."

Allowances for the denial of access to particular public schools are guided by provisions in the Quebec Education Act, pertaining to school choice and school capacity. As a parent, because I have a valid certificate of eligibility for English language education for my children, I can enrol them in any public school within either of the two (French or English) jurisdictional school boards: "Each year, every school board shall enroll students in its schools in keeping with the choice of each student's parents or the choice of the student, if of full age" (Education Act, CQLR 2018, c. I-13.3, s. 239). Even so, the act is clear that "if the number of applications for enrollment in a school exceeds the capacity of the school, enrollment shall be effected according to the criteria established by the school board after consultation with the parents' committee" (Education Act, CQLR 1977, c. I-13.3, s. 239). The act further stipulates that enrolment criteria prioritize students who reside in close proximity to the school and that criteria for participation in special programs may not be used to exclude students from the school of their choice. That being said, the act also outlines specific conditions whereby exclusionary criteria may in fact be pursued by a school: "By way of exception, at the request of a group of parents and after consulting with the parents' committee, a school board may, with the Minister's approval, establish a school for the purposes of a specific project other than a religious project, subject to the conditions and for the period determined by the Minister. The school board may determine the criteria for the enrollment of the students in that school" (Education Act, CQLR 1977, c. I-13.3, s. 240). In other words, where parents organize to designate a school as a special project school, the board is then legally empowered to create and employ any selective criteria they see fit. It therefore becomes well within the rights of a publicly funded school to deny a child entry on the basis of poor "fit." Unsurprisingly given these context factors, the distribution of educational opportunities and exclusions is highly gendered, classed, and racialized across the city. A 2016 report by the Conseil supérieur de l'education du Quebec finds "the difference in achievement between students from schools in disadvantaged areas and those in affluent ones continues to be markedly more significant in Québec than in other Canadian provinces or territories ... analysis also shows that the stratification of the offer in compulsory education – brought about by a proliferation of selective special programs and private schools – is leading to an unequal treatment that tends to favour the more fortunate" (Conseil Súperior de l'Education, 2016, p. 1). In what follows, I explore how the policy matrix outlined above influences the movement of newcomer students, many of whom are racialized, and in some cases contributes to their exclusion within the education system more broadly.

I interviewed Ashan in 2016, when he was an MA student at McGill University. He arrived in Montreal from Sri Lanka during childhood and was placed in one of the Welcome Classes in the public system.

> A: Yeah, so I had, I had went to a welcoming school, which was French ... It was like, three months-ish, and yeah, it was just, like, a welcome school ... For a lot of immigrant kids. A lot of the friends I made were from Mexico, from Spain, Romania, Honduras, and I was there for maybe two and a half months-ish. Yeah, it was fun. I have fond memories of that school. I learned French – a little bit of it, at least. And it was a great time ... But there was this issue of, like, language and what school I was gonna go to because there were specific laws about who gets to go to English schools in Montreal. Since my parents weren't educated in Canada, like, it meant I had to go to a French school, but my mom was like, "No, I want you to go to an English school."

Ashan has positive memories of the welcoming class and the friends he made there, and he observes that he learned "a little bit of" French. But two months of immersion does not provide a young person with the French fluency required to navigate and be effective in a highly competitive French language secondary school system. Ashan arrived during middle childhood – right around the time when decisions about eligibility for secondary school programs are being made. Even after a year in intensive language immersion, it would have been nearly impossible for him to effectively demonstrate disciplinary content knowledge acquisition at the secondary level (Cummins, 2000). Given the role education plays in subsequent access to resources and opportunities, as well as the exclusionary contexts produced by the Charter of the French Language and the Quebec Education Act, Ashan's parents sought to have him educated elsewhere.

Policy moves meant to improve the integration of immigrants in Quebec can actually serve to diminish the educational (as well as future labour market) opportunities for newcomers, who cannot meet the eligibility requirements for the public school board in their desired language of instruction.[3] Ashan's parents recognized that in order for him to access post-secondary education and job opportunities down the road, they needed to find a way for him to continue his education in English – the language of instruction at his boarding school in Sri Lanka. For Ashan to attend school in English, however, his parents had to send him out of province (or pay unsubsidized English private school fees in Montreal). First, he boarded with friends and later he attended an Islamic Seminary school in a nearby Ontario town:

> So then we had to figure out a way, so we actually traveled to Toronto and my parents were kind of trying to negotiate with another family to see if I could stay with them in Toronto so I could go to an English school. We actually met a family because we knew them from Sri Lanka, and they were here in Toronto. I remember this meeting happening, cuz, like, I met these people and it was a big family. The kids were much bigger than me ... I was, like, a tinier person. And they were kinda, like, rambunctious kids and my mom didn't feel comfortable leaving me there cuz she felt like I was gonna get bullied or whatever, and so she was like, "Maybe Toronto is not the option." So then I ended up going to, like, a private school in Ontario ... Not a boarding school. I stayed at another person's

---

3 Of course, access to English language instruction would not address other linguistic barriers people face. Almost half of Montreal students do not cite either French or English as their native language. Across the city of Montreal, 42.69 per cent of students are allophone (whose native language is neither French, nor English, nor an Indigenous language) (Comité de gestion de la taxe scolaire, 2016 In Courtmanche, 2017).

house in Cornwall while doing that ... I don't think I really understood what was happening back then. I was kinda – as a kid, I was kinda used to not living at home, cuz even in Sri Lanka, I went to a boarding school, and so for me it was kinda like, "Oh, it's normal to have, like, my interactions with my parents were once a month-ish," and that kinda reality, yeah, I've sort of accepted. So I didn't really think hard about it. [Later, when they moved me to] the seminary school ... I feel like my parents put me in a situation, at least now, that I wasn't prepared for. Cuz like, my parents didn't really know what they were sending me into.

In Ashan's case, his family was able to mobilize a range of economic and social resources so that he could continue his schooling in English after immigrating to Quebec. In doing so, however, they also had to make a number of sacrifices – sending Ashan to live with another family in Ontario and later enrolling him in a religious private school that was affordable, but that had unforeseen implications for Ashan's life. Although his parents were able to ensure Ashan had access to English language instruction in secondary school, they had to work creatively with what was accessible, affordable, and within the confines of the laws in Quebec. The choice to send Ashan to a private Islamic seminary in Ontario reflects his mother's quick and creative navigation of the Canadian education systems, rather than a strong desire to educate Ashan in the Islamic faith (in Sri Lanka, he attended an Anglican school).[4] Ashan himself quickly learned that he was not a typical seminary student. He explains that the school largely served as a form of punishment and reform for Muslim youth who – according to their parents – had gone astray. As such, the school was somewhat of a strange fit for a quiet and studious young Ashan, who'd had no previous Islamic faith-based instruction:

A: I wasn't really brought up Islamically. Like, my dad is Muslim, and he's not very religious at all. My mom came from a very Hindu family. So in terms of Islamic knowledge of – or the ways of being as a Muslim – like I had no clue, right? I was going in as someone who was Muslim by name, basically, right? And you go in there, and it's kids who've been raised up as Muslim their whole lives and they kinda understood what the rules were, what the expectations were, and I was sort of, like, thrust into that

4 According to the school's website, tuition and board for the seminary school is $3,000 per year, which is far less than the cost of private school tuition and boarding fees at any other Ontario private schools. In comparison, the cost of tuition, room, and board for the top twenty private schools in Ontario range from $17,600 to $42,620 per year (Our Kids, 2014). In Ontario, private schools do not receive public funding.

kind of environment, and I was just trying to figure it out. But I was also this kid that never really wanted to fail at anything I did, so I just put my head down, whatever, as much as possible, and just sort of got through ... [Eventually, I learned] Islamic seminaries in general are where parents kinda send their kids when they're kinda, like, fed up with them. So it's kinda like a miniprison kinda thing, so, like –

NN: A reform school?

A: Yeah! Exactly. So when you get tired of your kid [or] your kid's getting arrested, it's like, "Okay, let's send them to the seminary" and it's [the Seminary's] problem now and we'll just leave them there forever because no one really gets kicked out, you just have to run away from seminary.

NN: Do people do that? Were people running away from seminary?

A: Yeah ... I never ran away, but the kids I was with – it wasn't a very, like the environment itself wasn't conducive to learning. It was – it was a lot of people sort of interested in deviance and that kind of lifestyle because for them this is – they're there against their will and they want to stick it to their parents, stick it to the school ... it was, you know, kids who were just not, you know, accepted within society and they just throw 'em in there. And I remember, like, going there and my mom was, like, she's showing off my art work and my report cards and like, "this is the kind of kid you're getting," and I remember, like, the administration being really confused, [wondering] "Why are you sending this kid here?"

The experience at the seminary was life-altering for Ashan, who faced racism and Islamophobia from residents of the town where the school is located, immigration officials at the border when he and his friends would try to cross into the United States in their seminary uniforms, and people on city buses when he would ride in his traditional religious clothing. The seminary experience was also powerfully positive, shaping his profound religious faith and his subsequent work as an Imam. After graduating from the seminary, Ashan went on to attend a public English language undergraduate university and is currently finishing his MA at McGill. While it would be naive to pretend to be able to predict Ashan's educational trajectory had he stayed in Quebec, there are a few things I feel confident about claiming. Had Ashan proceeded with his secondary education in the public school system in Quebec, he would have been required to attend a French public school without entrance requirements, because he would have been unable to sit a French exam. In Quebec, only 51 per cent of boys in the French public school system graduated from high school on time, with boys from the privately subsidized English system graduating at a higher rate of 70 per cent (Ministère de l'Éducation et de l'Enseignement supérieur, 2017). (As I explain later, though, many go on to finish in the adult system.) According to the Fraser Institute rankings, seventeen of the twenty lowest ranking schools (based on academic performance data) in Montreal are public schools (without special project status), largely in poor neighbourhoods across the city (Fraser Institute, 2017). Given the rates of secondary school completion for young men in public French language schools, and given Ashan's lack of French language proficiency, it is reasonable to think his parents made a good choice for him. His experiences are important to include because they remind us that a single set of policy and institutional conditions will produce a range of outcomes at the level of the population. Different scenarios and consequences materialize as policy and institutional relations intersect with the other conditions of a young person's life.

While Ashan's experience is unique compared to anyone else I spoke with in Montreal, a second language education colleague assures me that it is not uncommon for immigrant parents to send children to attend public schools in Ontario, when they are coming from countries where the colonial language of educational instruction was English (Sarkar, personal communication, 2018). But the French language and education laws in Quebec have produced very different outcomes the lives of other young people I interviewed who immigrated to Canada during adolescence. In addition to my interview with Ashan, I interviewed a young woman named Imani who'd immigrated to Montreal with refugee status during adolescence; as well, a graduate student and youth research assistant coconducted a focus group with a number of newly arrived adolescent refugees – all of whom participated in a Welcome Class to learn French. When I met Imani she was preparing to write her final General Educational Development (GED) tests at an adult education outreach site in a West Island suburb. Like I had done with young people in Toronto, I asked her how she happened to be going to school at this alternative site. She explains that she transferred from a French public high school: "I was going to a high school, C-school, and then after I wanted to change schools. I didn't like the school, so I wanted to go to another school. The one that was close to my house was [the adult education program], and it's an English adult school. I'm more comfortable with English than French, so yeah." I prompt her to explain why she was in a French school in the first place, if she is more comfortable in English: "Because when I got here, I couldn't go to adult school – I didn't know about adult school – and I couldn't go to a high school that is English because my parents weren't born here, and they didn't go to an English school, something like that, and so they said we have to go to a French high school … We'd been in Uganda ten years from Tanzania. We were in Uganda as refugees in a refugee camp." Like Ashan, Imani is ineligible for English language instruction at the secondary level because neither of her parents is a Canadian citizen who received elementary instruction in English in Canada (Charter of the French Language, CQLR 1977, c. C-11, s. 72). When someone arrives in Quebec as a refugee or an immigrant without Canadian citizenship, they are not eligible to apply for the certificate of eligibility required to participate in one of the English school boards. While people with a range of ethnic and racial backgrounds immigrate to Quebec, in the last fifty years the majority have arrived from Haiti, Latin America, Southeast Asia, Lebanon, and countries from North-West Africa (Berthiaume, Corbo, & Montreuil, 2014). In some instances, young people arriving as immigrants have been directly placed into Welcome Classes, despite having received formal instruction in schools in French in countries such as Haiti (Maynard, 2017). Other young people who immigrate to Montreal during adolescence describe being placed in the city's Welcome Classes only to age out of the system (i.e., reach sixteen years of age) before achieving the language proficiency that would enable their participation in the secondary school system (Baffoe, 2006). Participants in Baffoe's study sense that these programs – particularly where they are oriented to adolescents – create a pedagogical context that significantly disadvantages the educational participation of immigrant youth. Coupled with experiences of systemic and overt racism across the education system, young Black people (Zellars, 2017) and immigrant and refugee youth (Baffoe, 2006) are disadvantaged in and by the education system in Montreal, experiencing more punitive and exclusionary interactions with educators and school administrators than their White peers. In this chapter I attempt to show how education programs designed to promote the integration of immigrants into the dominant cultural, linguistic, and political-economic organization of life of Quebec often serve to Other and exclude them.

For Imani, the stint in the Welcome Class punctuated an already discontinuous educational trajectory. Growing up in a refugee camp, Imani did not participate in formal schooling until she was twelve years old:

I: In the refugee camp, there was school, but it's not like school. You don't have like a class. You just sit under the tree and play, just like to bring us around not to have to stay home. You don't learn nothing. Nobody knows how to write. That's where I was going until my parents got a job and sent us to a school in town, not the refugee camp. Yeah, and I was the oldest in class. I didn't know how to read or even write my name and no English. Then whenever they tell me to read, I would just be like scared and I don't know what to say ... It was like in a primary school, and it starts from Primary 1 up to Primary 7. Because I didn't know nothing, I was supposed to start from Primary 1. But I was really old for that. The teachers decided they should put me in Primary 3 at least. I didn't know nothing to be there in that class, but they said I'll catch up … I did that from twelve to fourteen. Then I didn't go to school again and I sat home for a year and a half.

NN: Because?

I: Because we were expecting to come here. They were like telling us, "You're about to go," and my parents said, "Okay, we don't have enough money, so we're going to a new school in Canada."

For most of Imani's life, she had no access to formal education. Where she was able to participate in schooling, she did well, progressing quickly to catch up with similar-aged peers. But due to the cost to attend a school outside of the refugee camp and uncertainties associated with the immigration process, her parents were reluctant to continue to send her and her siblings. When she arrived in Montreal, she was fifteen years old, and she entered the public education system through a Welcome Class, which initially she found "comfortable": "They put us in a class of everybody doesn't know [French], and we all have to learn, so it was not bad. It was comfortable … [But then] There was a fight at the school. I was involved in the fight … I was in a [Classe] d'accueil, and the students [who wanted to fight me] were in a regular class." Despite Imani's age and educational history – namely, that she had received no formal education until early adolescence, at which point she nearly completed the entire primary school curriculum in English over two years – she is placed in a Welcome Class until she demonstrates the French language proficiency required to attend public school in French. Like Ashan, Imani describes the Welcome Class itself as comfortable; unfortunately, interactions between students in the Welcome Class and those in the mainstream French Language public school where it is situated remain fraught. Imani describes an experience of targeting and racially motivated harassment from other students in the mainstream school, which educators and school security personnel fail to address. The inaction from school staff is particularly problematic given Imani's recent arrival, her unfamiliarity with state systems in Canada (as well as her legal rights to, for instance, live free from discrimination), and the availability of evidence (built through her social media feeds) that she was violently targeted by a group of students in the mainstream school.

In our interview, Imani describes a conflict that began on Facebook after she posted a video and tagged a boy from her class in the post. The video and the post were viewed by the young man's girlfriend, who then posted on her own Facebook page: "We're going to beat this bitch's ass tomorrow." From here, the whole thing blew up into a series of racist and threatening posts, status updates, and tags that eventually numbered over five hundred comments. All the while, Imani was also receiving personal messages conveying hateful things about her race and her ethnicity and threatening her with violence:

> The messages, the stuff they were saying were more bad than the fight ... Really bad [things] about my parents, about me. I had braids and like blue strips on the braids. Yeah, and they were calling me "blue head," and then they laughed. I blocked that guy who posted the status and the friend who now posted the status, because that way they couldn't tag me. She posted a new status that said they're going to beat the blue head. And now everybody – I didn't know nobody. I only know people in my class at that school, but the whole school, they say, "We're going to take you back to Africa and then you're going to die there with hunger."

Imani spoke with her sister and her friends about the messages she'd been receiving. In our interview, she explained that there had been fights at the refugee camp as well – fights that often led to serious injury and sometimes resulted in death. As such, when she started to receive threats over social media, she was quite afraid. In speaking with friends, she was advised that fights in Canada rarely led to serious injury and that the police would intervene and keep her safe. She assumed that the worst of the violence was limited to what she was experiencing online, and she went to school anticipating that things would blow over:

> I didn't expect the fight. I had come like three minutes late and going to get the stuff from my locker and go to class. The first bell had gone. The bus came late for some reason, so everybody was running. A lot of people were already at school, and the girls were waiting. My sister picked her stuff and ran. We are already late for class. Everybody was just running on their own. And the one girl came [and peeked] and saw that I'm there and she went and told the rest of girls. There were four girls and they came and they started fighting. Yeah. Then the rest of students who are passing by, like a lot, they came and saw the fight going on, and they stood there. They came, and they saw it and started cheering and taking videos. Yeah. And they pulled off my braids. I had braids that attached to my hair. They pulled. It came off with my real hair too. It was everywhere. They picked it and put it in the garbage. My friend came because the boys were picking

it up and asking, "What is this?" Then one of my friends, she was trying to push off the girls, but she was just one and she couldn't. So [the other girl] put the braids in the trash bins there. The security guy at school came and took us in the detention room, and he just left us, all of us there. We sat and they called our parents. My sister called my mum, and my mum came ... They gave us the equal punishment. And the lady was there. She saw the messages, what had happened and everything, and she just says that I should tell my parents, we should go and tell the police, and it had nothing to do with the school, but it's on my parents supposedly to go to the police ... the teacher when the fight happened, she was more focusing, one of the teachers, on me and like I was the cause of the fight, and the four girls who were fighting me. And there the video, the cameras were there and boys, the videos, boys that were sharing online, she saw it. And she was saying that "I know in Africa you experienced so much violence and stuff." I experienced violence, but I'm not the one who was fighting.

While the four girls attacked Imani, yanking off her hair extensions and putting them into the garbage, the other students in the school "started cheering and taking videos." The videos were quickly uploaded to social media sites by the young men who were filming, creating a public record of the fight, which could have been used as evidence that Imani had been targeted by the other young women. But in the end, all of the young women – including Imani – were given equal punishment for fighting, and Imani's experiences were patronizingly dismissed by the teacher as the result of a cultural clash. Indeed, the responding teacher suggests the problem is an inability on Imani's part to leave a violent Africa behind as she integrates into a peaceful Quebec: "I know in Africa you experienced so much violence and stuff." Instead of treating the incident as bullying, racism, or an assault, it was treated like a playground fight and Imani and her family were advised to follow-up with the police. Unfortunately, when Imani did report the incident to the police, it took them more than two months to respond: "I went to the police after, and then they called me after two months. I was really mad when I went there, and after two months it was just like, 'Okay' ... they called me and said, 'Do you still want to continue your case?' I told him, 'No, just leave it.'"

Other Black young people in Montreal share similar stories of racially motivated taunts, threats, and bullying by White students, which are left unaddressed by White teachers or, worse, resulted in their own punishment (Baffoe, 2006). In Imani's case, not all of the young women who assaulted her were White – which only superficially complicates what is clearly an example of explicit and systemic racism. As Imani's own experiences and insights reveal, White supremacy and anti-Black racism are pervasive. After an experience in the Welcome Class where a friend from Pakistan is pressed by other young Pakistani women about why she would hang around with a "Black girl,"[5] Imani reflects on the ways anti-Black racism – particularly as it intersects with class-based oppression – shapes standards of beauty more broadly: "Like in my country, a lot of people bleach their skin. There is like bleaching products. They do it, and when you're darker, it means you're poor, you can't get money to buy the bleaching products." The fact that not all of the young women who assaulted Imani are White does not diminish the racist overtures of the social media posts, the young women's physical actions (e.g., pulling off her braids and throwing them into the garbage), or the passive aggressive racism and lack of action demonstrated by Imani's teachers.

There is provincial legislation in place to support the prevention of violence in schools in Quebec. In 2012, Bill 56: An Act to Prevent and Stop Bullying and Violence in Schools was adopted as Law 19 in Quebec's National Assembly as an amendment to Quebec's Education Act. The purpose of this bill is "to prevent and stop all forms of bullying and violence targeting a student, a teacher or any other school staff member" (Quebec Education Act, Bill 56, 2012, p. 4). But policy and legislation are inert – only gaining the capacity to coordinate insofar as people are willing to enact and enforce them; furthermore, and as others have already noted (Walton, 2005; Ringrose & Renold, 2010), school bullying discourses often paper over and distract from the more insidious and systemic forms of racial- and gender-based violence that shape public education in Canada.

Here, it is worth revisiting Rosewood's youth worker Warren's observations about the damage done by well-intentioned teachers. In their failure to see, hear, and connect with the actual young people in their classrooms, they rely on objectified, single-dimensional personas – racialized and sensationalized caricatures of Blackness and youth – portrayed on the twenty-four-hour news station to code and interpret the conduct of their students in reductive and racially biased ways. Similar sense-making practices are employed by the mostly White

---

5 The full quotation from the interview is: "Why do you talk to her? That's why boys don't talk to you. She's ugly, she's Black. When you talk to Black girls, then the boys won't talk to you."

teachers that make up the teaching staff in Quebec schools, who rely on the post-racial discourses about Quebec culture and values to sublimate and sidestep conversations about racism. With reference to her own children's education, Zellars (2017) observes "steely silences that operate to ignore and 'invisibilize' anti-Black violence against Black children in the French language system and, as a result, render the pain of encountered racial violence 'unrecognizable'" (Zellars, 2017, p. 23).

In the end, Imani never returned to the Welcome Class. Having reached sixteen years of age, she learned she was eligible to participate in the adult education system. She transferred to an English language program where she finished the entire secondary school curriculum over the next two years and ultimately graduated as the class valedictorian – this despite a series of additional challenges she encountered as a result of the move into the adult system. As a student in the adult education system, Imani had to pay fees: "Sixty dollars, yeah [every semester]. We pay sixty dollars and then we have to buy books too." The school fees, coupled with other incidental costs (e.g., for skin lotion and clothes), proved too much for the family's small budget, and so Imani and her sister were asked to move out. Her sister was the only one of eight children who had a job, but the money she made doing part-time minimum wage shift work (as a personal support worker) only covered the school and book fees for herself and Imani. Their parents (also students), who needed help with the rent, felt that the two young women were not pulling their weight. Imani and her sister moved out – first opting to stay with a friend from their new school and ultimately into a temporary (or transitional) supportive housing environment for youth (a Maison des jeunes) – and continued to work towards the completion of their secondary school credits. But faced with the prospect of securing their own food and housing and a growing sense of vulnerability, accentuated by the fight at school and their subsequent loss of housing, both young women ended up navigating the provincial mental health system with the support of a teacher:

When we came here, we were expecting to be safe. But after that happened [at school] and the rest of the stuff that I was seeing happening, it's just I feel safe, but not really my sister. For her, she really doesn't feel safe. She can't really walk at night. It's just like normally it gets dark, she's in the house. Just there, yeah, just like before. There [in the refugee camp], what happened was really not something that would have bothered me, but because I didn't expect it to happen *here* it was just like, "Oh, this could happen here too." It was never in my dreams that I saw something. Like coming here is like heaven, and everybody comes and like dreams, "I'm going to heaven. There is all nice stuff and rich." But I told my friends, some of them that I have on Facebook, I say, "Well, that's not what is here," and they don't believe me. But when they come, then [they will see]. I don't want to break their dreams too, because when you're there [living in the refugee camp], some people, what keeps them alive is the hope of getting to come here one day. They just look at all the good things here. I don't want to start just telling them, "Okay, it's all bad. There is nothing. Some of you could even die, if you were to come here." I didn't tell them exactly what happened, but I told them not to have so much hope of coming here.

During the interview Imani elaborated about what made the refugee camps so dangerous: "Because they rape people. They rape girls. Because you have to go to get water. You go at like seven in the morning and you probably come back at eight or nine [at night] to just find water. And it's really dark. It's far from where you live to go find water." The idea of being raped after being separated from the group of children who have gone to find water seemed ordinary to Imani. But the loss of hope – the abasement of her dreams – because she "didn't expect it [the violence and police inaction] to happen *here*" was devastating, unleashing a deep-seeded fear in her sister who continues to suffer from night terrors and whom Imani must meet at the bus at the end of each late-night shift.

The education system pivots around the construction of young people in a single dimension. From a policy point of view, the point of intervention was Imani's French language deficiencies – a unidimensional vantage point, which obscures all of the other strengths, resources, and challenges that were shaping Imani's life and her experiences in school. By hiving off a particular aspect of a young person's life, it becomes possible to design, administer, and account for an intervention that targets this bureaucratic illusion – a distinctive segment of a young person's life that requires attention. But the social relations of experience are complex and intersecting and only artificially can a single strand be teased out for the purposes of an institutional intervention. As such, young people whose experiences, aptitudes, conduct, dispositions, and mannerisms obviously and consistently defy the unidimensional standards through which the education system has been normed, will be described using catch-all phrases such as "hard to serve," "complex needs," or "at risk." The lack of precision associated with these terms – a function of the disconnect between the normative categories and interventions that the state and its institutions employ and the varied experiences of actual young people – means they can be filled with meaning and used to initiate (or not) a range of different institutional processes.

Youth "At Risk"

Once framed institutionally as non-normative (i.e., as a behavioural youth, a youth with special needs, or a youth risk), a range of tactics are accessible to adults seeking to teach young people in schools. Many are interventions that can be brought in to mainstream classrooms to ensure young people can function more effectively and communicate what they know to teachers (e.g., my daughter can use noise-cancelling headphones to help her concentrate and glasses to help with visual efficiency). In other instances, young people are removed from mainstream programs and taught in segregated classrooms for young people who have been judged to be out of sync with the normative organization and everyday relations of the public-school system. Rosewood's School Away from School program represents one such alternative program for youth who are – for a range of reasons – seen to be unsuitable candidates for mainstream high school. Unlike other alternative programs, young people and their families do not elect to attend school at Rosewood; rather, they are enrolled there by school staff.

Recall that the first interviews I did were with young people learning at Rosewood, and I simply asked them how they ended up there. Officially, young people described being moved out of mainstream programs for attendance or disciplinary issues. But as young people elaborated on these moves, a complex social world came into view, which complicated this official narrative about why a young person is sent to Rosewood. I start with one of the most popular explanations we heard (the explanation with which I started chapter 4): young people are not consistently attending school and/or are coming to school late. As I've already suggested, the focus on attendance as an indicator of academic risk reflects national preoccupation with correlations between education and economic data (OECD, 2010; World Bank, 2007). What becomes clear as young people talk is that a whole bunch of other things underpin the statistical indications of academic risk – captured in these attendance data – which our current systems do not effectively address.

Solely moving young people out of mainstream schools and into alternative settings will not improve the myriad conditions that shape young people's educational trajectories, including the regularity with which they come to school. In the interview below, graduate research assistant Alison and I ask a young woman (Rebeca) how she came to Rosewood. This interview took place in April. I had met Rebeca the fall prior, when she was at Rosewood for the first time; she came and went numerous times over the course of this research. She was sixteen at the time of this interview and had yet to complete her grade 9 or 10 credits. As the interview was warming up, I asked Rebeca if she remembered meeting me and my son – a baby at the time – who I was still nursing and therefore regularly accompanied me to Rosewood. She nodded vaguely, and I couldn't tell if she was just being polite. I asked what had been going on in her life since we'd last seen each other, and she answered:

> REBECA: I don't know. I was doing this assessment with a CTYS [City of Toronto Youth Services] worker, and it was like – it was like an assessment about my feelings, I guess, or whatever. And I guess I stopped coming to school because it was the same time around when my brother passed, and so it just affected me. And it only started affecting me now, I guess … he passed in 2005 but I was younger. But I'm only reacting to it now.
> NAOMI: So what were you doing on your days when you weren't here?
> REBECA: I was just out smoking, drinking, being with my friends. Acting like a teenager.

From here, Alison invited Rebeca to describe herself. Quietly, and with much prompting from Alison, Rebeca explained that she used to run track and play soccer, but not since she started smoking three years ago. At this point in the conversation, she told us that she lived with her sister, who is twenty-one, and has five other siblings as well as a brother "who has passed." Later in the interview she told us that she was actually living with a friend. When prompted about whether there were words related to race, gender, or culture she might use to talk about herself, Rebeca explained her "background [Jamaican and Grenadian], where my mom and my dad's from," is important to how she thinks about herself. When Alison asked her how she ended up at Rosewood, Rebeca began by offering brief, soft-spoken responses. I include the back and forth, to give the reader a sense of the pacing of the conversation the slow-going illumination of detail:

> ALISON: And so how did you come to Rosewood?
> REBECA: From my mainstream school.
> ALISON: And how did that happen?

REBECA: They suggested me to come here before I started going back to school there. So I have to finish credits here before I start going back there.

ALISON: Who suggested that you come here? Do you know? Your principal or vice-principal?

REBECA: It was the social worker at the school.

ALISON: And did you see the social worker regularly? Were you –

REBECA: Sometimes.

ALISON: – in a relationship with her?

REBECA: Sometimes.

. . .

ALISON: So she suggested Rosewood? And how did you feel about that?

REBECA: At first I didn't want to, but then after I just said, "Okay, I'll try."

NAOMI: How come she made that suggestion?

REBECA: Because I wasn't going to school regularly.

ALISON: So it was attendance issues.

REBECA: Yeah, and I don't like a lot of students. Like I don't like a lot of people around me or just I won't talk. I won't do nothing. I just leave … I was going to school in Hamilton, but then my aunt broke my bail because her husband didn't like me, and me and her husband got into an argument. And yeah, so then she broke my bail because he said if she doesn't break my bail then he's going to leave her or whatever. So she had to. Then my mom came and bailed me out again, and that's when my stepdad bailed me out after.

ALISON: So you were in Hamilton and then you ended up back in Toronto, and you went back to the school, like your last high school?

REBECA: Yeah, but I was on house arrest.

ALISON: House arrest. And did that school year go okay? I guess there was some attendance issues so maybe you weren't going to school.

REBECA: I ran away.

ALISON: You ran away from –?

REBECA: Home and school. Yeah, it was after school. I left and I went to my cousin's house, and I was gone for like four or three months. And then I was at my cousin's house and the house got raided and I got arrested. And then that's when my stepdad bailed me out.

Officially, Rebeca is learning at Rosewood because of "attendance issues," as Alison – a teacher herself – notes during the interview. But as Alison and I slowly tease out the details of Rebeca's story with her, we discover considerable instability in Rebeca's life, including a number of moves in a short period of time – living with her mother, her aunt, her mother again, her sister, her cousin, and a friend – and experiences running away from home. As we are given further insight into Rebeca's life, we learn she had been charged and released under the Youth Criminal Justice Act numerous times over the last four years. Like Rebeca does above, other young people with youth criminal justice records talked nonchalantly with us about being bailed or breaking bail. They are referring to the conditions of their release – not only after having been charged with an offence (and often before) but also in some cases after going to trial. When Rebeca talked about her aunt, her mother, and/or her stepfather bailing her, she is commenting on their willingness (or not) to take responsibility for her upon her release from custody. According to the Youth Criminal Justice Act:

> A young person who has been arrested may be placed in the care of a responsible person instead of being detained in custody if a youth justice court or a justice is satisfied that
>
> (a) the young person would, but for this subsection, be detained in custody under section 515 (judicial interim release) of the Criminal Code;
> (b) the person is willing and able to take care of and exercise control over the young person; and
> (c) the young person is willing to be placed in the care of that person.

(Youth Criminal Justice Act, S.C. 2002, c.1, s. 31[1])

To avoid detention, young people involved in the youth criminal justice system rely on the presence and willingness of caring adults in their lives to state before the courts that they are "willing and able to take care of and exercise control over" them, as a condition of their release. In her explanation to Alison, Rebeca described living in Hamilton with her aunt who initially agreed and later revoked her responsibility for Rebeca's care and control upon release from custody. After this, she returned to live with her mother in Toronto under house arrest, but when she ran away, she ended up with further charges for breaching the conditions of her release. Later in the interview, Rebeca explained that she'd actually been under house arrest in Hamilton as well due to a series of offences and administration of justice charges (or breaches of the conditions of her probation/release). Not unlike other interviews I've done with young people who have had lengthy histories of involvement with the youth criminal justice system (Nichols, 2014), it is difficult to situate Rebeca's story chronologically. As the interview opens up, however, it becomes clear that regular school attendance is not the most pressing concern in her life.

A year prior to our interview with her, Rebeca was living in Hamilton serving out a house arrest under her aunt's custody and supervision. Given the racialized distribution of policing resources in Toronto (Maynard, 2017; Nichols, Fisher, & Braimoh, submitted; Wortley & Tanner, 2003), the over-representation of Black and Indigenous youth in Ontario's criminal justice system (Rankin & Winsa, 2013; Maynard, 2017), and the fifteen interviews we conducted in Ontario's largest jail, I heard a lot about house arrest from the young people we interviewed in the largely black-Caribbean-diasporic neighbourhood where research for Schools and Safety took place. One of our youth researchers was on house arrest during the first summer of data collection, and I wrote the notice, which he carried on his person, indicating that he was participating in a paid summer school co-operative education program, under my supervision. When young people talk about being on house arrest, it either means that they are pretrial and living under the most stringent of bail conditions or that they have been charged, found guilty of an offence, and sentenced, but that they are serving out this sentence in the community. House arrest is accompanied with very strict conditions (e.g., you can only leave your house to go to school or work), including regular supervision by a probation officer. The racialized disproportionality of stop-and-search practices (e.g., that young Black men experience police stops at a rate of 3.4 times that of their population in Toronto [Rankin & Winsa, 2012]) increases the likelihood that a Black youth will receive administration of justice for failing to comply with the conditions of their release.

In Rebeca's case, she was serving out a conditional sentence (or house arrest) in Hamilton because this is where an adult (her aunt) agreed, in writing, to be legally responsible for her custody and control after she received an obstruction of justice charge (for giving an officer a fake name) and an administration of justice charge (for failing to comply with the conditions of her probation by spending time in the company of her coaccused offender and missing curfew). Rebeca continued the story in her own words, as Alison and I tried to follow along:

REBECA: I was in a hotel [in Oshawa], and then I got pulled over on the highway. That hotel was under investigation for child prostitution, but I didn't know. And then me and my cousins were trying to leave that same night because we found out [the hotel was under investigation] after the girl brought us there and then so we tried to leave, but the Go Station was closed, so we couldn't leave. And so we stayed overnight but we stayed in a different room, but they [the police] were watching it already. So when we left to go to drive us back to Toronto (because we were in Whitby or something like that. I think. Yeah, it was Oshawa), and we were on the highway in between Pickering and I can't remember … They pulled us over and then they asked for our, like, identification or whatever. But I was coaccused with my cousin, and I was *with* my cousin, and this other girl was on the run. And so, like, she gave a false name, but then my cousin gave her real name, but I gave a fake name.

NAOMI: Because you weren't supposed to be with your cousin?

REBECA: Yeah and because she gave her real name, my picture popped up from before because I got arrested before with her. And they arrested all three of us because they found out who the other girl was. She got arrested too.

NAOMI: What was she running from?

REBECA: Her group home.

NAOMI: Were you running from a group home too?

REBECA: No. I was just on curfew and I was with my cousin and we were coaccused, so, yeah … and because I broke bail and got arrested.

ALISON: So you broke bail, got arrested, and how did you end up in Hamilton?

REBECA: Because my aunt bailed me out again. Because my mom bailed me out – my mom bailed me out again and then my aunt had to bail me out because my mom couldn't bail me out. And then my stepdad bailed me out.

There is a recursivity to Rebeca's narrative that makes it difficult to follow her story. She is in Toronto, then Hamilton, then Toronto again. She is living with her mother, her aunt, her cousin, her sister, and at the end of the interview she tells us she's now living with a friend. At one point, the house she is living in (with her cousin) is raided by the police. And although she describes being arrested numerous times in this account, her experiences with the youth criminal justice system predate her explanation of coming to school at Rosewood. When I asked if she'd ever spent time in detention or custody outside the home, she tells us that she was detained several times while awaiting trial:

REBECA: I went to one in Peterborough. I went to one in Brampton.

NAOMI: Like for a long time? No, just short, like two weeks sort of thing? [Rebeca nods] So you don't do school or anything when you're there?

REBECA: No.

NAOMI: When you're waiting for court?

REBECA: Yeah.

NAOMI: Peterborough, Brampton. So just two?

REBECA: Peterborough, Brampton, one in Oshawa, and I can't remember the other one.

Between twelve and sixteen years of age, Rebeca's life is punctuated by instability that manifests as "attendance issues" and difficulty obtaining credits, but this focus on attendance and credits misses the mark. Considering that she has bounced from institution to institution and city to city throughout her adolescence, it is unsurprising that Rebeca has failed to consistently attend.

In this regard, she reminds me of a bright young woman named Stella who I met at a homeless shelter about a decade ago. Stella didn't finish grade 9 because she was in and out of secure and open custody facilities, inpatient mental facilities, and group homes between ages fourteen and seventeen (Nichols, 2014). Stella was "known to police" and repeatedly charged with failing to comply with her probation order (especially the mandated curfew), but Stella was not Black, which means she was less likely to be "randomly" stopped by police than Rebeca. Wortley and Tanner's (2003) study of non-criminally involved youth in Toronto revealed that more than one-third of Black youth had been stopped by police, compared to less than one-tenth of White youth – a difference of approximately 25 per cent. This single interview with Rebeca does not offer enough insight into her life to allow me to trace out all the differences and similarities in the two women's stories of their schooling and other institutional relationships. I want to focus here on a few that I think are important.

The first is that while both young women were court ordered to undergo a range of interventions, only Stella participated in mental health diversion programs, including a range of Intensive Support and Supervision programming and multiple mental health interventions. Rebeca, on the other hand, describes periods of incarceration and supervised custody (by family members) in the community with some basic access to counselling and employment programming through the City of Toronto Youth Services. Further, while both women experience housing precarity, it doesn't sound like Rebeca ever engaged with the range of housing services for youth that Stella relied on. Instead, she – like other youth I worked with in her neighbourhood – describes crashing in houses that are raided by the police. My relationship with Stella developed over a year, and eventually we became reasonably close, so I know more about her life and experiences than I do about Rebeca's. But I am struck by two important similarities, in addition to the differences I've just listed: first, even where young people are ultimately mandated to attend school (e.g., when under house arrest), youth criminal justice

interventions exacerbated attendance issues and educational discon-
nections, rather than enabling their resolution; and second, neither
young woman felt she was understood/heard by the people who were
ostensibly trying to help her.

Research suggests that there is a racialized dimension to the disconnect between what schools offer and what young women need
and want. In 2014, two groundbreaking US policy studies argued that
young Black women in schools have been oversurveilled, overpoliced,
and underserved by the education system (African American Policy
Forum and Columbia Center for Intersectionality and Policy Studies,
2014; National Association for the Advancement of Colored People
and National Women's Law Centre, 2014). When Alison and I ask what
might have been a useful intervention for her, the clear impression she
offers is that we are asking her the wrong questions:

> ALISON: So, if you're not in class anymore, because that was an issue, right?
> You stopped coming sometimes. What advice would you have to staff at
> the school to help better support?
> REBECA: I don't know.
> ALISON: Is there anything that the school could have done, do you think?
> Or was it just too much stuff outside?
> REBECA: It was just myself.
> ALISON: Just yourself.
> NAOMI: Is it because we don't get it?
> REBECA: Yeah.
> NAOMI: What part are we really missing?
> REBECA: A lot.

It is in the observation that Alison and I don't get it that we get some
insight into the chasm between the imagined student against which the
public education system has been normed and the actual conditions of
Rebeca's life. This discord is what impacts her attendance.

Elsewhere, and drawing on Griffith and Smith's (2005) work on
mothering and schooling, I've written about the institutional and policy processes through which racialized young people are constructed as
non-normative (Nichols, 2018) within the public education system. The
policy matrix through which school safety and improvement are pursued by some (e.g., the White teachers in schools serving Black youth)
produces the conditions of dislocation experienced by others (e.g., the
Black youth, who are transferred for failing to attend). Of course, it's
not quite as reductively Manichean as I've just suggested; but I want
to be clear that the same set of state processes will produce disparate

effects in actual people's lives, and that these disparate effects reflect and entrench the intersecting and interconstitutive social relations of class, race, and gender. Through the provision and management of public sector resources and punishments, the state (re)produces historically entrenched racialized, classed, and gendered disproportionalities, as well as the systems of classification and categorization that shape the objectified (or shared) modes of consciousness whereby people come to make sense of these trends in relation to a sense of self and others.

Not only does the singular focus on school attendance make it difficult to pay attention (institutionally) to the diverse and actual circumstances of young people's lives making school attendance difficult, but some principals approach non-attendance from a punitive standpoint, using it as a threat and/or justification for removal – again to the benefit of some at the expense of others. Kayla, a student success teacher we interviewed, observes how a piecemeal, superficial, and punitive approach to "at-risk" students simply contributes to their systemic disadvantage:

> K: Like, I think where we have piecemeal or programs here, there, and everywhere, are they working? What is the point? What is the intended outcome? What are trying to address here? … So if we have, like, this group of at-risk kids, certain policies that don't actually – you're not going to solve the problem with that policy, right.
>
> AF: So can you give me an example?
>
> K: The attendance policy at our school. It's completely restrictive. And so [if] you're late, you're [recorded as] absent … the point is, is that you might be able to deal with the kids who are – like, you're preaching to the converted with this policy. You're going to be able to attract the kids that are already kind of attending, but kind of falling off. But the real attendance issues are not going to be responded by a detention, a call home. The issues are so much bigger than that. And so when you kind of set a mindset for that [punitive approach], then people don't use the thinking of mitigating factors and the supportive ways [of addressing the roots of the problem].

While truancy officers have been rebranded as attendance counsellors in Ontario, the approach to school attendance retains the historically punitive orientation. When asked about school attendance, Brad, a young Black (Guianese and Trinidadian) man we interviewed in jail, recalled, "The principal said 'if you skip school, you're out.' He said, 'you can't come back again.' I was like seventeen at the time. I was kicked out for good. He transferred me to [a Safe and Caring Schools learning centre]." Think back to Jani's intake, suspension, and re-intake. A cluster of institutional activity backgrounds each move into or out of a program. Each of these institutional junctures increases the likelihood that important information will not accompany the young person as she or he is moved to yet another site. Notably, the moves amplify the sense that "you are nobody" and that the problems you are experiencing are a function of personal and familial deficits.

Negotiating, Coordinating, and Enabling Access to Education

As well as transfers for poor attendance and below-target rates of credit accumulation, the youth we interviewed also describe ambiguous disciplinary exclusions from mainstream programs that were neither suspensions nor expulsions. Tyrone provides us an exemplary explanation for the type of educational relocations we heard most frequently about from youth. Shortly after having started at a new school, he tells us:

> I got into a school, I got into a fight with a kid, and then the principal didn't suspend me. He told me not to come back to school and then I stayed home for five days. He didn't tell none of my family. I just stayed home and then came back … And then after … he just told me not to come back to school and I was out of school for two months until last week … [my principal] was trying to find me an alternative school for two months … I kept calling him, calling him. My grandma called him, my mom called him … and he's like, "Oh, we're trying to find you, we're going to try to place you at Rosewood." He said that in January, he's going to place me here last January. I wasn't here in January. February flew by, I kept calling.

Initially, these moves perplexed me, procedurally. The youth were not being de-enrolled for poor attendance (e.g., like David or Marianna) or being suspended or expelled for disciplinary issues. Rather, the youth were simply being told they were no longer welcome on campus. Eventually, I discovered that these school removals and transfers were institutionally sanctioned alternatives to school suspensions and expulsions.

When I was at Rosewood in January 2018, youth worker (Warren) and the new executive director (Shae) described receiving daily calls from vice-principals, probation officers, and parents looking for places for young people to complete their schoolwork – despite the School Away from School program at Rosewood being officially defunded by the TDSB in 2017. When Shae and Warren established a grass-roots space for youth to work independently towards the completion of secondary school credits, with mentorship from youth workers in the absence of teachers, they discovered that many of the youth showing up on their doorsteps still had active status at the sending school, despite being told they are no longer welcome there. This, they found, was most often the case for young people who were eighteen or close to eighteen – the age at which, in Ontario, it is no longer a violation of the Education Act to restrict access to education (in Quebec, the age is sixteen). But young people are also unofficially moved out of mainstream programs at other times in their educational histories upon the discretion of educational administrators.

Samir, a Black youth we interviewed at Rosewood in 2014, explains how this sort of thing happens, in his own words. When I ask how he ended up at Rosewood, he begins by telling me it took him a month to get back into school, after a period in a provincial detention centre: "My mum was calling the TDSB, calling my school, trying to make them transfer me to a school. No schools would accept me." Once admitted to a school, it is under strict conditions regarding school attendance, and Samir describes being summarily removed to Rosewood when court proceedings required that he miss two mornings of school:

> SAMIR: So then I think [the Safe Schools placement coordinator] got me into E-school, and I went to E-school, and I was doing fine there. Like, I was actually doing fine. And I guess the principal never liked me and then she said I missed, like, they said if I missed any class, then I can't come back to the school. And I missed a class, but that was for court and I told them it was for court. And I gave them proof, but, like, she just didn't like me. She kicked me out. Because even on my credit summary, it says that, like, I didn't even miss – I only missed two classes and that was for court. And that was two morning classes ... like, basically I promised, saying if I missed any classes, unless it was for court, that they have the right to kick me out. Because, like, the school was much different, like, much different, much different.
>
> NN: I mean, what I'm curious about, I guess, is: Kids are being told that they're not allowed to come back, but they're not being expelled or suspended. What do the principals call it?
>
> SAMIR: No, she – like, she called – okay, right now that's still my school [E-school]. If I was to do anything here, let's say I go punch somebody in the face. The principal [of E-school] will make up how much days I get suspended from here for. Like, it's still my school, but it was just, like they just didn't want me in the school.

It is difficult to get young people who are coming out of detention (re)enrolled in a community school for a number of reasons, which I bring into view below. In addition to – or because of – Samir's mother's persistent effort to engage the school board, Samir explained that a school board staff member, the Safe Schools Transfer Coordinator for his quadrant, eventually "got him into" a school in a neighbourhood west of where he had been living. More than once in the interview, Samir described the school as "much different, like, much different." Having identified the schools in this quadrant that are in the nearby suburb Samir named, my best guess is that the school was one of the board's special status schools, serving young people on non-academic or advanced academic tracks. In both cases, special status designations might have enabled a more cautious stance on the part of the principal. After a quick call to the principal at Samir's previous high school, the receiving principal would have found out that Samir was not allowed to return there because conditions of his release from custody prevented him from attending school with his "assault victim."

At Rosewood, Samir's nickname was Trappa, which is slang for drug dealer. This name was not used ironically or in jest – as it would have been if Samir was pretending to be more involved in street work than he was. Samir came to school every day dressed in royal blue from head to toe, and the other young people gave him wide berth. Of course, none of these things reduce his rights to education – the only intervention consistently found to have a protective effect on young people involved in the youth criminal justice system. But the conditions of his expulsion from another school in the board, coupled with blatant allegiance to his gang (i.e., as manifested daily in his wardrobe choices), would go some distance to explain – although not justify – the principal's heightened surveillance of Samir's comings and goings.

Within this socially organized nexus of activity, Samir's subsequent placement at Rosewood is, as he notes, neither a suspension nor an expulsion. It is an exclusion, which is a new category of educational moves organized outside of the legislated school expulsion process. Ian, a Caring and Safe Schools educator in Toronto, explains:

[An] alternative placement is separate from suspension and expulsion. It could be an exclusion. So, for example, a principal has a student who has done some criminal activity over the summer – like, serious stuff, like a shooting or a stabbing or something like that. The principal finds out about it and says, "Look, this student is detrimental to the health of my school. Hasn't done anything on school grounds in order for me to suspend or expel them, but

I still think they're going to cause some harm here. I want them excluded."
Sends them to our program for assessment and support ... I think we've got
two A&S [Assessment and Support] kids right now ... And they're usually
really challenging kids. It's kind of a loophole. Suspensions and expulsions,
they're a legal process, but an exclusion is not.

While suspension and expulsion data are tracked and disaggregated
by race, the discretionary removal of students outside the bounds of an
official expulsion process is not tracked, and these processes are thus
subject to very little oversight. For example, when school exclusions
are not framed as expulsions, school administrators are not required
to conduct an investigation of the infraction and no expulsion hearing is scheduled. These hearings are meant to ensure young people
have access to justice and that disciplinary interventions are not being
implemented without full consideration of mitigating circumstances. I
certainly wouldn't advocate for increased expulsions and suspensions;
however, stories like Tyrone's and Samir's were all too common among
the students I interviewed in Safe and Caring Schools programs. When
youth are moved out of mainstream programs in off-the-record ways
it becomes difficult for young people and their parents or advocates to
challenge these moves using formal channels or for researchers to grasp
the extent to which exclusionary relations in schools disproportionately
impact the educational trajectories of young Black men and women.

Samir's story is not unique. The problem of access to education for
youth in conflict with the law is a systemic one, not only shaped by problematic intersections between education and the youth criminal justice
system but also through all of the intersecting criminalizing public sector interventions (that is, neighbourhood policing, immigration, child
protection, and school discipline) that disproportionately shape the
lives of Black youth in Canada (Maynard, 2017). These contemporary
relations are further nuanced by the considerable history of race-based
inequalities in access to housing, income, and quality education, as well
as the application of criminal legal system processes that have framed
the development of settler Canada from contact until the present
day (United Nations, Committee on Economic, Social and Cultural
Rights, 2016). At the root of the multiplicity of racializing/racialized,
gendering/gendered, and classing/class-based state interventions
noted above, one must also pay attention to the racialized "procedures
of differentiation, classification, and hierarchization" (Mbembe, 2017,
p. 24) objectified as, for example, data-led policing or school climate
surveys, that accompany "the ideology of security and the installation
of [corporate/public] mechanisms aimed at calculating and minimizing

risk and turning protection into the currency of citizenship" (Mbembe, 2017, p. 22). These social and political-economic processes underpin the removal and the eventual return of young people – like Samir and Jani – who have been singled out as representing a threat to the safety and inclusion of young people in school.

Coordinating access to education for young people like Samir, Tyrone, or Rebeca – that is, any young person who has been formally (e.g., due to criminal-legal charges or time spent in detention) and informally (e.g., through Safe Schools transfer processes) excluded from mainstream programs – poses a significant challenge for young people, their caregivers (often mothers and grandmothers), probation officers , youth workers, and educators at the sending institution (i.e., the Section 23 program in the youth justice facility). During one of my first visits to the secure custody youth justice facility where I ultimately interviewed educators and youth serving pre- and post-trial sentences, the principal, vice-principal and transitioning teacher with whom I spoke described the difficulties they faced seeking to coordinate a smooth transfer for young people coming out of custody. In my field notes from that early meeting, I record the transitioning teacher's reflection that he needed "a crystal ball" so that he could follow young people as they are released from custody and look to re-enter a school in their community. Because it is structured through the court system, custodial release isn't scheduled. Educators pursue information from the living unit managers and corrections social workers about court dates and possible release times to enable timetabling of academic schedules, but this information isn't always forthcoming – in part because having a court date does not necessarily mean a youth will be released from detention or custody. More often than not, a young person goes to court and simply doesn't come back, meaning someone like Leonardo (the teacher who wished he had a crystal ball) has difficulty supporting the young person to re-engage with school upon community re-entry. During an interview in 2014, the first principal at the school where I was doing this research (who retired later that year) described how her teachers had logged "thousands of hours of work" to develop

> student achievement forms, and they look somewhat like a progress report in that it's got the course code at the top, the credit value; there's a description from the Ministry of Education of the course. You can see each unit of study and you can see everything underneath that unit of study that must be completed before you move onto the next unit. And then there's another column where you can show what the kid got on that particular task or assignment, and then there's another column that

shows overall what their mark was for that unit, so it's very detailed. Then at the end of it there's a place for comments, strengths, areas of need, any accommodations. This is an area where we can put in the learning skills, exactly the same as you have on a report card. And then also what's really important when the student leaves before the course is finished, is it'll show, okay, the student has completed 58 per cent of the course to date. This is their mark. Of that 58 per cent, they've so far achieved 75 per cent. That's their grade. So that way, when they leave we send those off to wherever the student's going.

The problem is that despite all the work that goes into producing the comprehensive individualized student achievement forms, they are most often used by people *inside* the jail, when young people return to complete subsequent detentions. For the student achievement forms to be useful outside the jail, young people have to carry them on their person or Leonardo needs that crystal ball. The school staff in the jail have reached out to local probation officers as a potential link between the school in the jail and those schools on the outside, but during our conversation Leonardo observed that his phone "is not exactly ringing off the hook." Further, principals in schools across the Greater Toronto Area are reluctant to enrol young people coming out of detention or custody, and often do so – like in Samir's case – with significant conditions and only after considerable work on the parts of parents (almost always mothers and grandmothers), POs, Safe Schools coordinators, and often the youth themselves to negotiate the transfer. During my interview with Raina – the former principal at the school in the jail – I asked how the transfer process worked from the standpoint of mainstream school principals, since she had been a mainstream school principal for far longer than she'd been the principal at the school in the jail. Despite what I'd heard from teachers and administrators in community schools about the difficulties coordinating mid-semester transfers, Raina observed:

> Well it's the same as someone who moves into the area, right? I mean Peel [for example] is a very transient region because a lot of housing is being built. And when I've met with groups of probation officers and teachers and other Section 23 people and principals, I've said, "When you have a student who arrives on your doorstep in mid-November because their parents' house just closed on the weekend, you don't turn them away and say, 'Oh sorry, come back on February 1st.'" You accommodate them. So, there's really no difference here. What you do is, in a regular school, the guidance counsellor would call the previous school, find out what courses

the student was enrolled in, see if we can match those courses. And most of the time you're not in exactly the same place, so what we would do is we would get from the previous school estimated marks, and then what we would do is just try to match the program as best we could.

Raina makes two important observations above. First, the resistance youth face from principals when they seek to re-enrol after a period in detention does not reflect legitimate logistical or organizational barriers – although this is often what youth are told. Second, the onus is on the receiving school to call the sending school (in the jail or wherever a young person has been learning) and ask for an updated student achievement form to be sent.

Between 2012 and 2018 when I was doing research for this and other projects, I consistently encountered teachers – particularly in the small off-site alternative learning centres like the one at Rosewood – who describe receiving very little information about the young people they were asked to teach. When a provincial student record (for example) did arrive, it was typically months after the young person him or herself. None of these teachers knew it was their responsibility or even within their purview to phone and request this information directly from a sending institution. And because many young people have been detained and participated in "Section 23" educational programs (that is, educational programs administered in cooperation by the Ministry of Education and the Ministry of Health and Long-term Care, or the Ministry of Education and the Ministry of Children and Youth) in one school board, only to seek re-entry in another board, the work of coordinating the transfer of information regarding student progress is significant. So, while it is unjust that Samir waited for a month to get a school to enrol him upon release from custody, given the lack of a rights-based approach to personal administrative data (e.g., one's own student record), barriers to information sharing across youth-serving systems and geographic regions, limitations on where Samir could attend (i.e., not with a "victim" or "coaccused"), and stigma faced by young people with youth criminal justice records, it is unsurprising that Samir faced difficulties gaining access and conditions upon admission.

Conclusion

The problem with the range of educational and intersecting social and criminological interventions highlighted in this chapter is that each time a young person is moved temporarily out of the mainstream system – for example, because they are building up language skills required to participate, are detained in a youth justice facility, or have been expelled or moved discretionarily to finish a semester at a site like Rosewood – the process of negotiating and coordinating access to mainstream sites begins again once they have met the conditions for their reintegration. Each time a young person is moved, aspects of their educational progress and social histories fail to accompany them from site to site. Furthermore, young people, their parents (typically mothers and grandmothers), school administrators, and educators expend considerable emotional, physical, and bureaucratic labour participating in and coordinating these moves. This labour and the racialized/ing, classed/ing, and gendered/ing exclusionary effects of school-based relocation processes are profound for the young people, captive in a system that continues to fail to meet their needs. Depending on who is reading this book, it might sound like a stretch when I now suggest that all of these institutional barriers are systemically producing race, class, and gender inequalities. (Others will see the connection right away.) I will simply remind the reader that the range of interventions, which undeniably and systematically entrench Black youth in relations of economic marginality, surveillance, and control, have been developed and implemented under the banner of – and with the explicit aim to promote – community and school safety.

Materially and conceptually the outcome of this move is to associate Samir (Tyrone, Rebeca, and all of the other Black youth who largely make up the target population at Rosewood and the school in the jail – both exemplary school/community safety interventions) with unsafety. They are the people the police describe – in contrast to civilians or the community – as "the criminal element." In so doing, their objectification as less-than-human is meant to be read in post-racial, post-class, and post-gendered terms. Public, private, and public-private efforts to calculate and manage risk distract from the racial, gendered, and classed distribution of these interventions and the developmental contexts they produce in young people's lives. They also pose practical problems for researchers, who are seeking to map the extent of the problem and are advocating for justice for children and youth.

Chapter Six

State Surveillance and School Discipline

Research conducted over the last two decades has shined a light on the disproportionate use and effects of punitive school discipline policies on the lives and educational trajectories of young Black men and women (Advancement Project, 2011; Bhattacharjee, 2003; Gilborn, 2005; Greggory, Skiba, & Noguera, 2010; Maynard, 2017; Morris & Perry, 2016, 2017; Ofer, 2011/2012; Rios, 2011; Ruck & Wortley, 2002; Skiba, Eckes, & Brown, 2009/2010; Skiba et al., 2014; Wun, 2016). The research demonstrates how the racialized distribution of exclusionary school disciplinary practices are implicated in racialized patterns recorded in academic achievement and youth justice data. In this final chapter, I explore how suspension and expulsion practices are coordinated by educators and school administrators and experienced by young people across Ontario and Quebec. Taken together, chapters 4 and 5 reveal the institutional and policy relations that background the following "joke" shared with Andy (one of the youth researchers) by a young Black man named Morris about the race-based organization of the school system and school discipline, in particular: "I used to make a joke, because they'd call a bunch of kids down to the office, and I'd be like, 'It's all the Black kids.' And then again, the whole school was all Black kids anyway."

Across Canada, Black and Indigenous men and women are over-represented in adult correctional institutions and Black youth are more likely to report negative interactions with the police in their neighbourhoods (Wortley & Owusu-Bempah, 2011). In Ontario, Black and Indigenous young men are over-represented in youth justice facilities at rates four to five times higher than in the general population (Rankin, Winsa, & Ng, 2013). Research from across the US and Canada consistently documents racial disproportionality in incarceration rates (Alexander, 2012; Rios, 2011; Maynard, 2017) and school suspension and expulsions (Hines-Datiri, 2015; Galabuzi, 2014; Morris & Perry,

2016, 2017; Skiba et al., 2014). As school disciplinary processes and the youth justice system intersect (e.g., where conditions for mandatory suspensions, pending expulsion are also conditions warranting youth criminal justice charges), researchers have described young people as participating in a school-to-prison pipeline (Allen & White-Smith, 2014). Indeed, the neighbourhoods in Toronto with the highest rates of school suspensions are also neighbourhoods with high rates of incarceration (Rankin & Contenta, 2009). But the continued use of the term "school-to-prison pipeline" obscures the precise ways that schools contribute to racialized, classed, and gendered patterns of criminality. In order to see what's actually going on, one needs to train a lens on the institutional policies and practices through which school discipline and special education services interconnect with criminal legal processes.

Young people serving long-term suspensions (i.e., suspensions for five to twenty days) and/or expulsions (i.e., permanent removal from a school or a school board) require that parents, educators, school administrators, and sometimes also probation officers and youth workers coordinate the movement of a young person into and out of at least one but often a number of sites (particularly where the removal from school is associated with a criminal charge). As was made apparent in chapter 5, these moves are difficult for educators, parents, and other adults in young people's lives to coordinate in a smooth and timely manner, and they can be highly disruptive to young people's learning. With reference to young people experiencing homelessness and those who are described as "highly mobile," Moore (2013) argues that "frequent school changes are increasingly detrimental" (p. 8) to student success and well-being. Any supports students may have had at a sending school (e.g., from counsellors, youth workers, friends, and teachers) are lost and have to be re-established in a new setting (Courtney et al., 2014).

The research design for Schools and Safety was influenced by a research and knowledge mobilization project that I had participated in with Greater Toronto Area Safe Schools educators working in Long-Term Suspension and Expulsion programs (sometimes colloquially described as Safe Schools programs). From educators, I learned about the importance of these programs for young people because their designation as educational programs (not schools) enabled the provision of holistic wrap-around social and educational supports (Nichols, Griffith, & Fisher, in press). During this early work, I also learned about the complex of institutional and policy relations surrounding school discipline processes, which link to other complexes of institutional activity (e.g., processes in the youth criminal justice sector).

For example, many of the conditions for mandatory expulsion (e.g., selling drugs) are also conditions that warrant youth criminal justice charges. Other youth incur charges that are originally unrelated to school but end up impacting their educational trajectories (as Rebeca's story in chapter 5 illuminates). For youth who are navigating the youth justice system, the number of missed school days because of delays in the court system, relocations due to conditions (e.g., specifying that one cannot attend school with one's "coaccused"), and/or time spent in a youth justice facility further disrupt their schooling experiences. Thus, the institutional processes linking schools and community safety diminish young people's generally tenuous attachments to school, entrenching patterns of instability in lives (like Rebeca's) that have already been characterized by uncertainty up until that point. Most problematically, Black and Indigenous young men and women are subject to these intersecting relations of exclusion at rates higher than one would anticipate finding in the general population. This means the processes are not simply exclusionary but they are fundamentally productive of race, class, and gender – both as categories enabling classification and governance and as objectified (or shared) forms of consciousness influencing how young people see themselves in relation to others.

Safe Schools Policy Background: Ontario and Quebec

This section serves as a brief policy primer and outlines the key policy and legislative moves that have shaped the policy, practice, and programmatic landscapes in Ontario and Quebec and, consequently, the experiences of young people and educators in these two provinces.

Ontario

In Ontario, school disciplinary processes are regulated by the Ontario Education Act. In 2000, Bill 81 (colloquially described as the Safe Schools Act) amended the Education Act, regulating and providing new policy guidance around school discipline. The Safe Schools Act extended the power to suspend students to teachers and specified a number of actions that required non-discretionary suspensions and expulsions. It also set the stage for the minister of education to establish a provincial code of conduct. While codes of conduct aren't law, they can be written into law in ways that make them quite powerful; for example, by naming code of conduct violations as grounds for suspension or expulsion. The provincial code of conduct provided a more detailed account of particular student actions that warrant suspensions, as well a framework for increasing police involvement in schools. Bill 81 has had a disproportionately negative impact on Black and Indigenous youth and young people with disabilities; in 2007, pertinent parts of this act (sections 306–311) that address suspension and expulsion processes were repealed and amended under Bill 212.

Bill 212 introduced a series of mediating interventions meant to counter the disproportionately negative effects of Bill 81 on young people who are Black, Indigenous, and/or learning-disabled. Progressive discipline policies and a mandate to consider mitigating circumstances (e.g., the presence of a learning disability) were one such intervention. School expulsion programs for students who had been expelled from the school board were another mediating intervention. A third was the introduction of expulsion investigations and hearings – a move that was meant to ensure young people had access to justice throughout the disciplinary process. Since Bill 212, actions that previously required a mandatory expulsion now require a mandatory suspension, pending an investigation, hearing, and decision to expel or not. Young people who are suspended for up to twenty days or expelled are moved into alternative education sites that fall within a board's Safe Schools portfolio or, in some instances, Section 23 programs in youth justice or mental health facilities. The activities requiring a mandatory suspension under Bill 212 are the same ones that originally necessitated a mandatory expulsion:

310. (1) A principal shall suspend a pupil if he or she believes that the pupil has engaged in any of the following activities while at school, at a school-related activity or in other circumstances where engaging in the activity will have an impact on the school climate:

1. Possessing a weapon, including possessing a firearm.
2. Using a weapon to cause or to threaten bodily harm to another person.
3. Committing physical assault on another person that causes bodily harm requiring treatment by a medical practitioner.
4. Committing sexual assault.
5. Trafficking in weapons or in illegal drugs.
6. Committing robbery.
7. Giving alcohol to a minor.
8. Any other activity that, under a policy of a board, is an activity for which a principal must suspend a pupil and, therefore in accordance with this Part, conduct an investigation to determine whether to recommend to the board that the pupil be expelled.

(S.O. 2007, Ch. 14 ss. 310[1], Bill 212, An Act to Amend the Education Act in Respect of Behaviour, Discipline and Safety)

Once a young person is suspended and moved into a Long-Term Suspension and Expulsion program, the principal is supposed to investigate and determine whether or not to recommend an expulsion to the board. If an expulsion is recommended, a hearing is scheduled with the school board discipline committee, which is comprised of at least three trustees empowered to act on behalf of the board. The hearing is meant to improve young people's access to justice in the traditional sense – that is, timely access to judicial processes. But based on historical legacies of racialized injustice (Maynard, 2017), many youth and families have little faith that our traditional judiciary processes will lead to a just outcome for them, and so they opt not to participate. Instead they sign "minutes of settlement," thereby agreeing to the principal's account of what happened and his or her recommended disciplinary actions. Unfortunately, these agreements often contain a clause that prevents them from making any future claims against the board, including a human rights complaint. The "minutes of settlement" can also have legal implications if the young person is charged for his or her offence. Except for the last item on this list, all of the other actions requiring a non-discretionary suspension also require that that principal report the incident to the police – who, relative to the provincial code of conduct, were (until 2017) already present in many schools as school resource officers.

Bill 212 was important because it eliminated non-discretionary expulsions and required that boards provide programs for suspended and expelled students to continue learning, while behavioural issues were addressed. Another important change was the addition of bullying to the list of activities that warrant a discretionary suspension. In 2012, Bill 13 (the Accepting Schools Act) amended the Education Act again, providing a definition of bullying and a framework for identifying, responding to, and preventing bullying in schools. This most recent set of amendments are important – they set the stage for the implementation of climate surveys and the development of a provincial equity and inclusive education strategy. The amendments and the interventions that accompany them were pursued to ensure the safety of young people disproportionately subject to school violence – for example, gender and sexual minority youth. But they have simultaneously enabled the heightened surveillance and removal of other young people (largely young Black men) deemed to undermine a safe school climate. Amendments to the act remain steeped in and further entrench the safe/unsafe, victim/perpetrator binaries that shape the criminal legal system. The series of interventions, implemented with respect to Bill 212 and Bill 13, have reshaped the educational work of administrators and young people whose conduct is deemed to undermine a safe and positive school climate. Significantly, expulsions continue to disproportionately impact young Black men. Drawing on disaggregated expulsion and census data, Toronto District School Board researchers conclude that "self-identified Black students accounted for almost half (48%) of the 2013 expulsions" that were analysed for ethno-racial trends between 2011 and 2016 (Zheng & De Jesus, 2017, p. 25).

Quebec

In Quebec, like in Ontario, school disciplinary processes are also regulated by the provincial Education Act. But in stark contrast to the centralized approaches to school discipline in Ontario, in Quebec school discipline is primarily organized at a local level, where the principal of each individual school develops and imposes a school discipline culture / set of practices in relation to a locally developed code of conduct (Quebec Education Act, 1988, Section 76). According to the Quebec Education Act and in relation to the behaviour outlined in a school's code of conduct, principals may suspend students who do not comply with the school's rules, especially regarding bullying and violence. In 2012 Bill 56: An Act to Prevent and Stop Bullying and Violence in Schools was adopted as Law 19 in Quebec's National Assembly as an amendment to the Education Act. Bill 56 requires that every school in the province have a plan to prevent and stop bullying and violence. This plan must include prevention, confidential reporting, collaboration, support, and follow-up measures, among other objectives. While a principal *may* suspend students found to commit acts of bullying or violence, a suspension is not a mandated response. If repeated acts of bullying and violence are documented, the principal has grounds to expel or relocate a student: "In case of further acts of bullying or violence, a student may be asked to change schools or be expelled from the school board" (Bill 56, 2012, p. 7). Ultimately, the decision to expel a student is made at the school board level, upon the request of the principal to the council of commissioners (Bill 56, 2012, p. 7).

At the board level, the response to school safety varies. Three French school boards and two English boards operate on the East and West island of Montreal, and each of these boards has their own locally developed policy. I am most familiar with the policies of the English Montreal School Board (EMSB) – the English school board for the city of Montreal – where the research in Montreal occurred. In 2000, the EMSB adopted the Safe Schools and Centres Policy, which is not legally binding but lays out board-level recommendations and commitments regarding school safety and discipline. In 2012, building from the Safe Schools and Centres Policy and in accordance with Bill 56, every school board has continued to develop and broaden their safe school policy for its schools for youth, centres for adults, vocational centres, students, and employees. For instance, the EMSB's Safe Physical and Cyber Environment Policy states that there should be a strong safety and prevention focus in schools to ensure that "every member of its community has a right to learn and work in a safe physical and cyber environment" (2012, p. 1). But as Imani's experiences of being the victim of racist bullying in her school illuminate, the establishment of board-level policies does not necessarily lead to their uptake and use in schools.

Key Differences/Similarities

While the discourse of Safe Schools and the practice of creating school safety plans is shared across the two policy contexts, a key difference between the Quebec and Ontario policy landscapes reflects degrees of centralization. Across Quebec, school administrators have increased scope of professional discretion compared to their Ontario counterparts, in terms of decisions to suspend, expel, or relocate (Quebec)/ transfer (Ontario) students. Other key differences include: the age of compulsory schooling, which is sixteen in Quebec and eighteen in Ontario; the educational infrastructure surrounding Safe Schools initiatives (e.g., there are no Safe Schools programs, educators, and administrators in Montreal); and a lack of board-level research on the outcomes of various disciplinary interventions on particular groups of students in Montreal, compared to Toronto. Finally, intersectoral reporting requirements across the two provinces differ, with the impetus to report expulsions to Child Protection Services limited to Quebec. This additional reporting requirement may explain why expulsions in Quebec are rare (Cheff, 2018) and why administrators seek out other forms of punishment (most often suspensions and relocations) for youth. This brief policy overview sets up the remainder of this chapter, which centres young people's experiences and knowledge of school discipline processes in both provincial contexts.

"Then I Got Suspended": Young People's Experiences of School Discipline in Montreal and Toronto

Like the previous chapters, this one delves deeper into the institutional contexts shaping school discipline in Ontario because school disciplinary practices were one of the central foci of the original study. But the topic of exclusionary discipline (suspensions and expulsions) were front of mind during my early days of engaging with young people in Montreal. These young people were quick to point to their own and their friends' experiences of absurd and overtly racist exclusionary disciplinary actions in Montreal schools – for example, young Black women who were sent home from school with code of conduct violations (i.e., school uniform) because their hair was left natural. In fact, one of the early music videos produced by the group was recorded at their high school and explicitly questioned the justness and purpose of school suspensions, after Khaled (the youngest member of the group) was suspended from school and David was de-enrolled. In an in-depth interview I did with David in 2016, I asked him to think back on the approach to school discipline he observed in his high school (before he was de-enrolled), reflecting on other conversations we'd had as a team about what they had felt were unjust locker searches:

> D: You know there's like this rule in high school where if you skip three detentions, they in-school suspend you. It's not really a suspension, but you stay in school for the whole day. You can't go outside for lunch, and you stay in this room. That's the only time [I was suspended].
>
> NN: … Other people, in conversations we've had with the group, they've talked about a sort of sense of the principal and other administrators sort of identifying people as suspicious and then following up on them all the time and asking them to come down for these visits in the office. Did that ever happen to you?
>
> D: No, no.
>
> NN: But you saw that happening?
>
> D: I saw it happen a lot.
>
> NN: Who did it happen to?
>
> D: Some of my friends, actually – my close friend.
>
> NN: Yeah? Why? Why those guys?
>
> D: The way they brought themselves – like, how they wore their clothes, I guess. You can see that they were profiling them. It was like, "Oh, yeah, he's a drug dealer. Let's check his locker. Let's check his phone."
>
> NN: So, a suspicion of drugs because of how kids dress – like, gangsta? Like, what's the …

D: Yeah, yeah. Like, maybe baggy pants and oversized shirt.

NN: Did race matter in how people were deemed suspicious?

D: Yeah, sometimes. I have some friends that were, like, harassed ... The authorities in high school is mostly the vice-principal. Because the principal just stays in his office, but it was mostly the vice-principal, like, always walking in the hallways, checking people's lockers.

David observed that young people at his public high school were identified as suspicious and targeted for locker and phone searches based on their appearance. I pressed him to elaborate on what he meant by this, and David explained, "The way they brought themselves – like, how they wore their clothes, I guess. You can see that they were profiling them." In an in-depth interview I conducted with Alon (another young man on our research team who had gone to the same high school as David), he made similar observations about who got targeted and "blacklisted" by school administrators in their school and why. Earlier in the conversation, and prior to the topic of school discipline, Alon had been talking about school – his experiences of disconnection from his teachers and the subject matter, as well as his desires for help, which remained unaddressed. I prompted him (like I did with David above and in light of Sampling Youth Development's explicit orientation to relations of race, class, and gender) to consider whether race – and other categories of identity – mattered in his analysis of his own schooling experiences: "And did race matter at all in your schooling? Did language? We've talked a lot about those categories and how they can hold us back or shape how people see us. Class, economics, struggles at home – did any of that matter to how you experienced school?" And to my prompting Alon (who is a person of colour with Filipino ethnicity) responded, "Lots of gender stuff and race ... But mostly gender because race is, like – it's more of a quiet thing." Later in the interview, I invited Alon to unpack this idea – that race is "more of a quiet thing" with me further, and this is where he makes the connection to school discipline at his high school:

NAOMI: I want to go back to something you mentioned in passing, which is about race being a quiet issue in high school. What do you mean by that?

ALON: Like, you don't really hear about it all the time, but the ones who are usually pointed out for drugs and stealing are usually the kids of colour.

NAOMI: Pointed out by principals and teachers?

ALON: Yeah ... it happened to me, actually. So, I had my friend, Jacob; we were very good friends. And they had nothing on Jacob, and they started picking on me because I was his very good friend. They started calling me to the office and stuff, and they're like, "Do you do drugs, blah, blah, blah?" And I'm like, "Yeah, I smoked weed, and that's all." They're like, "Okay." And then after, they mentioned my friend's name, tried making me rat on him. I was like, "No, dude. What's the reason? Why am I here?" I feel like they use the strategies that police use …

NAOMI: Why they would call you to the office? What was their reason?

ALON: Like, suspicions from teachers. Yeah. I remember this one time I was in ethics class, and I was very tired. I think, yeah, I was skating outside during lunchtime, and then after I went back inside, and I had ethics. And my ethics teacher, she said that I looked high. And I wasn't high, and she put me on the suspicion list. I don't smoke. I don't like smoking anymore … Whenever something bad would happen, they'd just call the police … [it was] always [for] drugs. Once it comes to drugs, they kick you out. They don't really help you. They just send you to places where other people do drugs too.

Whether or not administrators at Alon and David's school actually had a "suspicion list" of young people who were suspected of using or selling drugs in school is less relevant to the argument put forward in this chapter than the institutional practices the young men point to in their school and the ways these mirror the practices young people witness and administrators describe taking on in Ontario.

In the contexts of school disciplinary norms, reshaped by the adoption of Safe Schools policies and legislation across North America (Bhattacharjee, 2003; Brent, 2007), administrators are increasingly engaged in practices of surveillance, interrogation, and something that Alon and David describe as "profiling," "harassing," or "pointing out" particular youth on the bases of their appearance – how they dress, how they "brought themselves," and the colour of their skin. Race-based differences in the school-based disciplinary practices have a long legacy in Canadian schools (Zellars, 2017); but under the post-racial banners of zero tolerance and Safe Schools, race becomes a "more of quiet thing" and racism or racial profiling become difficult to prove. Furthermore, in the aftermath of the implementation of zero-tolerance-styled Safe Schools policies in Ontario, which led to high rates of expulsion among Black and learning-disabled youth and an Ontario Human Rights Commission complaint against the TDSB as well as the Ontario Ministry of Education (OHRC, n.d.), young people are, as the previous chapter illuminates and David and Alon both point to, being moved out of mainstream school programs and into other sites without having been formally expelled.

In fact, in the English Montreal School Board, the Safe Schools and Centres Policy offers explicit grounds for the "relocation" (not expulsion) of students:

> Every student subject to compulsory school attendance [i.e., any young person who is under 16 years of age] may be relocated if, while under the supervision of the Board or while on Board property or any adjacent property, he/she:
>
> a. is found in possession of a firearm, prohibited weapon or replica thereof;
> b. commits an act of violence with a weapon of any kind;
> c. is found in possession of narcotics and/or alcohol for the purpose of selling or using. (pp. 3–4)

Alon and David (as well as Khaled and Eva, the two other young people on our research team) all signalled that the vice-principal of their school was targeting young people suspected of using drugs at school (as well as a young person found with a water gun in his locker) in order to justify their relocation to alternative settings. Think back to chapter 3, where I signalled the evidential practices backgrounding the removal of students whose credit accrual, standardized test scores, and attendance rates suggest a school is struggling, as well as the free-choice marketized approach to schooling that characterized the city of Montreal. The school that Alon, David, Khaled, and Eva were attending when I met them is a public English language high school, without any special admission requirements. The website states that the school is "truly public in that it strives to admit all those who apply without requiring an entrance exam." With no way to select for particular students during admissions, one way to improve school rankings is to relocate struggling students once they've been admitted. In this context, David's relocation to an alternative outreach program during his last year of secondary school, as well as our youth research team's insistence that youth of colour were targeted for suspicion of possession of drugs (not to provide the students with addictions support, as Alon observes, but to ensure justification for their removal), suggest ways schools participate in systemically racist and racializing practices, under the depoliticized banner of school improvement. Indeed, the Fraser Institute's Report Card Rankings for schools in the city suggest that the school has been on an "improving" trend over the last five years. The rankings are based on standardized test results, "rate of delay" (i.e., credit accrual pace), rates of failure, and gender differences in language and math results. A considerable amount of discretion is afforded to school principals in Montreal, regarding the development and implementation of the school's code of conduct and the disciplinary practices through which it is enforced.

The Safe Schools and Centres Policy also specifies a list of student actions that *may* prompt an expulsion, and many of these activities overlap with the list warranting school removal, thus illuminating the distinctive role that principal discretion plays in Montreal schools as compared to Toronto:

Expulsion may result from the following:

a. aggravated assault, rape or sexual harassment;
b. the possession of a knife with the intent to harm or maim another person;
c. extortion and/or taxing;
d. repeated acts of bullying and/or intimidation;
e. acts of violence motivated by race, sexual orientation, religious and/or language issues;
f. any act endangering the lives of others. (EMSB, n.d., Safe Schools and Centres Policy, p. 4).

Even where a student has engaged in one of the above-named activities, it remains within the principal's discretion whether to have the young person expelled. In other words, unlike in Ontario, there are no grounds for mandatory suspensions and expulsions. In the EMSB's Safe Schools and Centres policy, detentions and in-school suspensions are the recommended disciplinary strategies, with expulsions considered only after other strategies have failed.

Unlike Ontario, where a complex procedural, policy, programmatic, and legislative network guides disciplinary practices, and where long-term suspensions, pending expulsion are mandated in certain instances, Quebec has no overarching provincial legislation pertaining to school discipline other than the principal's mandate to establish – with the approval of the school governing board – a code of conduct for their school (Education Act, CQLR 1977, c. I-13.3, s. 76). One of my MA supervisees and a vice-principal in a Montreal high school recently completed a thesis about how administrators learn to discipline students after discovering there are very few board-level or provincial policies that guide disciplinary practices; she was advised by the board's research ethics committee that her research topic was irrelevant since school discipline is a matter of common sense.

This belief among school board staff that one simply learns to discipline students through experience and the premise that knowledge about school discipline is common sense stands in stark contrast to young people's own critiques that excluding young people from school is nonsensical. An excerpt from an interview between one of our youth research team members and two young Black men is representational of this particular point of view. After asking where the two men learn best, the interviewer asks:

I: Have you guys had any negative school experiences?
P1: Yes.
P2: For sure.
I: You guys wanna talk about one?
P2: Well, we have been discriminated against, racially profiled, mistreated. Apparently, we were a threat to society at one point.
P1: Yes, just because we were a group of friends who all played basketball together, so we hung out and we all grew up in the same neighbourhood, so we were all close together. They assumed we were a gang.
P2: They kicked us out the gym.
P1: Yo, bro, they suspended us. Make us come and do community service.
P2: What did you expect? All we do is play basketball.
P1: All we do is play ball. Of course, we're gonna be crowded in the gym. We're all basketball players, man.
P2: They kicked us out the gym.
P1: Like, come on, you kicked us out the gym
I: So, how did this situation make you feel?
P1: It made it worse.
. . .
P2: Because pretty much the gym made us stay out of trouble.
P1: Basically, because when we were all together in the gym, [over-talking] give us something to do. Like, yo, we were all playing basketball.
I: [laughs] Yeah, and they took the one thing that …
P1: Yeah, [over-talking] because, yo, legit, that's what we did. We were all together. We weren't in the hallway causing no troubles, but, yeah, you want to kick us out the gym, then where else are we supposed to go?
P2: We have nothing to do.
P1: So, now, we're just crowded in the hallway, and you made it even worse.

This overwhelming sense of incredulity about the use of exclusionary discipline practices in schools permeated conversations with members of our research team and the young people they interviewed. While the numbers of young people who indicated they'd been suspended or expelled from school were much lower in Montreal than Toronto, all of the people who referenced suspensions and expulsions were young Black men and women. More than simply a conceptual disconnect between White administrators and Black students, the reliance on principal discretion in the implementation of school-based disciplinary practices opens up the entire process to the forms of racial bias that Michelle Alexander (2012) documents in *The New Jim Crow*.

The use of professional discretion coupled with open-ended policy constructs, such as "suspicious activity" to legitimize the targeted surveillance of young Black men and women, has a long history in the US and Canadian criminal legal systems (e.g., street-level stop-and-search practices engaged by police) and the types of school-based surveillance practices young people describe in schools (e.g., targeted locker searches and lists of suspicious students). As Alexander illuminates, it is the openness of the concept coupled with long-held (and often unconscious) racial bias among those for whom the notion coordinates their practice, which shapes the overpolicing of Black bodies and sets the stage for their over-representation in carceral contexts – and, as my own work reveals, among youth pushed to the margins of the education system.

Like the police activate concepts like "suspicious activity" in order to justify a particular course of action on the streets, school principals rely on "code of conduct violations" to warrant particular institutionally mandated sequences of action in schools. Statistically speaking, most school suspensions (28.2 per cent in Toronto) are acts "considered by the school principal to be a breach of the Board's or a school's code of conduct," which specifies acceptable norms for speech, dress, and activity (Toronto District School Board, 2013a, p. 12). The ambiguity of the "code of conduct violation" category used by school administrators to initiate school disciplinary processes is similar to the "fits the description" or "suspicious activity" categories used by the police. In either case, the categories are sufficiently open that they can be filled with bits of information that enable their use to accomplish the what-happens-next in a particular institutional sequence of action (Griffith & Smith, 2014). Use of these categories requires and institutionalizes an interpretive process on the part of the principal or the officer who will use prior evidence (e.g., a history of documented infractions) and other socially constructed knowledge to activate the category as part of what will become a textually regulated procedure (Griffith & Smith, 2014).

For example, when I ask Tonette to tell me how she ended up in one of Toronto's "Safe Schools" programs for suspended and expelled youth, she says:

I got expelled. I used to go to a school in Scarborough, X Secondary School, and I got expelled from that school ... Because if I wasn't wearing my uniform and stuff, I would get suspensions. All those little things. The suspensions add up, right? And I was going there since grade 9. So since grade 9 to grade 11, whatever suspensions or whatever it was – like, I never got in a physical fight or anything. It's just the suspensions ... And then they said I had my last string or whatever ... My last strike, yeah. And basically, I blew that last strike ... I was expelled for walking on another school property ... I went to, whatever, Y Secondary School, and I got expelled for being on the property.

Like in Quebec, school disciplinary processes in Ontario are regulated by the provincial Education Act. In 2000, Bill 81 (colloquially described as the Safe Schools Act) amended the Education Act, regulating and providing new policy guidance around school discipline. It has, as I noted earlier, been amended twice more since then – in 2007 by Bill 212 (the Progressive Discipline and School Safety Act) and in 2012 by Bill 13 (the Safe and Accepting Schools Act). The policy and practice changes associated with the Progressive Discipline and School Safety Act are visible in Tonette's story above. Progressive discipline policies are a provincially mandated response to criticism of "zero tolerance" policies, which have been found to disproportionately impact Black students and other racialized student groups in North American schools (Bhattacharjee, 2003; Galabuzi, 2014; Gregory et al., 2010; Morris & Perry, 2016; Ofer, 2011/2012; Rios, 2011; Ruck & Wortley, 2002; Skiba, Eckes, & Brown, 2009/2010; Skiba et al., 2014). A 2013 TDSB student and parent census found that White secondary school students represent 2.9 per cent of school suspensions but 29 per cent of the student population, while Black students represent 8.6 per cent of school suspensions and 12 per cent of the student population (TDSB, 2013). The most recent report by the TDSB suggests 48 per cent of school expulsions are experienced by Black youth (Zheng & De Jesus, 2017). But these quantitative data tell us little about the processes through which they are generated or whether they have been influenced by more recent policy shifts associated with progressive discipline.

The TDSB Progressive Discipline and Promoting Positive Student Behaviour policy outlines a process for ensuring that the disciplinary response "will be in proportion to the severity of the behaviour leading to the discipline and the previous disciplinary history of the student" (Toronto District School Board, 2013b, sec. 3). Provincially mandated progressive discipline polices outline a scaled disciplinary response to address "inappropriate" student behaviour (Ontario Ministry of Education, 2012, p. 3) These policy shifts result in interrelated shifts in practice. A principal's recommendation to expel a student is mediated by the Education Act, a school board's progressive discipline framework, and a school's code of conduct – as these three documents work together. An administrator can establish grounds for expulsion based on a review of a student's disciplinary records and careful documentation of code of conduct violations. An administrator's work to establish grounds for expulsion requires extensive documentation of code of conduct violations and the appropriate use of progressive discipline techniques. This work organization lies beneath Tonette's sense that her suspensions "add up," and the experiences of surveillance described by young people when moved into a new school through a Safe Schools transfer or after a period in a youth justice facility.

Young people I interviewed explained that administrators seem to be waiting for them to make a mistake so that there is a reason to move them on again: "I kind a felt like he [my principal] was always trying to see if I was doing anything bad. Trying to get me for the smallest things. Like there was no fights or nothing. I think he was just out for me, still" (Darnell). The shared sense that school principals pay more attention to some young people's actions than others is shaped by progressive discipline policies. The polices were introduced as a way to diminish the use of expulsions for minor or first-time code of conduct violations and ensure educators pay attention to "mitigating factors" (Ontario Ministry of Education, 2012) when making disciplinary decisions. But as these policies and practices get hooked into the work organization of schooling they facilitate the emergence of new relations of surveillance through which administrators are able to produce the evidence they need to justify a particular disciplinary action. The observational evidence produced by school administrators ultimately becomes part of the historical justification for removing young people from mainstream schools.

School Discipline, Surveillance, and Educational (Under)Achievement

Disproportionality in expulsion rates among young Black men is important because exclusionary discipline (e.g., suspensions and expulsions) impedes academic development and contributes to racial disparities in achievement (Morris & Perry, 2016). When one begins to examine how expulsion processes are organized institutionally, further insights into this relation come into view. In an interview, Ian, a teacher who works in a Caring and Safe Schools program in Toronto, explains to graduate research assistant, Alison, what an expulsion means for a young person:

IAN: There are only two types of expulsions. There are expulsions from one school and expulsions from all schools. Expulsions from one school (I'll start there), [mean] they're not allowed to return to their school. But, depending on the time of year, they can go to another school right away. So, if they get expelled from one school in February, say, at the beginning of semester two, then they can return to another school and our quad administers place them right away. If it's around this time, and they get expelled from one school, they'll usually stay with us [in a Caring and Safe Schools program] until the end of the semester and then they'll get Safe Schools transferred in September.

ALISON: And what about the expulsion from the board?

IAN: Yeah, that's all schools. That means the student is not allowed to go to any schools in Ontario, except for private schools. And they must stay with us for a minimum of one semester, and they must get our stamp of approval before they can return to a regular school … They have to demonstrate improved behaviour, and they can't demonstrate any of the behaviours that got them there. And we have to sign off on the behaviours that the principal has wanted us to work on. So, they've checked off on their ESAP, for example.

School expulsions require that a young person is removed from mainstream programming temporarily, while they await the coordination of a Safe Schools transfer to another school within the school board or indefinitely until the student demonstrates that he or she has met the criteria outlined in their Expelled Students Action Plan (ESAP) (Zheng & De Jesus, 2017). Although Safe and Caring Schools program educators are responsible for monitoring and assessing demonstrations of improved behaviour, as per the conditions of a student's ESAP, the ESAP itself is produced by the school principal from the expelling school. It is not uncommon for the ESAP to arrive well after the student is expelled (Rankin & Contenta, 2009). In addition to lag times for the arrival of ESAP paperwork, my own research with Safe Schools educators in programs across the GTA suggests sending schools do not tend to provide documents and resources (e.g., progress reports, outlining work-to-date on a course, or bridging assignments) that allow for a smooth transition from the sending school to the receiving program. These findings correspond with what Rankin and Contenta found in their 2009 investigation. For these and other reasons (e.g., that the program's central focus is on behavioural changes and the reality that most students have already fallen behind the four credit per term target), credit accumulation rates in Long-Term Suspension and Expulsion programs are quite low (Zheng & De Jesus, 2017). Poor academic performance is not a condition justifying an expulsion under the Education Act; however, timely credit accrual (as well as attendance and punctuality) can be ESAP criteria that students need to meet in order to return to mainstream programming. As such, Rankin and Contenta found that between "February 2008 and April 2009, only 29 per cent of students who participated in a TDSB expulsion program returned to regular schools. Fifty-four per cent were still in the program while 17 per cent withdrew, entered a treatment centre, or are in custody" (2009).

Expulsions are serious disciplinary acts, with the potential to significantly disrupt a young person's educational trajectory. Given that education remains one of the most potentially protective interventions for young people (e.g., in terms of health promotion and criminological prevention [Cutler, Huang, & Lleras-Muney, 2015; McMurtry & Young, 2008]), it makes good empirical sense to limit the use of punishments that undermine connections to school. However, amendments to the Safe Schools Act in Ontario also paved the way for the emergence of other exclusionary processes (the ambiguous exclusions describe by David in Montreal and Samir and Tyrone in Toronto) whereby principals formally and legally relocate (but not expel) young people from schools, as well board-level disciplinary practices enabled by alignments between a board's code of conduct and the Education Act: "Any other activity that is an activity for which a principal may suspend a pupil under a policy of the board" (Education Act, R.S.O. 1990, c. E.2, s. 306.1; s. 310.1). These changes have significantly altered the work of school administrators. The onus to investigate any student action warranting expulsion has produced (as Tonette's story illuminates) conditions of intensive surveillance in schools, which continue to disproportionately influence young Black men from poor neighbourhoods. School administrators, responsible for investigating and punishing student behaviour, are increasingly undertaking work that resembles the outreach and investigative work done by police. Administrators describe reviewing camera footage and taking statements from "victims" and "perpetrators." Where footage isn't available, they draw on other evidences – statements from students, staff, Ontario Student Records, observations – to make a case about a student.

Todd, a vice-principal at a Toronto school in one of the city's NIAs (i.e., municipally designated vulnerable neighbourhoods, containing large numbers of people living in poverty) describes how the growing number of students moved into his school through safe school transfers shapes the nature and focus of his administrative work. The Safe

Schools transfers, themselves, represent considerable administrative work – meeting with the student, often parent(s) or guardian(s), Safe Schools administrators, and other staff; reviewing the student's records and coordinating new timetables with the guidance department; and then ensuring that the youth is integrated into the new environment and not engaging in the activities that warranted the transfer in the first place. Todd explains that public perceptions about lack of safety at his school have led to lower enrolment numbers over the years. The impetus to keep enrolment numbers up means that his school admits higher numbers of Safe Schools and other transfers from schools and programs in the board, increasing the numbers of students in his school who have been suspended or expelled, have youth criminal justice charges preventing them from staying at the current school, or who have been proactively relocated due to attendance and/or disciplinary issues.

Safe Schools educator, Ian, explains how the Safe Schools transfer process works in general and how the process works when the focus is on reintegrating a young person after the conditions of their ESAP have been satisfied:

> IAN: Okay, so once we put the stamp of approval on lifting their expulsion from all schools, the quad administrator comes in, meets with the student. Depending on the kid, sometimes they say, "Give me a list of three schools. Where do you want to go? I'll see what I can do." Now, schools can only take a limited number of what's called Safe Schools transfers per year … [The number of transfers] depends on the school and the principal. The principal can start to not answer the phone when the quad administrators call, right? … But that's Safe Schools transfers, not just expulsion lists …
> ALISON: Your kids would not be considered a Safe School transfer when they're coming from your program?
> IAN: Uh, I think technically not. Technically not … But it's the same type of MO of kid, like, an at-risk kid, a behavioural kid. So, principals are wary of that. And yeah, that's a stigma right there. A kid comes into the school, gets grilled by the principal, feels like he's got a target on his back, the teachers get informed, and sometimes they're out the door before they step in the door.

Indeed, the readmission process for expelled youth, who have been able to consistently meet the objectives outlined in their ESAP, begins with an application by the student, "in writing to the principal of the expulsion program requesting that the student return to a school of the Board" (Zheng & De Jesus, 2017, p. 21). It is then up to the school principal in the Long-Term Suspension and Expulsion program who filled out the ESAP to negotiate re-entry for the student. Once a receiving school has been identified and prior to being readmitted to school, a re-entry plan (including a progress report) is developed by educators in the Long-Term Suspension and Expulsion program (Zheng & De Jesus, 2017). Most often, students are re-entering at a new school, and so, in addition to the plan, a re-entry meeting (like the one that Jani, the student at Rosewood, participated in when she sought re-entry to the program there) is usually coordinated with a new school. A number of communicative and coordinative tasks surround the removal of young people from one site and reintegration in another.

In a limited number of work hours, Vice-Principal Todd describes being unable to put the energy he'd like to toward the development of a new health certificate program because of the time that is invested in coordinating school transfers and addressing disciplinary issues at his school – disciplinary issues he associates with the large number of Safe School transfer students at his school. By way of an example, he talks about the work that he was required to put into investigating allegations of a gun on school grounds. Other scholars (e.g., Manicom, 1995) have observed how different uses of teacher time shape unequal outcomes in school. For example, in some schools, teachers dedicate the majority of their workday to curriculum development enrichment activities; elsewhere, teachers dedicate much of their workdays to filling health and wellness gaps required for their students to learn. A similar relation comes into view in Todd's description of his own work. In schools where educational leaders spend much of the workday producing the evidence required to enable institutional responses to school problems (e.g., investigating and resolving disciplinary issues), there is less administrative time available for community engagement, professional mentorship and development, or program creation. Although Todd is most passionate about developing a new health and wellness certificate program for students, an invitation to walk the interviewer through a typical workday reveals that the majority of his time is spent dealing with issues related to safety. Todd explains:

> I led the whole investigation. I had forty police in here doing what I was asking them to do ... So I kind of felt a bit odd. I'm leading an investigation, "Now go down to this locker. Open that locker up." We went down and looked and spent the afternoon looking for the weapon, which we never found. The school was in lockdown for the rest of the afternoon. And

finally they released the kids at about 3:30 p.m., let the kids go home, and one of the kids went into the boys' bathroom on the third floor and found the [replica] gun hidden upstairs on the third floor ... The kids get what's called a twenty-day pending. It's short for the safe in schools twenty-day pending, which means they're immediately suspended for twenty days, which typically we can't do. You can't suspend a kid if you don't know what they've done, but this is pending an investigation. So we're allowed to suspend for twenty days. The investigation must be finished within five [days]. It's like a police investigation. We find witnesses and take statements. We take statements from the perpetrators. Everything's written down ... Our investigation in this case was pretty clear-cut. I can see everything on camera, and we ended up with a gun at the end of the day.

The character of Todd's work differs significantly from other schools in the city. Because of the high number of disciplinary issues at his school and mandated by the Education Act, Todd "must conduct a school-based investigation into incidents that are brought to his or her attention where a suspension or expulsion could be issued" (Zheng & De Jesus, 2017, p. 17). As such, rather than spending time interacting with staff, students, and parents, Todd is reviewing camera footage, conducting interviews with students and staff, and supporting a police investigation. Once the young men were arrested and taken to the station, he has five days to conduct his own internal investigation in order to determine whether to expel the youth. Meanwhile, the principal is taking care of all the paperwork surrounding the school's "hold and secure" procedure, which is put into action after a weapon is reported. And both administrators are fielding calls from parents, concerned for their children's safety and threatening to put them in a different school. Every time an incident occurs that warrants a non-discretionary suspension, pending an investigation to determine grounds for expulsion, school administrators' work shifts to accommodate the collection and use of evidence to justify a decision about expulsion. The investigative work that administrators are called to do draws them into professional discourses and practices that shift how they see their work and understand their relations with youth and parents in the neighbourhood.

It also enables the coordination of work processes between school administrators and the police. As is common when young people have engaged in activities that necessitate a mandatory long-term suspension, pending expulsion, Todd worked with the police throughout the investigation ("I had forty police in here doing what I was asking them to do and it was a little bit odd ... I'm leading an investigation with,

'Now go down to this locker. Open that locker up'"). Most activities on this list are also violations of criminal law, requiring that a phone call to the police is one of the administrator's first moves, "And we phoned the police because [the student] said, 'I saw the gun. I can describe to you what it looks like.' The next move was phone the police. The police were here in literally twenty seconds" (Todd, interview, 2015). Numerous young people we interviewed described being called down to the principal's office, only to be met by police officers. Young people's rights during their interactions with the police are different than their rights when interacting with a school principal, but this distinction is not always clear to them – particularly where police are present in their schools in much the same way that educational authorities are. Prior to any conversation with the police, people are entitled to seek legal counsel. Young people (under the age of eighteen) are also entitled to have an adult present during these conversations. But unless these rights are made evident to youth, they may not see any problem in allowing their principal to serve in this capacity. Where this occurs, youth do not receive appropriate legal advice and adult guardianship at a crucial moment.

At the same time that a youth is participating in complex school-based disciplinary processes, he or she may also be required to navigate equally or more complex judicial ones. While first-time offenders may avoid a trial by participating in a community diversion process, other young people are required to interface directly with the court system. This process can be lengthy, requiring multiple absences from school in order to attend court and, in some cases, a stint in pretrial detention or conditions that impact where they can learn. Youth cannot, for instance, attend school with one of their co-accused while awaiting or participating in a trial. Sentencing will also result in changes to a young person's life and their learning. Periods in open or closed custody mean that they must switch schools again and often also switch school boards. Between Safe Schools processes and the justice system, youth in conflict with the law will be subject to many educational relocations and exclusions – starting and stopping a single credit on multiple occasions. Unfortunately, the progress a youth makes towards credit accumulation in one educational site seldom transfers with the youth as he or she is moved between programs, cities, and school boards. For any young person, this start-and-stop educational process is disruptive. For young people who are already disengaged from school, it can set the stage for complete disconnection – despite the inclusion of school participation in young people's probation orders. Further, "the more students are absent from school (e.g., on multiple short-term suspensions or to participate in court hearings), the more likely they are to drop out and get into trouble. More than 70 per cent of Canadian inmates did not complete high school, according to a recent study by a federal task force" (Rankin & Contenta, 2009). Compounding the instability caused by intersecting youth justice and Safe Schools interventions, many young people have experienced prior educational exclusions under the auspices of special education interventions, which disproportionately focus on behavioural disorders while failing to identify and address specific learning needs.

Institutionally Organized Intersections: Special Education and School Safety

Significantly, for many young people we interviewed in jail and in Safe Schools programs, experiences with long-term suspension and expulsion processes in high school can be charted back to elementary school, where they received numerous short-term suspensions and relocations to specialized behavioural programs, which created repeated disruptions in their schooling from a very young age. People in US prisons are three times more likely than the general population to report having a disability (McCauley, 2017). In the UK, rates of generalized (23–32 per cent) and specific (43–57 per cent) learning disabilities (e.g., dyslexia) are more common among incarcerated and detained youth compared to the general population (2–4 per cent and 10 per cent, respectively) (Hughes, Williams, Chitsabesan, Davies, & Mounce, 2012). State reports on the demographic characteristics of youth and adult "offenders" in Canada, however, do not capture this level of detail regarding the prevalence of disability among people in conflict with the law, which is unsurprising given the costs associated with neuropsychological or neurodevelopmental testing and the subsequent reliance on other forms of observational classification (e.g., behavioural disabilities) used in public institutions like schools.

When asked how many suspensions he experienced during elementary school, Dewain, a young Black man we interviewed in jail, tells us that he had a lot: "Over one hundred. When I was younger, I used to fight a lot. I was insecure. I didn't like writing or reading. If someone made fun of me, I'd fight them. Or if someone said at recess that my hair was nappy, I'd fight them." In this brief excerpt from my interview with Dewain, two important things stand out: the first pertains to school discipline and special education services and the second to experiences of racism in school. The two things are interconnected, and both issues raise concerns about the use of punitive and exclusionary school discipline practices, particularly in the primary grades. In his explanation for why he was suspended repeatedly throughout elementary school, Dewain reflects that he "used to fight a lot" because of educational insecurities, which he associates with not liking writing or reading. A focus on preventing further incidents of violence in schools – that is, a focus on creating conditions of safety and inclusion for everyone – would have addressed the conditions that interfered with the development of Dewain's literacy capacities; instead, his violent outbursts were met with punishment. It's important, at this juncture, to spend some time tracing out the deployment of school-based interventions that enable access to additional education resources and those that enable punishment and exclusion.

In Toronto, half of the analysed school expulsions between 2011 and 2016 were issued to students within the ambiguous category of "special education needs" (Zheng & De Jesus, 2017, p. 24), a term that remains undefined in the document. Learning disabilities and brain disorders (e.g., attention deficit hyperactivity disorder or ADHD) are diagnosed by certified psychiatrists, psychologists, and/or neuropsychologists in clinical settings, using standardized tasks and metrics. Securing access to these diagnostic services, if provided by the school, can take years; otherwise, access is only granted through private clinics with fees upwards of $3000. As my own experiences seeking supports for my daughter illuminate, once identified as having learning disability, a young person and/or their guardian can advocate for increased time and quiet spaces to complete tests, assessment strategies that decouple comprehension from reading, access to assistive technologies, and in-class special education resource supports. Unfortunately, most of the Individualized Education Plans (IEPs) for the young people attending school in the jail are for ambiguous "behavioural" disorders, more often associated with part- or full-time placement in Home School Program (HSP) and the self-contained Intensive Support Programs (ISP), respectively. As I will go on to explore below, the local development of IEPs for non-identified students follows a markedly classed, raced, and gendered pattern.

Antonio, one of the educators whom I interviewed at a youth jail in Ontario, noted that the educational assessments he conducted while the student was undergoing the fourteen-day intake process (that is, before being placed in a living unit and receiving a school timetable) included questions about the student's IEP: "A lot of the times, the kids don't know why they have an IEP. Normally, at that point, I would ask, 'Well, do you remember when it was given?' And normally I'll guess, 'Well, was it grade 4 or 5?' And usually that's the case. And if that's the case, I would guess, nine times out of ten, it's more behaviour-related" (Antonio, personal interview). Indeed, 40 per cent of new exceptionality designations in the Toronto District School Board are made in grades 5 through 8 (R.S. Brown & Parekh, 2010) and economically disadvantaged and racialized students are over-represented among language-related, mild intellectual delay, and behavioural exceptionalities (Clandfield, 2014). As a point of contrast, with regard to the learning disability category – where average or above-average intelligence quotient scores are accompanied by below average performative capacities, *and* where below average performance cannot be said to be primarily the result of socio-economic, cultural, or linguistic differences; student motivation; or teaching (Clandfield, 2014, p. 140) – economically advantaged, White, and male students are significantly over-represented (Brown & Parekh, 2010). These race, class, and gender disproportionalities are thought to result from race, class, and gender-based referral bias; differential degrees of access to private diagnostic and support services; and the Identification, Placement, and Review Committee (IPRC) process itself (Clandfield, 2014).

In order to lessen economic and human resource demands placed on the IPRC process, local in-school teams and school support teams, comprised of a school's own teachers and staff, were established by the TDSB to improve timely access to special education supports. The in-school team is framed as the first "tier of support" for young people who teachers have identified as struggling – that is, where "sound classroom instruction, based on what is usually successful for most students, has been unsuccessful for the student" (Toronto District School Board, 2016, p. 1). Interventions supported by the in-school team include the development and monitoring of an individualized learning profile and the implementation of strategies to support student learning. Where the intervention is deemed insufficient or ineffective, the "second tier of support" or the school support team is mobilized. The school support team includes the special education resource teachers at a school, as well as any of the following school board professionals from: special education, psychology, social work, attendance counselling, speech-language pathology, and occupational therapy and physiotherapy. The school support team can make referrals and/or produce an IEP for a young person – in the absence of official diagnoses (e.g., of a learning disability or neurobiological condition). Young people who receive an IEP through the school support team process are described as non-identified students on IEPs or IEP-only students, and in 2006 to 2007 they accounted for 48 per cent of students receiving special education support in the board (Brown & Parekh, 2013; Clandfield, 2014). Furthermore, while Black students made up 14.4 per cent of students in the TDSB in 2006 to 2007, they represented 28.7 per cent of students in the non-identified students or IEP-only category (Brown & Parekh, 2013). Students from the lowest and highest income neighbourhoods are similarly over-represented in the IEP-only and IPRC gifted categories, respectively.

Thus, while race, class, and gender bias are generally apparent with respect to referral, access, and diagnoses, where locally developed processes are in place, economically disadvantaged and Black young people are even more likely to be singled out as having ambiguous learning and behavioural challenges. These labels facilitate their removal into local special education programs: the partially integrated Home School Program and the self-contained Intensive Support Program. The significance of this trend is threefold: First, it suggests that discretionary decision-making leads to increasingly disproportionate outcomes along race, class, and/or gendered lines. Second, it suggests that the same institutional processes that create racialized, classed, and gendered advantage for one group (think back here to my own experiences seeking access to extra time and supports for my daughter by acquiring an official learning disability and neuropsychological diagnosis for her) produce disadvantages for others. Third, the safe/unsafe, victim/perpetrator binary distracts from the ways young people use violence in response to a system that has made them feel insecure and where they have, themselves, been exposed to racial and other forms of violence at the hands of others. In sum, young Black men from the city's poorest neighbourhoods are more likely to experience both exclusionary special education interventions *and* exclusionary punishments in the form of suspensions and expulsions – both interventions creating the types of instability associated with poor academic performance (Moore, 2013).

The Social Organization of Crisis Response

The second thing that jumps out from the two lines of text from Dewain's interview is that his elementary schooling experiences were shaped by racism (e.g., "someone said … my hair was nappy"). If the goal is actually to create positive and inclusive school climates, efforts must be made to reduce the use of exclusionary disciplinary processes that undermine fragile connections to school by responding to the underlying conditions (e.g., racism, economic polarity, stress) that shape the actions that manifest as playground and classroom violence. The underlying conditions that shape school violence are social and political-economic relations that operate globally but manifest locally as unequal educational, social, health, and criminological outcomes at the level of individual children, youth, and families. As such, educators, social workers, and health practitioners toiling exhaustively at the local level, without attending to the wider political-economic and social conditions within which this local work is occurring, find themselves trapped in crisis response mode, moving young people through interventions that clearly aren't working for them. Working in isolation from one another and out of sync with the ministries that govern their work, front-line educators, social workers, health workers, youth workers, psychologists and police officers cannot do much more than respond to the playground, classroom, and street-corner manifestations of the structural and systemic dislocations this book reveals.

While Dewain might not have actually been suspended one hundred times during elementary school, he was suspended often enough to have lost track. Many other young people I have interviewed for this book and my earlier work (Nichols, 2014) experienced punitive educational, youth criminal justice, and mental health interventions, which also failed to generate positive outcomes in their lives. Young people I've worked with and interviewed across Montreal and Toronto are unanimous that exclusionary discipline measures don't work – in fact, in many cases, they are seen by youth as an illogical response to issues of poor school attachment, which increases the time youth spend on the streets. Certainly, the experiences of young people who have become enmeshed in the youth justice system bear this out – the sheer number of hours in court and the ensuing youth justice interventions they experience make consistent school attendance impossible. But teachers and school principals are faced with pressure from all sides to continually demonstrate – based on aggregated school-based data – school improvement and a positive school climate. Their actions create conditions that favour the removal of individual students who make this difficult.

Intersectional Practices of Surveillance: Education, Child Protection, Policing, and Probation

Accentuating the impacts of increased exposure to institutional surveillance practices in schools, surveillance practices linked with other sectors (e.g., policing, child protection, and probation) also shape the lives of young people in highly disproportionate ways. For instance, in the United States child protection cases pivoting around suspicions of neglect are disproportionately opened for racialized young people living in poverty compared to rates for the general population (Eubanks, 2018). In Canada, Black and Indigenous young people are disproportionality represented among young people in all forms of state "care" (from foster care, group homes, and supervisory cases) (Government of Canada, 2016; Maloney, Jiang, Emily, Dalton, & Vaithianathan, 2017; Maynard, 2017; National Inquiry Into Missing and Murdered Indigenous Women and Girls, 2017; Ontario Association of Children's Aid Societies, 2015) compared to the general population. Furthermore, all aspects of the criminal-legal system (from frontline policing stop-and-search practices, to sentencing and probation) disproportionately impact the lives of Black and Indigenous men and women in Canada (Maynard, 2017; Wortley & Owusu-Bempah, 2011). The magnitude of the effects of the surveilling and punitive relations surrounding school can only be grasped when the wider arena of state practices is also kept in view. For young people whose lives are punctuated by interventions from all three systems – education, child protection, and the criminal legal system – the results are devastating.

In an interview with Andy, a young man named Fenton, a self-described Brown man of Guyanese ethnicity, described his experiences interacting with all three institutions throughout his adolescence. As he did so, the intersectional effects of the relations of surveillance he was participating in came clearly into view. The conversation began with Fenton's analysis of the economic and class-based relations, which underpin interactions between young people and the police in his neighbourhood:

And when you haven't even done nothing. You never even got in trouble with the law. They just want to say, "You live here? Yeah, we're going to profile you, too." It's ridiculous, bro. But at the end of the day, some cops have to realize they are regular people like us, too, you know? They're regular people. When they go to work, they go to work to put on their uniform. They finish work, they come out plain clothes driving a regular old car. They're no different than us. They probably just have a higher pay grade, or they're better than us, have a better car, have a better house, but they're no better than us ... You cooperate with certain police, they cooperate with you. But certain police, they're just jackasses ... They know how we live. They probably lived like that back in the days, too. But then they got up to a certain rank, they got their shit, got their badge, become a cop, started making more money, and then think they're better than people.

Fenton's response was prompted by Andy's observation that Fenton had been "affiliated" – as in affiliated with gang-related street work. To which Fenton responded that in terms of policing, your affiliations with the work matter less than your affiliation with poverty – a way of pointing to the presupposition (or naturalization) of class-based differences upon which he sees differential police practices resting. This recognition sets up his next analytic move of questioning the naturalized relation of power between those doing the policing and those being policed – "they are regular people like us." It's important to include the analytic insights young people share in these interviews – not as a research finding (as in, young people have analytic capacities that schools fail to recognize or amplify) but as an indication of the ways that young people's experiences in and observations of state institutions shape how they come to know and participate in the social relations of their lives.

But as Andy observed, and Fenton admitted, he *had* been "affiliated," and this meant that his relations with the police were not limited to the types of profiling he describes above. That being the case, even before Fenton became affiliated with street work and known to police, his life was punctuated by other relations of surveillance – those linking education with the child protection system in Ontario. Fenton's story begins when he was in early adolescence – a young man who liked school and trusted his teachers. This is a key juncture in terms of Fenton's evolving relationship with institutions of the state, which shape how everything else in in his life unfolds. Of course, the state doesn't *cause* Fenton to do the things he ends up doing in his life, but the actions themselves and their consequences are influenced by the multiple, overlapping relations of state surveillance that permeate and give shape to his life:

> FENTON: Some teachers, when they say they're going to keep shit confidential, they don't … I learned that shit from young, bro. That's how my family kind of got split up. That's how we kind of got into group homes and shit … Just because I told a teacher something and the teacher said, "Fenton, you know what? I'm going to hold it down. I'm not going to tell nobody." It was something serious, you know? It was about my dad being an alcoholic and him beating my mom and shit. Shit I grew up with. And then he went, told the Children's Aid. Children's Aid came –
> ANDY: Oh no!

FENTON: – and ripped our family apart. All of us. My little brother was a baby, my sister – a we all were babies. We're all kids. Just ripped us apart. And just because of that shit I look at my life different. And then ever since my mom passed away, too, shit changes. That's why I sort of messed up in school, too. Like, before I actually got, like, awards in school. I used to go in spelling bees, everything. And then I fell off.

Teachers are legally bound by a "duty to report" any suspicion or admission of child abuse (Child and Family Services Act, R.S.O. 1990, c. C11, s. 72). Many well-intentioned (White, middle-class) teachers imagine that reporting a suspected case of abuse to the state will result in better life outcomes for young people. Indeed, they are legally obliged to do so. Unfortunately, young people with histories of involvement in the child protection system experience poorer outcomes across a range of dimensions – education, health, housing, and labour market – than young people in the general population (Nichols et al., 2017). While these disproportionalities might come as a surprise to people in the White, middle-class majority – and particularly to those teachers who report suspicions of abuse to the state with the belief they do so in the best interests of children – people from neighbourhoods where state surveillance is more pronounced know all too well that interactions with the child protection system are unlikely to lead to protective outcomes for themselves or their children.

Note Andy's response to Fenton above. When Fenton explained that the teacher called the Children's Aid Society, Andy immediately interjected: "Oh no!" I'm reminded of the day Kenneth received a call from a neighbour letting him know that the Children's Aid was at his house, so that he could race home to help his mom; the interviews I did with the twins, Marianna and Monika (in chapter 3); and another interview I did with a young woman named, Diana, who explained: "Some teachers will friend you up and come off as, 'Oh, how are you? How's your family going? Is everything okay at home?' But when they're asking you that, they're *really* trying to find out are you being abused and stuff like that. They turn it against you and they're calling Children's Aid, whereas I just need somebody to talk to. I don't need you to report anything." These particular relations of surveillance are more insidious than the relations of policing Fenton spoke about earlier because they are framed in the guise of helpfulness. Across Ontario, Black and Indigenous people report greater surveillance, scrutiny, and long-term interference from child protection workers, and in Toronto Black children represent 40.8 per cent of those in state care but only 8.5 per cent of the population (OHRC, 2017). I will not speculate whether Black teachers who grew up in the neighbourhood would ignore the law requiring them to report a suspicion of abuse to the child protection system; but anyone who has experienced, observed, or even read about the history of racial bias in child protection – and the array of negative outcomes associated with involvement in this system – would not presume a child protection intervention to be a positive thing for a vulnerable youth.

As a consequence of the child welfare investigation, Fenton and his siblings were split up and placed into foster families. But fostering is seldom a permanent solution for young people the state has deemed to be in need of care, particularly when young people are – like Fenton was – in early adolescence (Nichols, 2014; Triseliotis, 2002). Not unlike the housing trajectories described by young people temporarily placed by in a youth homelessness shelter by the state during adolescence (Nichols, 2014, 2016), Fenton is placed in a number of different foster homes and group homes as he matures into adolescence. He explains all of this to Andy in the interview, and in so doing he brings the surveilling and dislocating relations of the state into view:

> Foster homes are actually much more freedom than group homes. Because group homes are for much worser kids and shit. Foster homes are like a regular home. She cooks, do what you need to. It's like you live there. It's your second home. There's one foster home in Markham and she's a great lady. She took care of us every day. She cooked for us. She just provided everything. Everything that we needed. She was good. But, like, there's some foster homes, they just want to be assholes for no reason. There was a foster home when I was in Ajax with my brother, and my brother didn't used to speak up for himself, you know? He's quiet all the time and shit. An' then I'm like, "Yo, what's wrong with these guys? These guys are taking advantage of my brother." So, I was the one who spoke up for him, and then just because I spoke up for him they started hearing my voice and they started saying, "No, we're going to move this guy. We're going to whip him away from his brother and put him somewhere else." And that's what they did … I don't like to see when somebody, especially when it's, like, my family, being disrespected. He's just being quiet because he's scared, you know? Foster homes are kind of good, but it's just, like, when you rip a brown guy and just put him into a fuckin' Black family, then the way that you're going to be raised, you're going to be raised different. You're going to be ripped off from your culture and put into something else. That's kind of the negative. They don't match up the kids.

The foster families with which Fenton was placed, did not, as he observes, share a racial and cultural background with him and his siblings – a disconnect that he describes as negative because you are "ripped off from your culture." Further, Fenton illuminates punishing relations of surveillance operating within the foster home itself ("because I spoke up for him, they started hearing my voice and they started saying, 'No, we're going to move this guy'"), where the punishment is Fenton's temporary separation from his brother. While any move to sever a kinship relation is deeply at odds with the provincial desire to support kinship care and the maintenance of familial supports (Ontario Association of Children's Aid Societies, 2018), I have heard too many stories from young people in too many different cities about the punitive practice of withholding access to family to imagine that these are misrepresentations on the parts of young people. Finally, I remind the reader that the movement of young people from home to home, city to city, and school to school also has negative repercussions for their performance in and connections to schooling, which Fenton's story illuminates for us.

As Fenton moves into adolescence, he is subject to more frequent and more significant moves, which dislocate him from his family, his community, and his schooling. As he tells the story, the origin of Fenton's disaffection from school is the breach of trust on the part of a teacher, whose promise to "hold [his secret] down" is at odds with his legal "duty to report." Beyond this violation of trust, the material instability arising from the child welfare intervention, further disrupted Fenton's connections to family, school, and community – the very circumstances of dislocation and disconnection that criminological research suggests lies at the roots of youth violence and criminal activity (McMurtry & Young, 2008; Wortley, 2008). By the time he was in high school, Fenton was facing a range of youth criminal justice charges, which, because of his lack of consistent guardianship, resulted in him being relocated to a group home in Brampton (under house arrest) after serving a pretrial detention at a provincial youth jail. Andy asked Fenton about his charges, and he explained: "I went in there for a couple things. I went in there for an assault. I went in there for a robbery, you know? Possession of an illegal firearm. But that one, I took that one[1] for a friend, you know? It wasn't even mine. I got caught with it, and I didn't even say nothing, I went down for it, you know? But that was it. And then possession of an illegal weapon – it was a knife. It wasn't a big deal." Until he was sixteen years of age, the state would have been responsible

---

1 When a young person references taking or swallowing a charge for a friend, it means that they were willingly charged for a crime their friend committed.

for taking care of and exercising control over Fenton upon release from custody. Recall from chapter 5 that when young people talk about being on house arrest, it either means that they are pretrial and living under the most stringent of bail conditions, or like Fenton, they have been charged, found guilty of an offence, and sentenced to house arrest (i.e., they are serving their sentence in the community). House arrest is accompanied with very strict conditions (e.g., you can only leave your house to go to school or work), including regular supervision by a probation officer. In Fenton's case, the charges also resulted in him being expelled from his mainstream school in Toronto: "Once I got charged while I was in J-school, they kicked me out and then that's why I moved to Brampton ... I came back, and then after I was done that, that's when I had to be transferred to a Safe School [program], and then I went to W-school." While Fenton was living in Brampton, the conditions of his community sentence meant that the only time he was supposed to be outside the group home was to attend school or to meet with his probation officer. With limited freedom of movement because of the conditions of his community sentence, Fenton tells Andy he was "slacking off," got caught skipping school, and ended up with further administration of justice charges or "breaches":

> when I was in B Secondary, I was charged, and I was kind of slacking off, you know? Because I had no freedom. So I used to skip, and I used to smoke, and I used to kind of forge signatures and shit on the tracking sheet. I got caught, bro ... The [school] calls in the group home, "Oh yeah, Fenton has missed fifteen days of school, sixteen days of school, where the fuck has he been?" They're like, "What? This guy brought the tracking sheet showing he's been at school. Where the fuck has he been?" Boom. Breached.

Earlier in the interview, Fenton had observed to Andy that probation and house arrest are a trap: "I was on probation and house arrest and all that shit's a trap. I've been on house arrest, I've been on probation, I've been on both. I breached a few times. That's [heavy sigh] life." Fenton's sense that probation and house arrest are "a trap" is shaped in part by the intersections of the child protection and youth criminal justice systems, which result in young people living in group homes receiving multiple administration of justice charges for "failing to abide" by the rules of their group homes (Nichols, 2014). Disciplinary infractions that would otherwise result in a loss of privileges (e.g., loss of TV access or autonomy) result in further charges for young people living in residential care settings:

It was basically like open custody. Everywhere I go I had a driver driving me to school, picking me up, driving me to my appointments. Everywhere I go. The only time I had some freedom was when I go to school. They drop me off at school and I had my tracking sheet and I had to sign in and out. So, I was on lock, basically, you know? Yeah, you basically did lose your freedom when you come out. You have to do all that shit. And I couldn't come home for, like, three months. Just because I got charged in front of my house, you know? When I came out, though, I had to come to my house, bro. I had to stay, like, two hundred metres, but I had to come to my house. I had no shoelaces – they took my shoelaces – I had no belt, I had no clothes. As soon as they came out [with my clothes], my social worker came, and she dropped me straight to the group home. She's like, "This is your address, and you have to stay here. You have to abide by the rules" … It's basically, like, lock-up. But there's no bars … Yeah, even as you go into the group home you have to pull out your pockets, and you have to empty all your pockets – everything – they search you to see if you bring anything in there … You could have no cell phones, no lighters, no zigzags, no weed. Nothing.

Fenton spent a year and a half serving out the term of his community sentence in that group home. From there, he returned to a group home in his neighbourhood with the conditions of his release outlined on his probation order and supervised by a probation officer. Known to the police in the neighbourhood – who were well aware of the conditions of his release – Fenton described multiple ongoing negative interactions with them as he sought to get his life together. Further, because he'd been expelled, he had to re-enter the Toronto District School System via a Safe Schools program, where his return to mainstream school were negotiated by the Safe Schools coordinator and a Safe Schools principal and then carefully monitored by the educators at his receiving school. In Fenton's case, he tried to re-enrol at his old secondary school (where he felt he had connections with teachers and students) without much success. The principal at C-school denied his requests to re-enrol: "But then after I got charged and shit they started dissin', you know? Trying to say, 'Yeah, you can't come back here because they think you're affiliated because of this, because of that.' I'm like, 'You know what? At least I'm trying.' It not like I didn't try, you know? I wake up one, two times, I'm like, 'Yeah, I feel when I go back to school I'm going to do this, I'm going to do this.' And then I go there, and they put me down." In the end, he enrolled at another school in the neighbourhood – W-school – a school where gang affiliations shape ongoing conflicts between students, which made Fenton's efforts to "mind his own business" more challenging: "A man's going to be wearing a red flag, or a man's going to be wearing a blue flag, and they're going to get a jumping. Just for a colour. That's the way fuckin' high school is. But when I went to school I just minded my own business, did my own thing, stayed by myself, and I had one, two friends. At the end of the day it's still trouble. Like, trouble that you try to avoid, but trouble comes to you." When Andy interviewed Fenton in 2014, he was living with his biological father again. He was in his early twenties, happy to be back in his old neighbourhood again, and hopeful that he and his dad would be able to secure a townhouse in one of the nearby Toronto Community Housing properties, so that his siblings could return home to live with them. He had not finished high school.

Conclusion

This chapter brings into view the relations that link the surveilling and punitive practices employed in Montreal and Toronto secondary schools to the wider web of institutional and policy relations within which young lives are unfolding. In schools, surveillance and documentary practices enable young people to be moved through suspensions, expulsions, relocations, and transfers, as well as through identification, placement, and review processes. As surveillance practices in schools intersect with neighbourhood policing on the streets and child protection interventions in homes, educational processes intersect with relocations coordinated by the youth criminal justice system (e.g., to open or closed custody environments) and/or the child protection system (e.g., to new group home environments, shelters, and foster homes).

Having been researching the ways various state institutions (dis)organize young people's lives for more than a decade, it seems clear to me that the more state institutions are involved in a young person's life, the more (dis)organized a life becomes. I have never sought to actively recruit people who have had negative interactions with state institutions, nor have interviews focused only on bringing a person's negative experiences into view. In fact, with Sampling Youth Development, Jessica Ruglis and I deliberately and actively sought to create questions that privileged young people's dreams, desires, and positive experiences in the public sphere. The work on Schools and Safety and Sampling Youth Development heeds Eve Tuck's critical warning about the epistemological, developmental, and political repercussions of documenting damage (Tuck, 2009). So, I need to remind the reader as I move towards the conclusion of this book that this is a book about public sector institutions that shape young people's lives, their sense of self, and their relations to others and to the state. In the vein of researching up (Brown & Strega, 2005), this chapter reveals how state institutions operate in young people's lives in ways that contribute to the maintenance of race, class, and gender inequalities.

Conclusion

The redistributive capacity of the state is linked to the provision and management of the public sector (e.g., welfare, social services, education, healthcare, child welfare, child and youth mental health services, immigrant settlement services, and public housing) (Jenson, 2013; Shields & Evans, 1998). The provision and management of public sector resources and interventions reflects the principles of bureaucratic organization (Weber, 1993) reimagined for contemporary managerial and neo-liberal contexts (Aucoin, 1995; Harvey, 2005). The characteristic principle of bureaucracy is "the abstract regularity of the execution of authority, which is a result of the demand for 'equality before the law' in the personal and functional sense" (Weber, 1993, p. 116). Bureaucratic forms of state organization were developed to level social and economic difference (Weber, 1993). But bureaucratic organization depends on general principles and standards, which reflect (and reinforce as universal) the values, expectations, and interests of dominant groups (Fanon, 2008; Foucault & Gordon, 1980; D.E. Smith, 1987, 2005). Normative standards – embedded in public sector legislation, policy, procedure, practices, programs, and, more recently, data processes, including evidence-led decision-making, administrative monitoring, and accounting processes – fundamentally shape the distribution of public sector resources and punishments access in highly unequal ways.

These inequalities are captured in disproportionality data, generated about service outcomes (for example, the disproportionate number of young Black men who are expelled from Toronto schools or who have Individualized Education Plans with behavioural diagnoses). The differential nature of service outcomes illuminates systemic patterns of exclusion and neglect, which institutions of the state have the authority and the responsibility to address. Indeed, a systematic effort to engender social and cultural change through law and legal structures, as these intersect with and are shaped by changing social norms and social institutions (Hughes, 2008; Mosher, 2008), is key to supporting different outcomes for young people whose lives are currently being shaped by central public sector institutions: education, child welfare, and youth justice. Efforts to change institutions and law matter, given the vast and ubiquitous ways these institutions punctuate young people's lives and development.

By holding in view both the ways that some people actively seek out and demand things of the state, as well as the ways that other people actively seek to avoid or resist state interventions, this book makes it clear that public institutions – and the discourses, practices, and processes they promulgate – are fundamentally implicated in the production of racial, class, and gender relations, even as dominant discourses proclaim that we have arrived in post-racial, post-class, and post-gender times. Young people learn to interact with public systems in the ways that they do, and these complexes of coordinated social action are contoured by and contour the social relations of blackness, whiteness, middle-classness, ableness, femininity, queerness, and so on. Beginning with young people's own accounts of their lives and experiences, this book reveals the myriad ways that state institutions, policies, processes, and programs deepen race, class, and gendered divides even as the discourse and practices of objective evidence-based governance suggests otherwise.

When evidence-based modes of governance and service delivery are investigated from the standpoints of actual and diverse people, differently positioned within and by state processes, the very modes of evidence upon which governing decisions rest are called into question. By grounding an investigation of institutional processes in the lives and experiences of actual – not imagined, theorized, or abstracted – youth, one begins to see how the evidential practices used in institutions both fail to account for their experiences and fail to improve the fit between the particularities of their lives and the general processes through which bureaucratic and managerial forms of organization unfold. Instead, we see how institutional processes can perpetuate – rather than disrupt – the status quo. Indeed, imperatives to monitor and compare school performance may end up incentivizing the removal or downward streaming of young people who fail to meet age and grade-based targets for credit accumulation. Coupled with the imposition of per-student or per-capita fund-distribution and the publication of performance results, the generation and use of data (by schools and by think tanks like the Fraser Institute) accentuate differences between have and have-not schools across a board. Similarly, while institutional monitoring activities enable demonstrations of compliance with policy, they do little to assess whether the things we are doing in schools are actually contributing to better educational and life outcomes for young people. They also fail to capture the ways that a young person's experiences in school are fundamentally conditioned by the activities and institutional foci of the other public sector organizations that influence young people's lives: child welfare, neighbourhood policing, social housing, youth justice, social assistance, and immigration.

One walks away from a study like this with the cynical view that all this work – to produce and monitor case files and school records, track student data, scrutinize call for service data, monitor "serious occurrences," and comply with legislation – contributes very little that is positive to the lives and development of young people. In fact, given the labour that goes into the generation and monitoring of institutional evidence, this work actually makes it more difficult to really listen to what children, youth, and families are saying they need to live the lives they want. My mind keeps settling on the case-conference re-intake meeting at Rosewood with Jani and her mom. I wonder how differently it might have unfolded if at that meeting – and at other times in Jani's life – people had recognized Jani and her mother as knowledgable about their own lives and listened really carefully to what they were trying to tell them. I do not mean to undercut the importance of professional knowledge and expertise; rather, I am suggesting that we value and seek to develop the critical and empathic capacities of people who work on the front lines of public sector organizations, such that they are able to humanely and proactively respond to the insights people have to share.

Really listening to one another and valuing the contributions each person brings requires considerable time, energy, and a profound belief that all this work will make a positive difference. In current institutional conditions I am struck by a shared sense of exhaustion – among youth workers, critical educators, and young people themselves – because it feels like some youth are simply being moved from intervention to intervention until they reach the upper limits of provincial mandates for youth services and public education. At this point, they are promptly discharged into adult systems, many of which are ostensibly designed for people living in poverty but that further institutionalize mechanisms for state surveillance and criminalization. The longer I do this work, the clearer it is to me that governance processes serve the interests of institutions (e.g., by legitimating resources distribution and institutional practices) and those people who have historically benefited from the actions of the state – that is, White, middle- and upper-class families like my own. The young people's accounts that ground this book illuminate the interinstitutional and cross-sectoral policy "cracks" (or disjunctures) that organize how people relate to one another across institutional settings, producing socially organized patterns of inequality and exclusion, opportunity and advancement. Anarchist, queer, antioppressive, critical race, and feminist scholars have been pointing to the role state processes play in maintaining unequal social relations for decades. To this important conversation I hope this book adds specificity regarding the precise ways that state practices, programs, and policies entrench and normalize relations of privilege and marginalization.

My Next Moves

When I embarked on this research, I was optimistic that it would illuminate a clear path forward for those who work with/for youth in public sector organizations. Today, I am sceptical that the answer to state-generated and state-sustained inequalities should be sought solely through changes to the state – particularly a settler colonial state rooted in oppression and cultural genocide. I am curious these days – inspired by the candidacy papers of one of my doctoral supervisees (Jayne Malenfant) – about whether or not research can be *a form of* direction action, *serve the aims of* direct-action efforts, while also influencing policy and practice change in and across public sector institutions. More recently in a class presentation, two other doctoral supervisees (Goulet-Langlois & Megelas, 2019) proposed that we consider research as/in/with activism. My next moves will entail collective, grass-roots and inter-institutional efforts to open up governing systems to scrutiny and concerted community actions.

During the months wherein I was writing this book, I began paying greater attention to new shifts in governing relations, which I anticipate will heighten the divisive effects of the relations brought into visibility here. As governments turn towards data-led governance strategies – utilizing big data, open data, machine learning, algorithmic decision-making, and predictive public services (e.g., policing, child welfare) – the public sector is embracing methods of cold calculation that serve the aims of neo-liberal governance and increase the surveillance of already oversurveilled and criminalized groups (Eubanks, 2018). In this context governing processes and infrastructure are even less transparent and assessments of procedural fairness more difficult to undertake. Given that the effects of these new modes of governance will be magnified for those groups who have historically been the targets of and/or dependent on state systems (Eubanks, 2018), *and* given that exclusionary relations within interlocking state systems "can exacerbate and entrench [a person's] already marginal position in the political, social and economic structures of society" (Bhabha, 2004, p. 154), data-led governance and surveillance may represent the pressing social justice issue of our time.

Current evidential practices in state institutions – for example, auditing practices, as well as the generation and use of administrative and other institutional data to compare results across public sector departments and locales – are managerial technologies associated with a swath of public sector reforms, implemented in Canada and across the Western world under the banners of the "new public management" and evidence-based policy governance (Griffith & Smith, 2014; Nichols, 2014, 2017a; Nichols & Griffith, 2009). These managerial technologies have operationalized marketized approaches to the delivery and management of public sector services, which have flourished under neoliberal forms of governance. Where these earlier governing shifts meet advances in digital technology, new methods of surveillance, assessment, and classification are revolutionizing public life; techniques for collecting, organizing, and analyzing large data sets in the for-profit sector are increasingly being employed in public sector contexts – for example, health and social welfare (Gillingham & Graham, 2017). Furthermore, in the context of non-profit sector funding mechanisms and the pervasiveness of neo-liberal accounting rationalities, new evidential practices are reshaping civil society. As data collection, management, and use practices have proliferated across the public and private sectors, a range of new calculative, evaluative, and predictive technologies have begun to reshape governance processes within and across the public sector, as well as in civil society (Dencik, Hintz, & Cable, 2016; Gillingham & Graham, 2017; Nichols, 2017a, 2017b; Nichols & Braimoh, 2016). The effects of these moves are particularly pronounced for young people living in poverty – who, by virtue of their participation in public systems (e.g., education, child welfare), presence in public spaces, and dependence on civil sector organizations, are more likely to experience the consequences of the latest evidential turn.

To this end, my next move will be to work with a collective of youth and youth-serving organizations to open up the "black box" of evidence-based governance, such that state processes for generating and using evidence are brought under research scrutiny. Drawing on institutional ethnographic research strategies, the goal is to show how and where bias is built into public sector data collection and use practices and propose alternative public sector information generation-and-use pathways and then codesign equitable (participant generated) data-led interventions to improve the efficacy of organizations seeking to improve social and educational outcomes for young people they have historically failed to serve. By engaging in a research process, organized from the ground up and focused on changes to the social organization and use of knowledge in youth-serving institutions, my hope is that we can collectively devise ethical frameworks and practical strategies for using a range of data (e.g., lived experience, ethnographic, text-based, and statistical) to improve youth well-being and support institutional accountability to young people's concerns and aspirations.

References

Abada, T., & Lin, S. (2011). The educational attainments and labour market outcomes of the children of immigrants in Ontario. Higher Education Quality Council of Ontario.

An Act to Amend the Education Act in Respect of Behaviour, Discipline and Safety, Pub. L. No. 212. (2007). Retrieved from www.ontla.on.ca/web/bills/bills_detail.do?locale=en&BillID=1618

An Act to Amend the Education Act Respecting Pupil Learning to the Age of 18 and Equivalent Learning, Pub. L. No. 52. (2006). Retrieved from www.ontla.on.ca/web/bills/bills_detail.do?locale=en&BillID=339&isCurrent=false&detailPage=bills_detail_the_bill

Advisory Board on English Education. (2016). *Special education: Issues of inclusion and integration in the classroom.* Retrieved from www.education.gouv.qc.ca/fileadmin/site_web/documents/autres/organismes/CELA_avis-adaptation-scolaire_a.pdf

Ahmed, S. (2004). Declarations of whiteness: The non-performativity of anti-racism. *borderlands, 3*(2), 1–15.

Ahmed, S. (2007). A phenomenology of whiteness. *Feminist Theory, 8*(2), 149–68.

Ahmed, S. (2011). Happy futures, perhaps. In E.L. McCallum & M. Tuhkanen (Eds.), *Queer times, queer becomings* (pp. 159–82). Albany, NY: SUNY Press. Retrieved from http://research.gold.ac.uk/13931/

Alexander, M. (2012). *The new Jim Crow: Mass incarceration in the age of colorblindness.* New York, NY: The New Press.

Allen, Q., & White-Smith, K.A. (2014). "Just as bad as prisons": The challenge of dismantling the school-to-prison pipeline through teacher and community education. *Equity & Excellence in Education, 47*(4), 445–60. https://doi.org/10/gdds9w

Aucoin, P. (1995). *The new public management: Canada in comparative perspective.* Montreal, QC: McGill-Queen's University Press.

Baffoe, M. (2006). *Navigating two worlds: Culture and cultural adaptation of immigrant and refugee youth in a Quebec (Canadian) educational context.* Retrieved from http://digitool.library.mcgill.ca/R/?func=dbin-jump -full&object_id=102478&local_base=GEN01-MCG02

Bannerji, H. (1991). *Unsettling relations: The university as a site of feminist struggles.* Toronto, ON: Women's Press.

Bannerji, H. (1995). *Thinking through: Essays on feminism, Marxism, and anti-racism.* Toronto, ON: Women's Press.

Bhabha, H.K. (2004). *The location of culture.* New York, NY: Routledge.

Bhattacharjee, K. (2003). *The Ontario safe schools act: School discipline and discrimination.* Ontario Human Rights Commission. Retrieved from www.ohrc.on.ca/en/ontario-safe-schools-act-school-discipline-and -discrimination

Berthiaume, G., Corbo, C., & Montreuil, S. (2014). *Histoires d'immigrations au Québec.* Québec, QC: Press de l'Université du Québec. Retrieved from https://flipbook.cantook.net/?d=%2F%2Fwww.entrepotnumerique.com%2F flipbook%2Fpublications%2F22875.js&oid=7&c=&m=&l=fr&r=https://puq .ca&f=pdf

Bourdieu, P. (1990). *In other words: Essays towards a reflexive sociology.* Stanford, CA: Stanford University Press.

Bourdieu, P., & Passeron, J-C. (1977). *Reproduction in education, society and culture.* London: Sage.

Bradley, R.H., & Corwyn, R.F. (2002). Socioeconomic status and child development. *Annual Review of Psychology, 53*(1), 371–99.

Brent, D.A., & Silverstein, M. (2013). Shedding light on the long shadow of childhood adversity. *JAMA, 309*(17), 1777–8. https://doi.org/10/gdg3p8

Brent, R.H. (2007). *Safety and security in schools: Update on the safe schools act – beyond zero tolerance?* Presented at the 2007 OBA Institute of Continuing Legal Education: Update on the Safe Schools Act, Thomson Rogers. Retrieved from www.thomsonrogers.com/wp-content/uploads/2015/04 /Safety-and-Security-in-Schools-Update-on-the-Safe-Schools-Act-Beyond -Zero-Tolerance.pdf

Brown, L.A., & Strega, S. (2005). *Research as resistance: Critical, Indigenous and anti-oppressive approaches.* Toronto, ON: Canadian Scholars' Press.

Brown, R.S., & Parekh, G. (2010). *Special education: Structural overview and student demographics* (p. 73). Toronto, ON: Toronto District School Board. Retrieved from www.tdsb.on.ca/Portals/0/Community /Community%20Advisory%20committees/ICAC/research/SpecEd StructuralOverviewStudentDemo.pdf

Brown, R.S., & Parekh, G. (2013). *The intersection of disability, achievement, and equity: A system review of special education in the TDSB.* Toronto, ON: Toronto District School Board. Retrieved from www.tdsb.on.ca/Portals/research

/docs/reports/Intersection%20of%20Disability%20Achievement%20 and%20Equity.pdf

Buckingham, S. (2016). Trauma informed juvenile justice. *American Criminal Law Review, 53*, 641–92.

Butler-Kisber, L. (2010). *Qualitative inquiry: Thematic, narrative and arts-informed.* Thousand Oaks, CA: Sage.

Caldas, S.J., Bernier, S., & Marceau, R. (2009). Explanatory factors of the black achievement gap in Montreal's public and private schools: A multivariate analysis. *Education and Urban Society, 41*(2), 197–215.

Cammarota, J., & Ginwright, S. (2007). "Today we march, tomorrow we vote": Youth transforming despair into social justice. *Educational Foundations, 21*(1–2), 3.

CBC News. (2017, November 25). Quebec City police arrest 44 at far-right protest and counter-demonstration. Retrieved from www.cbc.ca/news /canada/montreal/quebec-city-police-arrest-44-at-far-right-protest-and -counter-demonstration-1.4419752

CBC News (2008, May 16). A timeline of residential schools, the Truth and Reconciliation Commission. Retrieved from www.cbc.ca/news /canada/a-timeline-of-residential-schools-the-truth-and-reconciliation -commission-1.724434

Commission des droits de la personne et des droits de la jeunesse, Gouvernement de Québec. (2011). Mémoire à la commission sur le Développement Social et la Diversité Montréalise et à la commission sur la Sécurité Publique de la Ville de Montréal dans le cadre de la Consultations sur la Lutte au Profilage Racial et au Profilage Social.

Césaire, A. (1972). *Discourse on colonialism.* New York, NY: Monthly Review Press.

Charter of the French Language, CQLR c. C-11 §. (1977). Retrieved from www.legisquebec.gouv.qc.ca/en/showdoc/cs/C-11

Cheff, N. (2018). Learning to discipline students in Montreal schools: An administrator's perspective (Unpublished master's thesis). Department of Integrated Studies in Education, McGill University.

Child and Family Services Act, R.S.O. c. C.11 §. (1990). Retrieved from https://nextcanada-westlaw-com.proxy3.library.mcgill.ca/Document /I10b717d59c7d63f0e0440003ba0d6c6d/View/FullText.html?originationContext= documenttoc&transitionType=CategoryPageItem&contextData=(sc.Default)

Clandfield, D. (2014). Special education and streaming. In G. Martell & D. Clandfield (Eds.), *Restacking the deck: Streaming by class, race and gender in Ontario schools* (Vol. 23). Beaconsfield, QC: Canadian Centre for Policy Alternatives. Retrieved from www.deslibris.ca/ID/448003

Contenta, S., Monsebraaten, L., & Rankin, J. (2014, December 11). Why are so many black children in foster and group homes? *The Toronto Star.* Retrieved

from https://www.thestar.com/news/canada/2014/12/11/why_are_so
_many_black_children_in_foster_and_group_homes.html

Courtemanche, F. (2017). Towards plurilingualism in Montréal French
schools: A critical discourse analysis of current governmental and school
board policies (Unpublished master's thesis). Department of Integrated
Studies in Education, McGill University.

Courtney, M., Maes, Nino, C., & Peters, E. (2014). System pathways into youth
homelessness. Retrieved from http://www.hereandnowwinnipeg.ca
/wp-content/uploads/2016/09/SystemPathways-SPCW-2014.pdf

Crehan, K. (2011). Gramsci's concept of common sense: A useful concept for
anthropologists? *Journal of Modern Italian Studies, 16*(2), 273–87. https://
doi.org/10.1080/1354571X.2011.542987

Crenshaw, K., Gotanda, N., Peller, G., & Thomas, K. (1995). *Critical race theory:
The key writings that formed the movement.* New York, NY: The New Press.

Cummins, J. (2000). *Language, power and pedagogy: Bilingual children in the
crossfire.* Toronto, ON: Multilingual Matters.

Cutler, D., Huang, W., & Lleras-Muney, A. (2015). When does education matter?
The protective effect of education for cohorts graduating in bad times. *Social
Science & Medicine, 127*, 63–73. https://doi.org/10/gdg3hw

Daniel, Y., & Bondy, K. (2008). Safe Schools and zero tolerance: Policy,
program and practice in Ontario. *Canadian Journal of Educational
Administration and Policy, 70*, 1–20.

Dei, G.J.S., Mazzuca, J., McIsaac, E. & Zine, J. (1997). *Reconstructing' dropout': A
critical ethnography of the dynamics of black students' disengagement from school.*
Toronto, ON: University of Toronto Press.

Dencik, L., Hintz, A., & Cable, J. (2016). Towards data justice? The ambiguity of
anti-surveillance resistance in political activism. *Big Data & Society, 3*(2), 1–12.

DeVault, M.L., & McCoy, L. (2006). Institutional ethnography: Using
interviews to investigate ruling relations. In D.E. Smith (Ed.), *Institutional
ethnography as practice* (pp. 15–44). Toronto, ON: Rowman & Littlefield.

Dhillon, J.K. (2017). *Prairie rising: Indigenous youth, decolonization, and the
politics of intervention.* Toronto, ON: University of Toronto Press.

Directions Evidence and Policy Research Group, LLP. (2014). *The Ontario
student achievement division student success strategy evidence of improvement
study* (p. 80). Ontario Ministry of Education. Retrieved from www.edu.gov
.on.ca/eng/research/EvidenceOfImprovementStudy.pdf

Donlon, T., Ekstrom, R.B., Lockheed, M. and Harris, A. (1977). Performance
consequences of sex bias in the content of major achievement batteries
(PR-77-11). Princeton, NJ: Educational Testing Services.

Duncan, G.J., Brooks-Gunn, J., & Klebanov, P.K. (1994). Economic deprivation
and early childhood development. *Child Development, 65*(2), 296–318.

Education Act, CQLR c. I-13.3 §. (1977). Retrieved from http://legisquebec
.gouv.qc.ca/en/ShowDoc/cs/I-13.3

Education Act, R.S.O. § c. E.2. (1990). Retrieved from www.ontario.ca/laws
/statute/90e02

Eubanks, V. (2018). *Automating inequality: How high-tech tools profile, police, and
punish the poor.* New York, NY: St. Martin's Press.

Fanon, F. (2008). *Black skin, white masks.* (R. Philcox, Trans.) New York, NY:
Grove (1952).

Fédération des Cégeps. (2006). *Finance CEGEPs according to their needs: Conclusions
of the task force of the fédération des cégeps on the financing of the public college
system.* Montréal, QC. Retrieved from www.fedecegeps.qc.ca/wp-content
/uploads/files/english/finance-v-web.pdf

Fine, M., & Ruglis, J. (2009). Circuits and consequences of dispossession: The
racialized realignment of the public sphere for US youth. *Transforming
anthropology, 17*(1), 20–33.

Foucault, M., & Gordon, C. (1980). *Power/knowledge: Selected interviews and
other writings, 1972–1977.* New York, NY: Pantheon Books.

Fraser Institute. (2017). *Report card on Quebec's secondary schools 2015/2016.*
Retrieved from http://quebec.compareschoolrankings.org/SchoolsBy
RankLocationName.aspx?schoolType=secondary&SortBy=RankThisYear

Freedle, R. (2003). Correcting the SAT's ethnic and social-class bias: A method
for reestimating SAT scores. *Harvard Educational Review, 73*(1), 1–43.

Gaetz, S. (2014). *Coming of age: Reimagining the response to youth homelessness
in Canada* (The Homeless Hub Report Series No. 11). Toronto, ON: The
Canadian Homelessness Research Network Press.

Galabuzi, G-E. (2014). Race and the streaming of Ontario's children and
youth. In G. Martell & D. Clandfield (Eds.), *Restacking the deck: Streaming
by class, race and gender in Ontario schools* (Vol. 23). Beaconsfield, QC:
Canadian Centre for Policy Alternatives. Retrieved from www.deslibris.ca
/ID/448003

Gilborn, D. (2005). Education policy as an act of white supremacy: Whiteness,
critical race theory and education reform. *Journal of Education Policy, 20*(4),
485–505.

Gilborn, D. (2008). Coincidence or conspiracy? Whiteness, policy and the
persistence of the Black/White achievement gap. *Educational Review, 60*(3),
229–48.

Gillingham, P., & Graham, T. (2017). Big data in social welfare: The
development of a critical perspective on social work's latest "electronic
turn." *Australian Social Work, 70*(2), 135–47.

Ginwright, S., & Cammarota, J. (2002). New terrain in youth development:
The promise of a social justice approach. *Social Justice, 29*(4), 82–95.

Ginwright, S., Cammarota, J., & Noguera, P. (2005). Youth, social justice, and communities: Toward a theory of urban youth policy. *Social Justice, 32*(3), 24–40.

Goddard, T., & Myers, R.R. (2016). Against evidence-based oppression: Marginalized youth and the politics of risk-based assessment and intervention. *Theoretical Criminology, 21*(2), 151–67. https://doi.org/10/f97kd8

Good, C., Aronson, J., & Inzlicht, M. (2003). Improving adolescents' standardized test performance: An intervention to reduce the effects of stereotype threat. *Journal of Applied Developmental Psychology, 24*(6), 645–62.

Gordon, A. (2017, November 22). TDSB votes down police presence in high schools. *The Toronto Star*. Retrieved from www.thestar.com/yourtoronto/education/2017/11/22/tdsb-votes-down-police-presence-in-high-schools.html

Government of Canada. (2016, April 13). *Living arrangements of Aboriginal children aged 14 and under*. Retrieved from www.statcan.gc.ca/pub/75-006-x/2016001/article/14547-eng.htm

Government of Quebec. (2009). Le financement de l'éducation préscolaire et de l'enseignement primaire et secondaire québécois - Année scolaire 2008-2009. Retrieved from http://www.education.gouv.qc.ca/references/publications/resultats-de-la-recherche/detail/article/le-financement-de-leducation-prescolaire-et-de-lenseignement-primaire-et-secondaire-quebecois-an/?no_cache=1&cHash=4f7686fa5cf4823fb244c1f27e220306

Gramsci, A. (1971). *Selections from the prison notebooks* (Q. Hoare & G. Nowell Smith, Eds.). London: Lawrence & Wishart.

Green, R.L., & Griffore, R.J. (1980). The impact of standardized testing on minority students. *The Journal of Negro Education, 49*(3), 238–52.

Green, T.D., Mcintosh, A.S., Cook-Morales, V.J., & Robinson-Zanartu, C. (2005). From old schools to tomorrow's schools: Psychoeducational assessment of African American students. *Remedial and Special Education, 26*(2), 82–92. https://doi.org/10/bppwrg

Gregory, A., Skiba, R.J., & Noguera, P.A. (2010). The achievement gap and the discipline gap: Two sides of the same coin? *Educational Researcher, 39*(1), 59–68. https://doi.org/10/bbhppx

Griffith, A.I., & Smith, D.E. (2005). *Mothering for schooling*. New York, NY: RoutledgeFalmer.

Griffith, A.I., & Smith, D.E. (2014). *Under new public management: Institutional ethnographies of changing front-line work*. Toronto, ON: University of Toronto Press.

Gutnick, D. (2017) Are Quebec's private schools creating a segregated society? CBC Radio. Retrieved from https://www.cbc.ca/radio/thesundayedition

/the-sunday-edition-october-29-2017-1.4374949/are-quebec-s-private-high
-schools-creating-a-segregated-society-1.4374965

Hacking, I. (2004). Between Michel Foucault and Erving Goffman: Between discourse in the abstract and face-to-face interaction. *Economy and Society, 33*(3), 277–302. https://doi.org/10.1080/03085140420000225671

Hall, S. (1986). The problem of ideology-Marxism without guarantees. *Journal of Communication Inquiry, 10*(2), 28–44. https://doi.org/10/drgd6g

Harvey, D. (2005). *A Brief History of Neoliberalism*. New York, NY: Oxford University Press, USA.

Hines-Datiri, D. (2015). When police intervene: Race, gender, and discipline of black male students at an urban high school. *Journal of Cases in Educational Leadership, 18*(2), 122–33. https://doi.org/10/gddxvk

Howard, P.S. (2006). On silence and dominant accountability: A critical anticolonial investigation of the antiracism classroom. In G.J.S. Dei & A. Kempf (Eds.), *Anti-colonialism and education: The politics of resistance* (pp. 42–63). Boston, MA: Brill | Sense Publishers.

Hughes, P. (2008). Law commissions and access to justice: What justice should we be talking about? *Osgoode Hall Law Journal, 46*(4), 773–806.

Hughes, N., Williams, H., Chitsabesan, P., Davies, R., & Mounce, L. (2012). *Nobody made the connection: The prevalence of neurodisability in young people who offend*. London: Children's Commissioner. Retrieved from www.childrens commissioner.gov.uk

James, C.E. (2011). Students "at Risk": Stereotypes and the Schooling of Black Boys. *Urban Education, 47*, 464–92.

James, C.E., & Turner, T. (2015). Fighting an uphill battle: Report on the consultations into the well-being of black youth in Peel Region. Mississauga, Ontario: F.A.C.E.S. of Peel Collaborative. Retrieved from http://www.unitedwaypeel.org/faces/images/fighting-an-uphill-battle -sm.pdf

James, C.E. & Turner, T. (2017). Towards Race Equity In Education: The Schooling of Black Students in the Greater Toronto Area. Toronto, ON: York University.

Jenson, Jane. (2013). Historical transformations of Canada's social architecture: Institutions, instruments, and ideas. In K. Banting & J. Myles (Eds.), *Inequality and the fading of distributive politics* (pp. 43–64). Vancouver, BC: UBC Press.

King, A., Warren, W., King, M., Brook, J., & Kocher, P. (2009). *Who doesn't go to post-secondary education*. Retrieved from www.collegesontario.org /research/who-doesnt-go-to-pse.pdf

Kirshner, B. (2010). Productive tensions in youth participatory action research. *Yearbook of the National Society for the Study of Education, 109*(1), 238–51.

Krishner, B., Hipolito-Delgado, C., & Zion, S. (2015). Sociopolitical development in educational systems: From margins to centre. *Urban Review, 47*, 803–8.

Lawrence, S.N., & Williams, T. (2006). Swallowed up: Drug couriers at the boarders of Canadian sentencing. *University of Toronto Law Journal, 56*, 285–332. https://doi.org/10/bw33xh

Lesko, N. (2001). *Act your age!: A cultural construction of adolescence.* New York, NY: Psychology Press.

Logical Outcomes. (2014). *This issue has been with us for ages: A community assessment of police contact carding in 31 division.* Retrieved from https://exchange.youthrex.com/report/issue-has-been-us-ages-community-assessment-police-contact-carding-31-division

Lorinc, J. (2018). Busted by big data: Algorithms could make cities safer – but they can't protect us from policing's worst instincts. *The Walrus.* Retrieved from https://thewalrus.ca/will-big-data-in-crime-fighting-create-a-new-era-of-racial-profiling

Magnuson, R. (1993). A profile of private schools in Quebec. *McGill Journal of Education/Revue des sciences de l'éducation de McGill, 28*(1).

Maloney, T., Jiang, N., Emily, P-H., Dalton, E., & Vaithianathan, R. (2017). Black-white differences in child maltreatment reports and foster care placements: A statistical decomposition using linked administrative data. *Maternal and Child Health Journal, 21*(3), 414–20.

Manicom, A. (1995). What's health got to do with it? Class, gender and teacher's work. In Campbell, M., & Manicom, A. (Eds.), *Knowledge, experience, and ruling: Studies in the social organization of knowledge* (pp. 135–48). Toronto, ON: University of Toronto Press.

Maraj-Grahame, K. (1998). Feminist organizing and the politics of inclusion. *Human Studies, 21*(4), 377–93.

Marx, K. (2010). *Karl Marx: Selected writings.* New York, NY: Classic Books International.

Marx, K., & O'Malley, J.J. (1970). *Critique of Hegel's "Philosophy of right."* Cambridge: Cambridge University Press.

Maynard, R. (2017). *Policing black lives: State violence in Canada from slavery to the present.* Black Point, NS: Fernwood.

Mbembe, A. (2017). *Critique of black reason.* Durham, NC: Duke University Press.

McCauley, E.J. (2017). The cumulative probability of arrest by age 28 years in the United States by disability status, race/ethnicity, and gender. *American Journal of Public Health, 107*(12), 1977–81.

McCoy, L. (2006). Keeping the institution within view: Working with interview accounts of everyday experience. In D.E. Smith (Ed.), *Institutional ethnography as practice* (pp. 109–26). Toronto, ON: Rowman & Littlefield.

McGill University. (2017–2018). Summer studies: Programs, courses, and university regulations, 2017–2018. Retrieved from www.mcgill.ca/study /2017-2018/files/study.2017-2018/summer_studies_2018_ecalendar.pdf

McMurtry, R., & Young, A. (2008). *The review of the roots of youth violence.* Toronto, ON: Queen's Printer for Ontario. Retrieved from www.children .gov.on.ca/htdocs/English/documents/youthandthelaw/rootsofyouth violence-vol1.pdf

Miller, J.R. (2012). Residential schools. In *The Canadian encyclopedia.* Retrieved from www.thecanadianencyclopedia.ca/en/article/residential-schools/

Ministère de l'Éducation et de l'Enseignement supérieur. (2017). *Diplomation et qualification par commission scolaire au secondaire.* Quebec: Gouvernement du Québec. Retrieved from www.education.gouv.qc.ca /fileadmin/site_web/documents/PSG/statistiques_info_decisionnelle /taux_diplomation_secondaire_CS_Edition2017_CD.PDF

A minority within a minority: Quebec's struggle to face racism. (2018, March 9). *The Current* [Radio program]. Toronto, ON: CBC Radio. Retrieved from www.cbc.ca/radio/thecurrent/the-current-for-march-9 -2018-1.4567875/a-minority-within-a-minority-quebec-s-struggle-to-face -racism-1.4567938

Moore, J. (2013). Teaching and classroom strategies for homeless and highly mobile students. National Centre for Homelessness Education. Retrieved from https://www.homelesshub.ca/resource/teaching-and-classroom -strategies-homeless-and-highly-mobile-students

Morris, E.W., & Perry, B.L. (2016). The punishment gap: School suspension and racial disparities in achievement. *Social Problems, 63*(1), 68–86. https:// doi.org/10/f8cthx

Morris, E.W., & Perry, B.L. (2017). Girls behaving badly? Race, gender, and subjective evaluation in the discipline of African American girls. *Sociology of Education, 90*(2), 127–48. https:// doi.org/10/f96nhv

Mosher, J. (2008). Lessons in Access to Justice: Racialized Youths and Ontario's Safe Schools. *Osgoode Hall Law Journal, 48,* 807–51.

National Inquiry into Missing and Murdered Indigenous Women and Girls. (2017). Interim report: The national inquiry into missing and murdered indigenous women and girls.

Ng, R. (1988). The politics of community services: Immigrant women, class, and state. Halifax, NS: Fernwood.

Ng, R. (1993). Racism, sexism, and nation building in Canada. In C. McCarthy & W. Crichlow (Eds.), Race, identity, and representation in education (pp. 50–9). New York, NY: Routledge

Nichols, N. (2008). Gimme shelter! Investigating the social service interface from the standpoint of youth. *Journal of Youth Studies, 11*(6), 685–99.

Nichols, N. (2014). Youth work: An institutional ethnography of youth homelessness. Toronto, ON: University of Toronto Press.

Nichols, N. (2016). Investigating the social relations of human service provision: Institutional ethnography and activism. *Journal of Comparative Social Work, 11*(1), 38–63.

Nichols, N. (2017a). Technologies of evidence: An institutional ethnography from the standpoints of "youth-at-risk." *Critical Social Policy, 37*(4), 604–24. https://doi.org/10/gctncw

Nichols, N. (2017b). The social organization of access to justice for youth in 'unsafe' urban neighbourhoods. *Social & Legal Studies, 27*(1), 79–96. https://doi.org/10/gc3cw5

Nichols, N. (2018). Producing youth "out of sync:" The intersectional social relations of educational inequality. *Journal of Youth Studies, 21*(1), 111–28. https://doi.org/10/gddxtm

Nichols, N., Anucha, U., Houwer, R., & Wood, M. (2013). Building equitable community-academic research collaborations: Learning together through tensions and contradictions. *Gateways: International Journal of Community Research and Engagement, 6*, 57–76. https://doi.org/10.5130/ijcre.v6i1.2822

Nichols, N., & Braimoh, J. (2016). Community safety, housing precariousness and processes of exclusion: An institutional ethnography from the standpoints of youth in an "unsafe" urban neighbourhood. *Critical Sociology, 44*(1), 157–72. https://doi.org/10/gcshcf

Nichols, N., Braimoh, J., & Fisher, A. (Submitted January 2018). "Vulnerable neighbourhoods," youth "at-risk," and safe schools – Explicating the intersecting social relations of race, gender and class. *Canadian Journal of Sociology.*

Nichols, N., Gaetz, S., Redman, M., French, D., Kidd, S., & Bill, O. (2017). *Child welfare and youth homelessness in Canada: A proposal for action.* Toronto, ON: Canadian Observatory on Homelessness Press.

Nichols, N., & Griffith, A.I. (2009). Talk, texts, and educational action: An institutional ethnography of policy in practice. *Cambridge Journal of Education, 39*(2), 241–55.

Nguyen, H.H.D., & Ryan, A.M. (2008). Does stereotype threat affect test performance of minorities and women? A meta-analysis of experimental evidence. *Journal of Applied Psychology, 93*(6), 1314–34.

OECD. (2010). *The high cost of low educational performance.* OECD Publishing. https://doi.org/10.1787/9789264077485-en

Ofer, U. (2011/2012). "Criminalizing the classroom: The rise of aggressive policing and zero tolerance discipline in New York City public schools." *NYLS Law Review 56*(4), 1373–411.

OHRC (Ontario Human Rights Commission). (2017). *Under suspicion: Research and consultation report on racial profiling in Ontario.* Toronto, ON: Author. Retrieved from www.ohrc.on.ca

OHRC (Ontario Human Rights Commission). (2018). *A collective impact: Interim report on the inquiry into racial profiling and racial discrimination of black persons by the Toronto police services.* Toronto, ON: Author. Retrieved from www.ohrc.on.ca

OHRC (Ontario Human Rights Commission). (n.d.). Human Rights settlement reached with Ministry of Education on Safe Schools. Retrieved from http://www.ohrc.on.ca/en/human-rights-settlement-reached-ministry-education-safe-schools

Omi, M., & Winant, H. (1994). *Racial formation in the United States: From the 1960s to the 1990s.* New York, NY: Routledge.

Ontario Association of Children's Aid Societies. (2015). *Race matters in the child welfare system.* Toronto, ON: Author. Retrieved from www.oacas.org/wp-content/uploads/2015/09/Race-Matters-African-Canadians-Project-August-2015.pdf

Ontario Association of Children's Aid Societies. (2018). Permanency. Retrieved from www.oacas.org/childrens-aid-child-protection/permanency/.

Ontario Ministry of Education. (2010). *Caring and safe schools in Ontario.* Toronto, ON: Author. Retrieved from www.edu.gov.on.ca/eng/general/elemsec/speced/Caring_Safe_School.pdf

Ontario Ministry of Education. (2012). *Progressive discipline and promoting positive student behaviour* (Policy/Program Memorandum No. 145). Toronto, ON: Author. Retrieved from www.edu.gov.on.ca/extra/eng/ppm/145.pdf

Ontario Ministry of Education. (2015). *Provincial model for a local police/school board protocol: 201.* Toronto, ON: Author. Retrieved from www.edu.gov.on.ca/eng/document/brochure/protocol/locprote.pdf

Our Kids. (2014) The most expensive private schools in Canada. Retrieved from https://www.ourkids.net/compare-schools/ranking-expensive-schools.php

Raby, R.C. (2002). A tangle of discourses: Girls negotiating adolescence. *Journal of Youth Studies, 5*(4), 425–48. https://doi.org/10/c8tj3b

Rankin, J., & Contenta, S. (2009, June 6). Suspended sentences: Forging a school-to-prison pipeline? *The Toronto Star.* Retrieved from www.thestar.com/news/gta/2009/06/06/suspended_sentences_forging_a_schooltoprison_pipeline.html

Rankin, J., & Winsa, P. (2012, March 9). Known to police: Toronto police stop and document black and brown people far more than whites. *Toronto Star, 9.*

Rankin, J., Winsa, P., & Ng, H. (2013, March 1). Unequal justice: Aboriginal and black inmates disproportionately fill Ontario jails. *The Toronto Star.* Retrieved from www.thestar.com/news/insight/2013/03/01/unequal_justice_aboriginal_and_black_inmates_disproportionately_fill_ontario_jails.html

Rankin, J., Winsa, P., Bailey, A., & Ng, H. (2014, July 26). Carding drops but proportion of blacks stopped by Toronto police rises. *The Toronto Star.* Retrieved from https://www.thestar.com/news/insight/2014/07/26/carding_drops_but_proportion_of_blacks_stopped_by_toronto_police_rises.html

Razack, S., Smith, M., & Thobani, S. (2010). *States of race: Critical race feminism for the 21st century*. Toronto, ON: Between the Lines.

Ringrose, J., & Renold, E. (2010). Normative cruelties and gender deviants: The performative effects of bully discourses for girls and boys in school. *British Educational Research Journal, 36*(4), 573–96.

Rios, V. (2011). *Punished: Policing the lives of black and Latino boys*. New York, NY: New York University Press.

Rocha, R. (2018). How many crimes happen near you. *CBC News*. Retrieved from https://newsinteractives.cbc.ca/montreal-crime/

Ruck, M.D., & Wortley, S. (2002). Racial and ethnic minority high school students' perceptions of school disciplinary practices: A look at some Canadian findings. *Journal of Youth and Adolescence, 31*(3), 185–95.

Said, E.W. (1979). *Orientalism*. New York, NY: Vintage Books.

Shields, J.M., & Evans, B.M. (1998). *Shrinking the state: Globalization and public administration "reform."* Halifax, NS: Fernwood.

Skiba, R.J., Simmons, A.B., Ritter, S., Gibb, A.C., Rausch, M.K., Cuadrado, J., & Chung, C-G. (2008). Achieving equity in special education: History, status, and current challenges. *Exceptional Children, 74*(3), 264–88.

Skiba, R.J., Eckes, S.E., & Brown, K.D. (2009/2010). African American disproportionality in school discipline: The divide between best evidence and legal remedy. *NYL Sch. L. Rev., 54*, 1071.

Skiba, R.J., Chung, C-G., Trachok, M., Baker, T.L., Sheya, A., & Hughes, R.L. (2014). Parsing disciplinary disproportionality: Contributions of infraction, student, and school characteristics to out-of-school suspension and expulsion. *American Educational Research Journal, 51*(4), 640–70.

Slate, J.R., Gray, P.L., & Jones, B. (2016). A clear lack of equity in disciplinary consequences for black girls in Texas: A statewide examination. *The Journal of Negro Education, 85*(3), 250–60. https://doi.org/10/gdds8b

Smaller, H. (2014). *Restacking the deck: Streaming by class, race and gender in Ontario schools* (Our Schools; Ourselves). Ottawa, ON: Canadian Centre for Policy Alternatives.

Smith, D.E. (1987). *The everyday world as problematic: A feminist sociology*. Boston, MA: UPNE

Smith, D.E. (1993). *Texts, facts, and femininity: Exploring the relations of ruling*. New York, NY: Routledge.

Smith, D.E. (1999). *Writing the social: Critique, theory, and investigations*. Toronto, ON: University of Toronto Press.

Smith, D.E. (2004). Ideology, science, and social relations: A reinterpretation of Marx's epistemology. In S. Carpenter & S. Mojab (Eds.), *Educating from Marx: Race, gender, and learning* (pp. 19–40). New York, NY: Palgrave Macmillan US. https://doi.org/10.1057/9780230370371_2

Smith, D.E. (2005). *Institutional ethnography: A sociology for people*. Toronto, ON: AltaMira Press.

Smith, D.E. (2006). *Institutional ethnography as practice.* Lanham, MD: Rowman & Littlefield.

Smith, G.W. (1990). Political activist ethnographer. *Social Problems, 37*(4), 629–48.

Solomon, R.P., & Palmer, H. (2004). Schooling in Babylon, Babylon in school: When racial profiling and zero tolerance converge. *Canadian Journal of Educational Administration and Policy, 33.* Retrieved from https://journalhosting.ucalgary.ca/index.php/cjeap/article/view/42713

Spivak, G.C. (1993). *Outside in the teaching machine.* New York, NY: Routledge.

Thobani, S. (2007). *Exalted subjects.* Toronto, ON: University of Toronto Press.

Thompson, E.P. (1966). *The making of the English working class.* London: Penguin UK.

Toronto District School Board. (2013a). *Board code of conduct* (Operational Procedure No. PR585). Retrieved from http://ppf.tdsb.on.ca/uploads/files/live/98/1714.pdf

Toronto District School Board. (2013b). *Progressive discipline and promoting positive student behaviour* (Operational Procedure No. PR702). Retrieved from http://ppf.tdsb.on.ca/uploads/files/live/98/1801.pdf

Toronto District School Board. (2014). *Caring and Safe Schools.* Retrieved from https://www.tdsb.on.ca/High-School/Caring-Safe-Schools

Toronto District School Board. (2016). *Special education: In-School Support Team (IST) and school support team model.* Toronto, ON: Author. Retrieved from www.tdsb.on.ca/portals/0/EarlyYears/SpecialEducation/IST-SST.pdf

Toronto District School Board. (2017a). *Learning Opportunities Index (LOI).* Toronto, ON: Author. Retrieved from www.tdsb.on.ca/Portals/research/docs/reports/LOI2017.pdf

Toronto District School Board. (2017b). *School resource officer program review* (Planning and Priorities Committee No. 11–17–3269). Toronto, ON: Author. Retrieved from www.tdsb.on.ca/Leadership/Boardroom/Agenda-Minutes/Type/A?Folder=Agenda%2f20171115&Filename=171115+School+Resource+Off+3269+FINAL.pdf

Toronto Police Service, Toronto District School Board, Toronto Catholic District School Board, Conseil scolaire de district catholique Centre-Sud, & Conseil scolaire Viamonde. (2011). *Police/school board protocol.* Toronto, ON: Author. Retrieved from www.torontopolice.on.ca/publications/files/misc/schoolprotocol.pdf

Triseliotis, J. (2002). Long-term foster care or adoption? The evidence examined. *Child & Family Social Work, 7*(1), 23–33. https://doi.org/10/d4vnwx

Tuck, E. (2009). Suspending damage: A letter to communities. *Harvard Educational Review, 79*(3), 409–28. https://doi.org/10.17763/haer.79.3.n0016675661t3n15

UBC (University of British Columbia). (2018a). Department of Psychology. Retrieved from https://psych.ubc.ca/graduate/prospective-students/admission-requirements/

UBC (University of British Columbia). (2018b). Department of Psychology. Retrieved from https://psych.ubc.ca/graduate/prospective-students/

UBC (University of British Columbia). (2018c). Department of Psychology. Retrieved from https://psych.ubc .ca/graduate/research-areas/clinical/admissions/

Vasudevan, L., & Campano, G. (2009). The social production of adolescent risk and the promise of adolescent literacies. *Review of Research in Education, 33*(1), 310–53. https://doi.org/10/c9mpkj

Walton, G. (2005). Bullying widespread: A critical analysis of research and public discourse on bullying. *Journal of School Violence, 4*(1), 91–118.

Warren, M.R., & Mapp, K.L. (2011). *A match on dry grass: Community organizing as a catalyst for school reform.* New York, NY: Oxford University Press.

Weber, M. 1993. "The Bureaucratic Machine." In C. Lemert (Ed.), *Social theory: The multicultural and classic readings.* Boulder, CO: Westview.

Winsa, P. (2014, November 12). Improper police "carding" continues in Jane-Finch area, survey finds. *The Toronto Star.* Retrieved from https://www.thestar.com/news/crime/2014/11/12/improper_police_carding_continues_in_janefinch_area_survey_finds.html

World Bank. (2007). *Education quality and economic growth.* The World Bank. https://doi.org/10.1596/978-0-8213-7058-2

Wortley, S. (2008). A province at the crossroads: Statistics on youth violence in Ontario. *The Review of the Roots of Youth Violence, 4,* 1–64.

Wortley, S., & Tanner, J. (2003). Data, denials, and confusion: The racial profiling debate in Toronto. *Canadian Journal of Criminology and Criminal Justice, 45*(3), 367–90.

Wortley, S., & Owusu-Bempah, A. (2011). The usual suspects: Police stop and search practices in Canada. *Policing and Society, 21*(4), 395–407. https://doi.org/10/c3bzvm

Wun, C. (2015). Against captivity: Black girls and school discipline policies in the afterlife of slavery. *Educational Policy, 30*(1), 171–96. https://doi.org/10/f749n6

Wun, C. (2016). Unaccounted foundations: Black girls, anti-Black racism, and punishment in schools. *Critical Sociology, 42*(4–5), 737–50.

Zellars, R. (2017). Blackness, exclusion, and the law in the history of Canada's public schools, Ontario and Québec, 1850–present (Unpublished PhD Thesis). Department of Integrated Studies in Education, McGill University.

Zheng, S., & De Jesus, S. (2017). *Expulsion decision-making process and expelled students' transition experience in the Toronto district school board's caring and safe schools programs and their graduation outcomes* (Research Report No. 16/17–15). Toronto, ON: Toronto District School Board. Retrieved from www.tdsb.on.ca/Portals/research/docs/reports/Student%20Expulsion%20Rpt%2030Mar17.pdf

Zoref, L., & Williams, P. (1980). A look at content bias in IQ tests. *Journal of Educational Measurement, 17*(4), 313–22. https://doi.org/10/fwnnp9

Index